JACK NICKLAUS

SIMPLY THE BEST!

The American Golfer titles may be purchased for business or promotional use or for special sales.
For information, please write to: Special Markets Department, The American Golfer, Inc.,
200 Railroad Avenue, Greenwich, Connecticut 06830.

THE AMERICAN GOLFER and its logo, its name in scripted letters, are trademarks of
The American Golfer, Inc.

FIRST EDITION

ISBN 1-888531-01-0

EAN 978-1-888531-01-5

Published by:
The American Golfer, Inc.
200 Railroad Avenue
Greenwich, Connecticut 06830
(203) 862-9720
FAX (203) 862-9724
email: imd@aol.com

ACKNOWLEDGMENTS

First and foremost, I would like to express our sincerest gratitude and deepest appreciation to our
contributing essayists — Dave Anderson, Arnold Palmer, Marino Paracenzo, Gary Player, Lee Trevino,
Jaime Diaz, Tom Watson, Dan Jenkins, Jack Whitaker, Jim Flick and Roger Schiffman.

I would especially like to thank Myra Gelband, a copy editor par excellence.

Thanks to Steve Indiveri whose background research for this book was incredibly complete. And thanks
to our office assistant Cori Lantz for her conscientious work in proofing the book and fact checking.

We would also like to single out Andy O'Brien, Scott Tolly, Julie Trimble and Jim Mandeville of the
Nicklaus Companies for their untold efforts and assistance.

And a very special thanks for the active cooperation and help from Steve Auch and Barbara Hartley
of The Jack Nicklaus Museum in Columbus, Ohio. Their efforts on our behalf were truly herculean.
Barbara's photography of Jack's medals used in the book add a great deal.

Thanks to Deane Beman and Johnny Miller for their insights and interviews. And also to Rick Vershure
and Phil Cardwell, golf professionals at Quaker Ridge Golf Club, for their guidance in depicting the
differences in Jack's swing over the years.

Much appreciation to Oksanna Babij for her truly marvelous art direction and also to her assistant
Jason Schmiedel.

Thanks to Walter Iooss, Jr. for the use of his photo of Jack and Arnie at Ligonier on pages 72-73 — one
of golf's truly great photos.

Thanks too to Cliff Schrock of *Golf Digest* for all of his help with the photos. A marvelous job well done.

Others we'd like to commend for their efforts on our behalf are Glenn Greenspan of the
Augusta National Golf Club; Julius Mason, Bob Denney and Lauren Demary of The PGA of America;
Marty Parkes and his staff from the USGA, Melannie Hauser, Peter Oosterhuis and Carol Mann.

Several organizations and individuals were responsible for providing many of the original photographs
accompanying these pages: specifically the United States Golf Association, Corbis-Bettmann,
Getty Images, The PGA of America, the PGA TOUR, The Associated Press, The Memorial Tournament,
Larry Hasak, Matt Ellis, Christian Iooss, Steve Szurlej, *Golf Digest*, John Kelly, The Jack Nicklaus
Museum, Historic Golf Photos/The Ron Watts Collection, *Sports Illustrated* and *The New York Times*.

This book could not have been published without the active assistance and cooperation of all those listed
above. Our sincerest thanks.

For Ashleigh

"…he is simply a mature and relaxed version of what he always was:
a midwestern boy of remarkable candor, quick wits, a pleasant touch of self-deprecating
humor, and an unflagging devotion to the traditions and courtesies of golf.
All that is formidable about him is what has put him where he is:
The unwavering industry to improve his game. His refusal to know that he knows.
His iron self-discipline. And the really terrifying self-confidence,
which rarely nowadays sharpens into cockiness,
of a golfer who is uncomfortable only when he is leading a tournament.
He is probably the only great golfer alive — or dead — who could
honestly have meant what he said to an English friend who casually asked him
what was his idea of the most rousing prospect in golf:
'Three holes to go, and you need two pars and a birdie to win.'"

—ALISTAIR COOKE
The New York Times Sunday Magazine, 1972

JACK NICKLAUS
SIMPLY THE BEST!

By Martin Davis

INTRODUCTIONS BY ARNOLD PALMER, GARY PLAYER, LEE TREVINO AND TOM WATSON ■ "HE ALWAYS MADE THE PUTT" BY DAVE ANDERSON, "TAKING PRECAUTIONS" BY DAN JENKINS AND "ALWAYS A PRESENCE" BY JACK WHITAKER ■ SWING ANALYSIS BY JIM FLICK ■ EDITED BY MYRA GELBAND

The American Golfer, Inc. • 200 Railroad Avenue • Greenwich, Connecticut 06830
tel 203-862-9720 • fax 203-862-9724 • e-mail imd@aol.com

Table of Contents

*Jack Nicklaus and his son, Jackie, during the final
round of the 1986 Masters.*

SIMPLY THE BEST!

By Martin Davis

One of the parlor games in golf is discussing the relative merits of the great golfers who have played at the very highest levels — Old Tom Morris, Young Tom, Ted Ray, the Great Triumverate of Harry Vardon, J.H. Taylor and James Braid, Gene Sarazen, Byron Nelson, Patty Berg, Babe Zaharias, Mickey Wright, Arnold Palmer, Gary Player, Lee Trevino, Tom Watson.

In golf we've been fortunate to suffer from an abundance of riches.

But when the discussion falls to who was the greatest player ever, three names invariably percolate to the top of the list — Bobby Jones, Ben Hogan and Jack Nicklaus.

In his book *Golf Between Two Wars*, Bernard Darwin refers to Bobby Jones, as "… the greatest of them all," and a case can be made for Jones heading the list. He was a life-long amateur who won 13 major golf tournaments in an eight-year period, including five U.S. Amateurs, four U.S. Opens, three British Opens and one British Amateur. Jones finished either first or second in every major he entered from the time he won his first in 1923 until he retired in 1930 an astonishing 80% of the time. In 1930 Jones captured the Grand Slam — then the two Amateur and the two Open championships of the major golf-playing nations, the United States and Great Britain — and fueled a fervor for the game that had begun with Francis Ouimet's victory in the 1913 U.S. Open against Vardon and Ray. It was such a monumental achievement that George Trevor of *The New York Sun* grandly called it "… the impregnable quadrilateral."

An equally strong case can be made for Ben Hogan, a winner of four U.S. Opens (some say five), two Masters, two PGAs and the only British Open he played in. Equally amazing, Hogan finished in the top 10 of each and every U.S. Open he played from the time he won his first tournament as a professional in 1940 to what was arguably his last hurrah in the 1960 Open. It is axiomatic in golf circles to say that the Hogan swing is the gold standard, even to this very day.

And then there's one Jack William Nicklaus, clearly the most dominating player — over a longer period of time — that the game has ever known. He not only won each of the professional Grand Slam tournaments once, he won them at least three times each. He dominated golf, as no one had ever done, for a span of almost 25 years.

All three set the standard of play by dominating their respective eras more completely than anyone ever had — Jones in the 1920s, Hogan in the late 1940s and early 1950s, and Jack from the early 1960s all the way up to the early 1980s.

Jones in 1930 with his Grand Slam trophies, from left: British Open, U.S. Amateur, British Amateur and U.S. Open.

Ben Hogan with a replica of the U.S. Open trophy and his championship medals.

Jack with the U.S. Amateur trophy in 1961. It was his second win in the Amateur and his second major.

Stewart Maiden,
also known as
"Kiltie the
Kingmaker",
with his standout
student Bob Jones.

Jack Grout keeps
an eye on his
prized pupil
Jack Nicklaus.

Interestingly, there are many similarities — some obvious, others surprising — among these titans of the game, perhaps more than have been widely recognized.

It goes without saying that each possessed rare physical ability and a finely honed technique. Jones was a great driver of the ball and became a superb putter. Hogan was perhaps the finest striker of the ball to this very day, and, at least in his prime, a deadly short putter and a fine lag putter. As for Jack, his driving was consistently both long and accurate — a lethal combination — his soaring long iron play was about the best ever and his putting was simply incredible, especially under the glare of a big tournament.

Each of the three had significant teachers with definitive ideas on what was important. Bob Jones was taught by East Lake's professional, Stewart Maiden, a diminutive and dour Scot. Hogan, most significantly, learned to weaken his grip and thus fade the ball, from teaching and tournament professional Henry Picard. Jack was taught by Jack Grout, who had been an assistant under Picard.

Henry Picard, in 1939, adjusts Ben Hogan's grip to a "weaker" one, so as to encourage a predominant fade.

Curiously, each of the three can trace the basic swing philosophy they were taught back to a common innovator and teacher of the golf swing: Alex Morrison. Maiden subscribed to much of what Morrison taught. Henry Picard spent eight days learning Morrison's swing fundamentals, hitting so many balls while practicing the distinctive ankle roll that is a key feature of the Morrison philosophy that his feet bled. And Jack Grout learned the basic Morrison principals firsthand from Picard.

In their salad days, the attitude of their competitors and the fans, as well, was that each man was the one to beat. When Jones played in the 1920s, the newspapers referred to him as Emperor Jones and would tout his play as "Jones against the field." (Such was his dominance that when the two greatest professionals of the era, Walter Hagen and Gene Sarazen, played in a major against Jones, neither finished better than 10th.) When Hogan played, all eyes were riveted intently on him and for several sublime years — from 1948 to 1953 — Hogan dominated, winning eight of the 10 majors he played in. When Jack competed, he was by far the odds-on favorite.

Jack and his
father, Charlie,
celebrate after
the 1965 Masters.

Each was strongly influenced by his father — Jones and Nicklaus in a highly positive fashion, Hogan perhaps more darkly, yet each was motivated by that relationship.

All three players are defined by their success in the U.S. Open, each officially winning four — the only players in the modern era to do so. (Willie Anderson, a Scottish pro, won four at the turn of the century in the early days of the game.)

Bob Jones and his
father celebrate
after the 1927
British Open.

Uniquely, each can also be defined by their long iron shots at critical times in major championships. Recall Jones's long iron out of the sand at Lytham in 1926 to win his first British Open (one Scottish writer called it "… the greatest shot in the history of British golf") or another off a sandy lie in the playoff at Inwood to set up his first national championship in 1923. Or Hogan's 1-iron to the 72nd hole at Merion in 1950, a scene that frames the most famous photograph in golf and perhaps the greatest comeback in the history of not

only golf, but in all of sport. Then there are Jack's thrilling long-iron shots in the final rounds in winning the biggest tournaments — the 1-iron which hit the flagstick on the par-3 17th hole at Pebble Beach in the 1972 U.S. Open; another 1-iron on the 15th at

> *"Jack's basic numbers are easy to remember. It's just a straight arithmetic progression — 1, 2, 3, 4, 5, 6, 7 — as in one NCAA Championship, two U.S. Amateurs, three British Opens, four U.S. Opens, five PGAs, six Masters and a member of seven winning Ryder Cup teams."*

Augusta in 1975; and yet another 1-iron 230 yards uphill to 22 feet on the 72nd hole at Baltusrol in 1967 for birdie and the Open scoring record; and finally a 4-iron, also at Augusta's 15th, in setting up his eagle putt in the 1986 Masters.

In an odd historical coincidence, dear old Merion played a significant role in each of their careers — Jones playing in his first national Open at age 16 with Harry Vardon and then in closing out the Grand Slam in 1930 on the 11th hole; Hogan's 1-iron on the 18th hole; and Jack's stupendous record-shattering play in the 1960 World Team Amateur and his play in the 1971 Open.

But for all these similarities, Jack's exploits eclipse those of the sainted Bobby Jones and the venerated Ben Hogan.

On even cursory investigation, Jack's record is over-whelming, simply mind numbing, so much so that if Frank Merriwell had written one of his novels based on Jack's career, it would have been dismissed as too fanciful.

Jack's basic numbers are easy to remember. It's just a straight arithmetic progression — 1, 2, 3, 4, 5, 6, 7 — as in one NCAA Championship, two U.S. Amateurs, three British Opens, four U.S. Opens, five PGAs, six Masters and a member of seven winning Ryder Cup teams. Then there are the 19 second-place finishes in the majors, the 73

Bob Jones comes out of the sand with a long iron on the 17th hole of the final round of the 1926 British Open. This shot has been referred to as "... the greatest shot in the history of British golf."

PGA Tour wins, the 11 international victories and one of the most enviable records in the Ryder Cup, 17-8-3, despite only playing in six Ryder Cup Matches.

So just what made Jack great, the very best of all time?

Start with great physical ability and superb athletic talent. Add to that a golf swing honed at an early age by Jack Grout. But many aspiring golfers — and successful ones, too — have also had superior physical talent, marvelous swings and fine coaching.

Yet Jack had something more. Something much more. It seems that all the truly greats do. It's something the chroniclers of sport call strength of mind — the ability to concentrate on the task at hand, the ability to set a course of action, a strategy to win, and then stick with it. It was his burning desire to succeed, coupled with his strategic thinking, that drove him to unbelievable heights. Jones had it, Hogan did, too, but Jack was able to sustain his mental toughness for a longer period of time.

Bob Jones once said, "Tournament golf is played in a five inch space. The space between your ears." And Jack played in this small space better than anyone else. He had the uncommon ability to close everything else out — concentrate on the task at hand — and to make adjustments in his swing and his strategy during a championship.

Dr. Joseph Parent, a noted sports psychologist and author, believes that Jack's mental prowess manifested itself in his inner knowledge of what he could accomplish, and conversely, the limits of his capabilities. This, along with his innate ability to both visualize shots (what Jack called "going to the movies") and not get down on himself when things did not go well on the golf course, combined to make Jack's mental game one of his great strengths.

> "*Bob Jones once said, 'Tournament golf is played in a five inch space. The space between your ears'. And Jack played in this small space better than anyone else.*"

One wag once said that Jack was a combination of Secretariat and Einstein — the great athlete combined with the great intellect — a tremendous winning combination. This analogy is apt.

Jack's only interest was in competing, testing himself, and winning. Second place was really of no interest. Mention the 19 second-place finishes in the majors — a record almost certain never to be broken — and he has little interest.

Johnny Miller tells a story that places Jack's golf intellect in perspective. Miller once asked Jack why he won the majority of his major championships by what seemed to be only a couple of strokes. Jack's answer was telling — he replied that his overarching strategy was to stay around the lead through the first 3½ rounds, so that he was in a position to win over the last nine holes. Jack wanted to let the other competitors play themselves out of the tournament, let them make the mistakes. In other words, he played strategically over the first three days, seldom going for difficult pins or charging putts, until the situation presented itself.

A look at the data clearly confirms Miller's observation. Jack won by up to three shots in 12 of his 18 professional majors and by four in three others, while only three were runaways. (In hindsight, Miller — an aggressive player who always seemed to go for difficult pins and charge putts — believes that if he had seriously adopted and employed Jack's strategic thinking, he would have won several more majors. Perhaps so.)

JACK'S MARGIN OF VICTORY IN THE MAJORS

The Masters	The U.S. Open	The British Open	The PGA
1963 – 1 stroke	1962 – Playoff	1966 – 1 stroke	1963 – 2 strokes
1965 – 9 strokes	1967 – 4 strokes	1970 – Playoff	1971 – 2 strokes
1966 – Playoff	1972 – 3 strokes	1978 – 2 strokes	1973 – 4 strokes
1972 – 3 strokes	1980 – 4 strokes		1975 – 5 strokes
1975 – 1 stroke			1980 – 7 strokes
1986 – 1 stroke			

Jack didn't win all the time — far from it — but much more so than anyone else ever has. Jack was a sportsman in the truest sense of the word. When he gave his all, in perhaps the greatest golf tournaments ever played — against Trevino at Merion in 1971 and again in 1972 at Muirfield, and then against Watson in 1977 at Turnberry and again at Pebble Beach in 1982 — and disappointingly came up short, he was the consummate sportsman because, in finishing second, he knew that he gave his maximum effort and he graciously congratulated his rival.

Jack won over a longer period of time of anyone who ever played a game — Satchel Paige excepted — against the finest group of players who won more major championships and more regular PGA Tour events than anyone before or since.

The breadth of players Jack played against is broad indeed, deeper than anyone else who has ever competed. Over the 27 years he dominated the golf world — from the 1960 Open, where he finished second as an amateur to Arnold Palmer, to his victory at the Masters in 1986 — Jack competed successfully against a panoply of golf history. It was the strongest group of competitors, with the greatest competitive records, any player in the history of the game has come up against.

Consider whom he competed against and the majors they won: Ben Hogan and Sam Snead (at the end of their careers, but still competitive in several majors with Jack), Arnold Palmer, Gary Player, Billy Casper, Lee Trevino, Raymond Floyd, Tom Watson, Hale Irwin, Johnny Miller, Seve Ballesteros and Greg Norman, all at the height of their careers. Among them there's a total of 65 professional major championships and a whopping 451 PGA Tour victories.

The Bob Jones Award presented by the USGA honors sportsmanship in golf. Jack received the award in 1975.

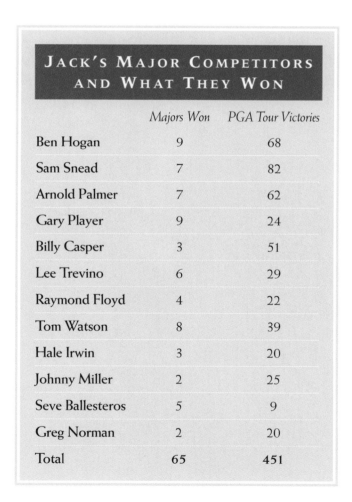

JACK'S MAJOR COMPETITORS AND WHAT THEY WON

	Majors Won	PGA Tour Victories
Ben Hogan	9	68
Sam Snead	7	82
Arnold Palmer	7	62
Gary Player	9	24
Billy Casper	3	51
Lee Trevino	6	29
Raymond Floyd	4	22
Tom Watson	8	39
Hale Irwin	3	20
Johnny Miller	2	25
Seve Ballesteros	5	9
Greg Norman	2	20
Total	65	451

Simply said, Jack won against the best players, with the most victories in the majors, at the most storied venues in the game, over the longest period of time. And he did it time and time again.

Without doubt, I think it is safe to say that Jack is simply the best. The best ever.

An Extraordinary Talent

You didn't have to be blessed with ESP to know that the kid was an extraordinary talent on the rise. You couldn't be rash enough to predict how high he might fly, but you knew it would be high. Clearly, this was someone special. If he had been a violinist, you knew you would see him on the concert stage. If he had been an artist, you knew his canvases would be in an exhibition some day soon. There is something that marks such talents. In sports, they are called "can't-misses." Of course, if there's one thing you learn it's that you have to restrain yourself in these things. The "can't-misses" sometimes miss horribly, sad to say. Goodness only knows what happens to them. Golf has an old saying: "The woods are full of long-hitters." I'd like to borrow from that truism and say the woods are also full of young can't-misses. But sometimes you are just so certain, and this was one of those times. And so I had no qualms about putting a big "can't-miss" stamp on this kid. That's how sure I was.

Jack Nicklaus was a hefty teenager when I first met him. It was in the late 1950s in Athens, Ohio, at an exhibition match honoring my good friend Dow Finsterwald, a hometown hero. We had already heard the tales about this big-hitting kid from Columbus. It seems that everyone is attracted by power, and that's what you heard about mostly, his power. About how he was hitting it farther than many touring pros. Then I saw for myself. They held a long-driving contest at the Finsterwald outing. Understand — I was one of the longer hitters on tour at the time, and I was about 10 years older than this teen-ager. I did out-drive him, but not by much.

Speaking of Jack Nicklaus the golfer, I'd have to say that if all there was to him was raw power, then we probably wouldn't have heard much more about him. He'd probably still be out in the woods with that crowd of other long-hitters. But he is worlds away from that. There is so much more to him as a golfer, as we have seen over the decades that have passed too fast. Let me sum up by saying — how about the pin-point irons? The deadly putting, almost from another world? Then oddly enough, Jack had perhaps just a so-so wedge. That was a running joke: His short game was weak because he didn't get to exercise it very much. His long game had already put him on the green, usually comfortably within birdie range. But there was one other thing about Jack and his game that impressed me more than anything he could do with his clubs. And the fans could never see it.

Jack and I were partners in the Finsterwald exhibition, and it was there — not on the practice tee — where I got my first real sense of where this kid was heading. He had the

By
Arnold Palmer
with
*Marino
Parascenzo*

Jack gets his first green jacket and a pat on the back from Arnold, the 1962 champion, after winning the 1963 Masters.

Even as a youngster, Jack's enormous power was evident.

BILL FOLEY-JACK NICKLAUS MUSEUM

game, all right. But what really set Jack apart had nothing to do with the mechanics of golf. It was his mind. As I've said many times, Jack was a different animal altogether, unlike any I had ever chased. It was uncanny how he could concentrate on the task at hand. I've never seen anyone who could stay focused the way he did. It was almost eerie. It was as though nothing else, and no one else, mattered. He was like a battlefield surgeon. I believe it was this quality that drove his great talent and made him such a giant of our game.

> "*Jack was always a gentleman, always courteous and friendly. And thanks to his father's influence, he always respected the traditions of the game. I could sense these things in him from the first time I met him, when he was just a youngster.*"

It came so easily to him, it was so natural for him, that you almost didn't notice it at first. I got a glimpse of it at the Finsterwald outing. I got a better look when I won the 1960 U.S. Open at Cherry Hills and Jack finished second as a 20-year-old amateur. But I got my best look in those early days in the 1962 U.S. Open at Oakmont, under what were very adverse conditions for Jack. Oakmont was practically a home course for me, and so Arnie's Army — local and otherwise — had turned out in full combat voice. And things became something of an embarrassment for me. I always welcomed support from the galleries, as everyone does, but not at the expense of competitors. This time, the army became overzealous and went from rooting for me to rooting openly against Jack. I wanted to stop it, but how do you tell all those people along the fairways and around the greens to mind their manners? I wanted to beat Jack, certainly. But I didn't want a victory with an asterisk on it: *Gallery-aided. Not in the record book and certainly not in my memories.

The Big Three — Arnold, Gary and Jack — became golf's standard bearers.

It didn't come to that. Jack went on to beat me in a playoff, making that U.S. Open his first victory as a professional. And this was the odd thing: Jack has long insisted he never heard the rude behavior of the fans. I'd always thought he was just being polite, but eventually I came to believe him. I believe he really did shut out distractions. But if you know Jack, you know that even if he had lost, he wouldn't have blamed the army.

Jack was always a gentleman, always courteous and friendly. And thanks to his father's influence, he always respected the traditions of the game. I could sense these things in him from the first time I met him, when he was just a youngster. I grew to know him better in a few tournaments where we saw each other, most notably that 1962 U.S. Open. Then I got to know him much, much better personally in 1964, when he and Gary Player and I were filming "Big Three Golf" for television. Things were so much more informal than in tournaments, and we all got to know each other better, and I liked Jack even more. That didn't mean I didn't want to beat him — him and Gary and all the rest.

A good deal has been made of the rivalry between Jack and me. It always amazes me that people are shocked to discover we were not like childhood playmates on the golf course. It should be obvious that the golf course was not a kiddies' playground, not for Jack and me, and not for any of the golfers. I've said it many times — Jack was my greatest competition in golf, both as a player and later in business. And Jack also has said many times that he felt the same way about me. Later, when I had passed my peak years, Jack felt the same about Johnny Miller and other younger players challenging him. This shouldn't surprise anyone. It's the way of life. But the competition has never blunted my admiration for Jack.

As our careers headed into the sunset years, first mine and later Jack's, that long-standing admiration bloomed into a close friendship. The two of us, often with Gary Player in a reunion of the so-called Big Three, have played a lot of tournament golf together in our senior years because it was thought it would be so enjoyable for the fans. Perhaps that was the case. But no one enjoyed it more than I did. We still are strong competitors, but now principally in our golf course design companies.

As partners, Jack and Arnold won the Canada Cup/World Cup three times and two other team championships.

To that, let me add that if we were still playing competitively, nothing would have changed. It would still be the same for me with our other great friends — Gary Player and Lee Trevino and all the rest. We all want to win.

Let me say this, too. I can't imagine golf without Jack Nicklaus. They are one and the same. If Jack had never picked up a golf club, it would still have been a great pleasure and honor just to call him my friend. But thank goodness for us and for our game, Jack did pick up a club.

The friendship between Arnold and Jack remains deep after nearly 50 years.

A GREAT COMPETITOR

*By
Gary Player*

We all recognize what a great golfer Jack Nicklaus was, but what probably impresses me most about him is what an outstanding family man he has always been, even when he was in the middle of winning tournaments.

It would be no surprise to see him rushing off to support one of his children in a sporting event somewhere in the country, even during a tournament — such was his desire to be a good father to his five children and husband to his wonderful wife, Barbara.

But, make no mistake, he was a fun guy to be around, too, and a great competitor. I remember once we were playing in the Australian Open together and staying at the same hotel. In the first round, Jack shot a magnificent 66, but I had a sparkling round where everything just went right and ended up with a 62. In the car on the way back to the hotel Jack asked, "How can I shoot 66 and be four shots behind you? Tomorrow I'm gonna whip that skinny butt of yours."

Well, the next day he went out and shot 63 to my 70. All of a sudden I was at 132 after 36 holes and three shots behind. In the car back to the hotel that day, I, of course, told him that I was going to whip his big butt the following day.

The next day we're playing and I miss a putt on the ninth for 28, then eagle the 10th. Next thing, Jack's caddie comes over from the hole behind to ask what my score was and I tell him that I'm 10 under. He goes away, and comes back a little later saying Jack wanted to know what my score was for the day, not for the tournament! Those were the days before big electronic scoreboards all over the course, but such was the friendly needle between Jack and myself that, even in the middle of a round, he wanted to find out how I was going just because of our friendly rivalry. I went on to shoot 62 and managed to beat Jack and win the tournament.

There was another time when Jack, Arnold Palmer and I were in Canada playing the Canadian Open. I remember we were sitting in our hotel after play one day with nothing to do. There was a big pitcher of iced tea on the table along with a few beers. For some reason, I thought it would be quite funny to shake up one of the beers and squirt it at Jack. Jack thought that was quite amusing, and the next thing you know he retaliated by drenching Arnold and me with the pitcher of iced tea. Boy, did we make a mess, but we were in fits of giggles.

At the 1975 Masters Jack collects the fifth of his green jackets from Gary, the 1974 champion.

ASSOCIATED PRESS

As Presidents Cup captains, Gary and Jack continue to compete against one another.

The suite we were in was in a terrible mess. We tidied up as best we could and the next day we trooped off to apologize to the manager and offer to make good on any damages. The manager was very good-natured about it all, realizing that we were just having fun.

> *"I have often referred to Jack as the greatest loser in golf. By that I mean he was as gracious in defeat as he was in victory — a sign of a great competitor. . . ."*

Over the years the three of us have spent quite a lot of time together, and we were all keen on promoting the game of golf, which took us to all corners of the globe. Even though we took our playing quite seriously, we really had some fun times together along the way.

In 1971 I stayed with Jack and Barbara at their home in Florida during the PGA Championship at PGA National. Going into the last round, Jack was one shot ahead of me and we were both playing exceptionally well. That morning Barbara had made scrambled eggs for breakfast and had put two plates on the table — one for me and one for Jack. I was already sitting at the breakfast table, while Jack was puttering around in another room. As Barbara turned her back, I quickly swapped the plates, just in case she had put something in my eggs so that I couldn't beat Jack. After we finished breakfast I told her what I did — we still laugh about that today!

It was very special growing up and playing in that era, having Jack as a fellow competitor, and I am proud to have been able to win tournaments playing among the likes of Jack, Arnold, Tom Watson and Lee Trevino.

I believe that Jack was the greatest player of his time, without a doubt. To compare him to players of different eras is, to me, a pointless exercise. Whether his record of 18 major championships is ever overtaken remains to be seen and, if it is, it will never make his remarkable achievements any less astonishing.

One happy consequence of Jack's recent retirement from playing competitive golf on the Senior circuit is that it has allowed him to focus his energies on his golf course design business and he is a wonderful designer. I have always said that to be able to design a golf course and leave something for future generations is a thrill and I am sure that Jack believes the same thing.

I have often referred to Jack as the greatest loser in golf. By that I mean he was as gracious in defeat as he was in victory — a sign of a great

Captains Nicklaus and Player agree to a tie at the 2003 Presidents Cup.

competitor, something which I have always respected in him. He would rather I refer to him as a gracious loser, but I know the former phrase winds him up, so for now we will stick to that.

The 2003 Presidents Cup played at The Links at Fancourt, in South Africa, was especially noteworthy for me. As a South African, I had always had to watch from a distance as years of Ryder Cup matches involving my fellow U.S. and British professionals took place. So to be appointed captain of the International Team for the Presidents Cup was an honor. Add to that the fact that the matches took place in my home country, on a course I had the privilege of designing, and you can understand how special an occasion it was. But most special was the fact that my old friend and rival Jack Nicklaus was my opposing captain, leading the U.S. side for the second time.

The Presidents Cup has always been played in a magnificent spirit. Under the leadership of Jack, the U.S. side played exactly the way we all believe golf matches should be played — sportsmanship is paramount, without forgetting the reason for being there, which is to win. When our matches were tied after regulation play and the playoff between Ernie Els and Tiger Woods was headed for darkness, it came as no surprise that Captain Nicklaus agreed to share the cup, because that is who he is: sporting and fair to the end. What a wonderful result. To me, those were among the most gratifying moments of my golfing career — and I did not even have a golf club in my hand.

I have enjoyed every moment with Jack on the golf course, but most important, I have enjoyed his friendship — a friendship that has lasted for decades. A friendship that, God willing, will continue for decades to come.

The Big Three make their first appearance at the 1962 World Series of Golf, at Firestone Country Club.

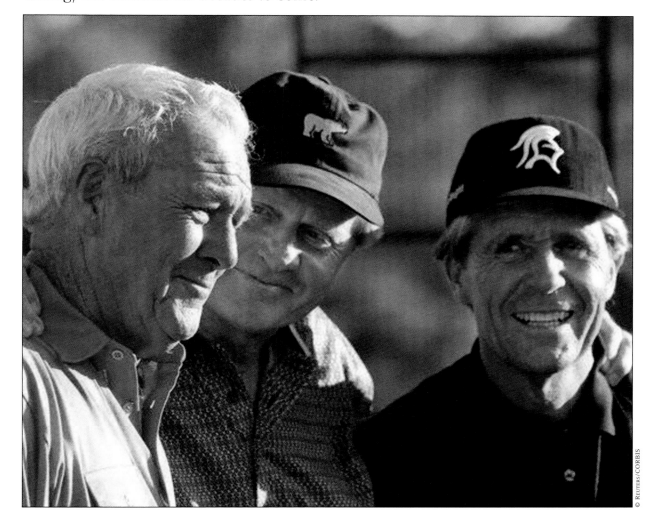

With 13 green jackets among them, the Big Three reunite for the first round of the 2000 Masters.

THE ULTIMATE MEASURE

*By
Lee Trevino
with
Jaime Diaz*

s I look back, I was so fortunate to go head-to-head against Jack Nicklaus in his absolute prime. I saw — like maybe no one else — history's best player at his very best.

Everyone always talks about how good Jack was mentally, but I want to tell you that physically, he was a tremendous athlete. He had size and strength and speed and great coordination. He was able to take that 42½-inch driver with a small 11-degree persimmon head, and the old balls, and turn those big hips and hit it 300 yards, which was just massive in our heyday. I tell people all the time that if you put a young Nicklaus in today's equipment, he would hit the ball 400 yards. He'd be chipping back to some of those greens.

He used all that ability with his long irons, too. It didn't matter how hard the greens were, because Jack could hit it so high and land it so soft. That was his biggest weapon at the majors. He was also the finest putter I ever saw. I'm not just talking about all those big putts he made. I mean year in year out, consistently brilliant putting. And never once did I see him get yippy on short ones. If the man had had a good wedge game, he would have won 40 majors. I'm serious.

Jack's win in the 1986 Masters said everything about him. That was pure greatness. At 46, Jack still had a little something extra. Which just tells you how much extra he started with. Probably more than anybody ever had.

I had some success against Jack in part because I never, ever thought I was as good as he was. But I also knew if my mind was right and I was playing my kind of course, I could stay close to him and maybe find a way to nip him.

I was lucky because my mind was usually right against Jack. For one thing, I got inspired playing against him. From where I came from, I always felt like I had won just by having the chance to play against him.

Also, I wanted to measure myself. See, until I got on the PGA Tour I never had a gauge. I never played amateur golf. Before I got on tour in my late 20s, I had only watched a few really top pros and played against very few of them. Sure, a lot of people around Dallas and El Paso told me I had talent, but to me that wasn't proof. That's why I practiced so much — probably too much — because I thought if I didn't, I'd fail. But I knew Jack was the real thing, the ultimate measure, and I really got up when we played in the same tournament, and especially when we played together. It always seemed to bring out the best in me.

Finally, I put myself in the underdog role. I'd learned that lowering other people's

ASSOCIATED PRESS

Lee and Jack before their 18-hole playoff at Merion, in which Lee prevailed.

Lee was ever the merry prankster, here famously messing around with a rubber snake at the 1971 U.S. Open at Merion.

expectations — and maybe my own — could take the pressure off. Against Jack, I always told everyone I was just happy to be able to compete against the best. I tried to make it like I had nothing to lose because I'd already won. Inside, I always felt like I had a chance, but I knew I had a better chance if I let myself relax.

> "*Honestly, I don't think my mind games ever had any effect on Jack. He's always been too solid and confident for that. That's why I always felt comfortable kidding him and messing with him. . . ."*

That's the way I approached my showdown with Jack at the 1971 U.S. Open at Merion. The golf gods shined on me that week. I loved that little course, I was playing well, and the greens were soft, which helped me hit my low-flighted irons at the pins. I got lucky when Jack barely missed a 12 footer for birdie on the last hole of regulation — it was just the kind of putt he always made. I felt like I was playing with house money, and when I beat him 68 to 71 the next day, that was the biggest thrill of my career. By the way, that rubber snake didn't scare Jack. I bogeyed the first hole, he parred it. Starting out, I was the nervous one.

Honestly, I don't think my mind games ever had any effect on Jack. He's always been too solid and confident for that. That's why I always felt comfortable kidding him and messing with him, whether it was about his swing or how slow he played or how he went from big boy to fashion model. I knew Jack would laugh and never take it as gamesmanship.

Nothing ever bothered him on the golf course. He had such a strong will that he always played his own game at his own pace. He'd stare at the target so long before pulling the trigger that we thought he'd fallen asleep. But when he was ready, he was readier than anyone's ever been. To make up for his slowness, he walked his playing partners into the ground. In the playoff at Merion, I tried to keep up because I needed somebody to talk to. But after three holes I was out of breath and I hung back the rest of the day. If you had put Jack on one of those treadmills we all use, he would have pulled about a 4.2. Today we call that speedwalking.

Jack was a meticulous course manager, almost to a fault. I remember playing with him in the final group at the 1974 PGA at Tanglewood. On the 17th, I three-putted for bogey, so instead of having a cushion on the last hole, now I'm sweating. It was a perfect time to jump on a guy, and if Jack had pulled out that driver and bombed it 300 and something, I probably would have fainted. Instead, he stuck to his game plan and hit his regular 3-wood in the fairway. I've got to say it relieved me, and I hit a good drive past him and held on to win.

See, even in the heat of battle there was something generous about Jack. We all saw it when he gave Tony Jacklin that putt in the 1969 Ryder Cup. At the very top of golf, you don't see too many guys willing to share or give up an edge. Jack was different. In early 1971, I was having some problems dealing with success, running around chasing money and getting burned out. One day in the locker room at Doral he asked me if I had a second to talk, and he sat me down. "Go ahead," he said, "keep clowning. I hope you never find out how good you are."

That meant the world to me. It was Jack who gave me what I needed most — the feeling that I really belonged. I started believing in myself more and I played the best golf of my life. Jack used to joke after I clipped him in a couple of majors in the next few years that he wished he'd kept his mouth shut, but I know he'd do the same thing again. Jack was such a champion that he always wanted your best. The better you played, the more he liked it. For him, that challenge was fun.

Jack could have been even better — won more majors, set more records. But rather than play more or practice more, he chose to spend more of his time with his family.

I benefited in two ways. In the short term, I won the Vardon Trophy five times, but I tell people at least four of them belong to Jack. He just never played enough rounds to qualify.

In the long term, Jack helped me be a better father. I remember when we were teamed up in the 1971 World Cup at PGA National in Palm Beach Gardens. After one of our practice rounds I said, "Man, we got to hit some balls." He said, "No, let's go." So I got in his car and we drove up A1A to watch one of his son Jackie's pee-wee football games. It made me think Charlie Nicklaus must have been a helluva dad, because his son sure was. I never knew my own father, and I learned to be a parent the hard way. But I've gained more appreciation for Jack's example as my wife and I have raised my youngest children, Daniel and Olivia.

I was so honored when Jack and Barbara made me the honoree of the Memorial Tournament in 2004. I remember when we were walking out to the podium and I said to Jack, "You go first. I was always following you." And he said, "Maybe, but you went past me a lot of times."

Moments like that are special. It means a great deal to me that Jack called me the most difficult of his contemporaries to beat, but I'm more proud that Jack Nicklaus is my friend. As much as I've always respected him as a golfer, I respect him even more as a man.

USGA President Hord Hardin presents the 1968 U.S. Open trophy to Trevino, at Oak Hill, as runner-up Nicklaus looks on.

"THIS IS WHAT IT'S ALL ABOUT"

By Tom Watson

When I was a boy of six, three events in my life combined to make golf my constant companion from then on.

The first event was the day my father presented me with two cut-down hickory-shafted clubs, one a 3-wood, the other a 5-iron. Those two clubs, along with a lot of fatherly instruction early on, introduced me to my future profession.

The second event was when my mother gave me my first "big book" to read, *All About Dinosaurs*. Reading opened up new worlds — not only of ancient beasts, and our universe, but also the history of golf's greatest players and moments through books and magazines such as *Down the Fairway* and *Golf World*.

Also unbeknownst to me as a six-year-old, the third event occurred, which I only read about four years later in *Golf World*. A story written about the then-current National Amateur champion, Jack Nicklaus, included a chronology of Jack's golfing accomplishments. What caught my attention was the fact that Jack had won the Ohio Open when he was 16 years old. To a highly competitive 10-year-old (me) that was a bigger victory than his National Amateur, because he not only beat Ohio's best amateurs, but he also beat its best professionals.

Jack turned professional after he took his second National Amateur championship in 1961, and I have to admit that I, along with just about every golfer I knew, was an Arnold Palmer fan. When Jack and Arnie tied after 72 holes to force a play-off in the 1962 National Open at Oakmont, we all waited in anticipation for our hero, Arnie, to beat the long-hitting kid with his flying right elbow (my dad's critical observation). In what was one of the most agonizing and disappointing Sunday afternoons of watching golf on television, I saw Jack handily beat my hero for his first professional victory. The proverbial Casey had struck out!

Looking back on that day, I see that Oakmont's stage was where the lead roles in the world of professional golf started to change. By 1968, Jack was the lone star, after thoroughly taking over as the best in the game with Arnie as best supporting actor.

I met Jack for the first time in 1966 when I was invited as a 16-year-old to play in an exhibition with him at Topeka Country Club. Watching him on that cold, windy March day, hitting high fades with his long irons and woods, I was inspired to copy his method. With a lot of help from my teacher, Stan Thirsk, I worked on emulating Jack's wide takeaway, steep backswing, and powerful lower leg drive on the downswing. The resulting left-to-right elevated ball flight proved to be

With Watson's longtime caddie, Bruce Edwards, looking on, Jack, runner-up, graciously greets Tom at the finish of the 1982 U.S. Open at Pebble Beach.

Jack congratulates Tom on winning the 1977 British Open.

GETTY IMAGES

one of the most important changes I ever made to my golf swing.

In 1971, I made my decision to pursue professional golf as my career. In making that decision, I asked the advice of a variety of people, and notably one question to a number of the local Kansas City golf professionals: What one thing should I do to ensure whatever success I was to achieve? Everyone responded with, "Watch the best players practice and compete. Learn from them."

So, I started watching the best, in particular Jack. I followed him in his large gallery for 18 holes in the 1972 Heritage Classic at Harbour Town Golf Links. And on that day I began to learn and understand firsthand what made Jack the best.

Probably the most valuable lesson on how to win was when I was paired with Jack in the final round of the 1974 Hawaiian Open. Frankly, Jack played horribly that day, but with just enough good shots at the right time, he came to the par-3 17th at Waialae Country Club with a one-shot lead. The flagstick was positioned back left in a

Jack congratulates Tom after Watson defeated him at Augusta in 1981.

ASSOCIATED PRESS

small area on the green, protected by difficult bunkers. Instead of aiming at the flagstick, he hit his ball to the front of the green with a shorter club, leaving himself a 50-foot putt, which he easily got down for a par. Walking up to the green, I asked him why he didn't go for the flagstick. His answer was, "The worst I can make is four, and that would still leave me tied for the lead, whereas going for the flag opened up a higher risk in making a five." The two lessons learned: Play the percentage shot when you don't have to be a hero, and you don't have to play your best to win a golf tournament.

In 1977, at the Open Championship at Turnberry, Jack and I had two short conversations during the final round — and I will always remember them. I was one stroke behind and waiting, seemingly forever, on the 14th tee for the huge crowd to reposition and cross in front of us. We were standing

> "*Jack, in my humble opinion, was simply the best at the mental aspect of the game. His great physical talent was a compliment to this mental focus — and resulting superiority.*"

next to each other, looking out towards Ailsa Craig through the dusty sunlight, when I quietly said to Jack in the silence, "This is what it's all about." "You bet it is," was Jack's response. Short, but it spoke volumes of the moment.

A miracle putt on the next hole, a birdie on 17, and a 7-iron to 2½ feet on the final hole left me one stroke ahead. Jack was on the edge of the 18th green with a must-make putt. As Jack has done so many times on a final hole in an important championship, he hit his long putt into the geometrical dead center of the cup for a birdie, forcing me to make that, now, "not-so-short" putt to win. When it went in, a rush I had never before experienced unleashed itself in a torrent of emotion. And as I thrust my arms into the air, I had but one thought — I just beat the best player in the game.

After a pause to let me savor that joyous moment, Jack took me by the shoulder and shook my hand. I put my arm around his waist, and as we walked off the green to the cheers of the crowd, he said, "I gave you my best shot, but it wasn't good enough." That was typical Jack: Class in the anguish of defeat.

In 1982, I won the tournament I most wanted to win, the National Open. The process of winning started as dreams I had when, as a Stanford student, I had the opportunity to play Pebble Beach a number of times (green fees were $10 back then). Usually, I played the course by myself and was first off in the morning, thanks to being in the good graces of Ray Parga, Pebble's starter. I always kept a strict score, and most of the time I pretended I was competing in the National Open and the man I had to beat was none other than Jack Nicklaus himself. The game within the game always started on the 15th tee, where I told myself I had to par in to win.

On that overcast June Sunday afternoon in 1982, there I stood on the 15th tee at Pebble Beach, playing in the National Open with a one-shot lead — on the man himself. 'Par in to win,' I told myself, just as I had years earlier, only this time it was for keeps.

It wasn't to be easy. After going par, bogey on 15 and 16, I was now in a tie. Then it happened — the chip-in for birdie at the par-3 17th, and to cap it off, another birdie on the final hole.

My dream — and all those solitary mornings playing the imaginary Jack Nicklaus — had literally been played out in real life. The National Open was mine. Looking back, I see now how much his formidable play, not only when he was on the course but even when he was not, inspired me in shaping my game and the way I think about golf.

From my first notice of Jack in that 1959 issue of *Golf World*, to playing with him in his final competitive round at the 2005 Open Championship at St. Andrews, I have been blessed with a warm and fruitful relationship with Jack and his family. During these many years, I have gratefully observed and learned from him so many fundamental lessons, both on and off the golf course, in victory and defeat.

Jack, in my humble opinion, was simply the best at the mental aspect of the game. His great physical talent was a compliment to this mental focus — and resulting superiority. Jack's understanding of how to play the game left little room for ambiguity or lack of confidence. I still see his greatest strength as his ability to break down a particular situation to its fundamental elements, understand the risk/reward of each element, then play, almost without fail, the proper shot.

This is why he is the greatest golfer to have graced our game.

Jack, it's been a privilege and a pleasure to have been in your company.

Comrades in arms as they walk off the 18th green at Turnberry.

The two adversaries and friends walk off the 18th green at St. Andrews in 2005, after Jack finishes his final round in the British Open.

Indian Wells, early 1960s.

He Always Made the Putt

...WELL, ALMOST ALWAYS

By Dave Anderson

For all of his endearing and enduring moments over nearly half a century, Jack Nicklaus will always be engraved onto the trophies of our minds for his farewell putt on the 18th green at St. Andrews during the 2005 British Open.

In a red sleeveless sweater over a white shirt, wearing navy blue slacks and white shoes, with his thinning blond hair fluttering in the breeze off the North Sea, he surveyed a 15-foot putt above the cup that meant nothing in the tournament but meant everything to him. He knew he would miss the 36-hole cut. He also knew he did not want to miss this putt. Not after the warm, loving applause unlike any other that had greeted this golfer unlike any other when he appeared on this stage. Not here at the home of golf where the game began six centuries ago. Not with his family and so many friends watching. Not with other pros watching. Not with Royal & Ancient blue blazers watching. And not with the millions who would watch it on television and the thousands who were watching from the nearby grandstands, homes, hotels, shops and the stone wall along the 18th hole in what the Scots call the Auld Grey Toon.

More important, not with himself watching.

Slowly and carefully he considered the putt's six-inch break to the right and the green's slightly downhill speed, then he glanced at the cup, looked down at the ball, hunched his shoulders into his familiar stance, set the blade of his putter, peeked at the cup again and tapped the ball. When the ball disappeared, 65-year-old Jack Nicklaus raised his putter and waved it as triumphantly as if he had won a fourth British Open.

"I knew that the hole would move where I hit it," he would say later with a laugh. "Every other putt going that way missed the hole, but this one gobbled it in."

Not that anyone should have been surprised that he made the putt. He always made the putt. Well, almost always. When the putt meant winning, especially a major, he made the putt much more often than not. Much more often than anybody else ever has. For all

Jack bids a fond farewell to adoring fans at St. Andrews.

Playing in his last major championship at the 2005 British Open, Jack Nicklaus acknowledges the crowd after his final putt on 18 at St. Andrews.

> *With his ability and quiet confidence, he never doubted that he would win when he was coming down the last holes of any tournament.*

his strength and length in the era before technology and exercise, for all the greens that he hit in regulation, he still had to make the important birdie or eagle putt at the important moment. And much more often than not, he made the putt.

"He was the best in the world when he needed it," Raymond Floyd once said.

One reason was the pleasure, rather than the fear, of the competitive pressure that tightened the throats of many of Jack's rivals, but never his throat, never his swing, never his putting stroke. He once described it as "an aggressive feeling rather than a pressure feeling," and he claimed that he never worried about it.

The bulky Jack in 1965 (inset) became the slimmer, stylish champion in 1970.

"You try to get the pressure on you," he said. "You want the pressure on you. You play with it. You enjoy it, because it means you're in contention, you have a chance to win."

Chisel those words on his tombstone. "It was me against myself," he once said, "and I embraced that." He changed his image from Fat Jack, the bulky rookie in a bucket hat who smoked, to the Golden Bear, the slender and stylish champion who did not smoke, but he never changed his mind-set as to what and how he thought about golf. With his ability and quiet confidence, he never doubted that he would win when he was coming down the last holes of any tournament.

"I just feel like I am the best player," he said when he indisputably was the best player. "I've got the best tools and I believe in myself more than the others believe in themselves. They are all scared of me — and I am going to take advantage of that. Just go do it."

Especially in the majors — the core of Jack Nicklaus's career as assembled here, after having written about him for four decades and having collected what originally appeared in *Golf Digest*, *Golf World*, *GOLF Magazine*, *Sports Illustrated* and other periodicals. As with all the truly great athletes, ego was an enhancing element in his success. Never loud or noisy, his ego was almost invisible but it flashed every so often when he didn't think anybody else was listening. He once was heard to mutter, "I've tried to separate myself from those other guys," meaning the every-day every-week pros out there. And after watching a television replay of his costly mistakes on the final holes of the 1974 Masters, he mumbled, "That's what some of those other guys do."

By "some of those other guys," he was not referring to Arnold Palmer, Gary Player, Billy Casper, Lee Trevino, Johnny Miller or Tom Watson — his prominent and primary rivals when he was at his best, all of whom beat him at one time or another. And he certainly wasn't referring to Tiger Woods, who later arrived with the

Golf's Big Three— Palmer, Player and Nicklaus — emerged in 1962.

talent and the time to someday surpass his record of 18 majors.

Jack recognized Tiger's potential the first time that he, along with Arnold Palmer, played a practice round with him at the 1995 Masters, when Tiger was a 19-year-old amateur as a Stanford University freshman. He predicted that Tiger would win 10 Masters, as many as he and Palmer had won — six for him, four for Arnold. By late 2001 he acknowledged that he would be "very surprised" if Tiger doesn't break his record of 18 majors. Not that more majors would necessarily put Tiger on a higher pedestal.

"Give them like equipment at the same age," said Hale Irwin, who won three U.S. Opens, "I'd still take Jack Nicklaus."

Following in their footsteps: In 1995 Nicklaus and Palmer play a practice round at the Masters with then-U.S. Amateur champion Tiger Woods.

When Jack was asked how he, at his best, would do against Tiger at his best in a hypothetical match, he didn't back off. "I don't know if I'd put my money on me or Tiger," he said. "Let's put it this way. I don't think he'd win every time."

As for "those other guys" among his contemporaries, some won a PGA Tour event every so often, even a major now and then, but none won anywhere near as many as he did. And whenever he won, it was invariably with his putting — the 12-footer on the 15th green and the 12-footer on the 17th green of the 1986 Masters that he won at age 46, the 20-footer on the 17th green of the 1980 U.S. Open at Baltusrol that he won in a four-day duel with Isao Aoki — to name three. Even with his record 19 second-place finishes in majors (48 in the top three, 56 in the top five and 73 in the top 10), only one missed makeable putt on the final holes still stings — the eight-footer on the 16th green of the 1972 British Open at Muirfield that cost him an 18-hole playoff with Lee Trevino and wrecked his bid for a Grand Slam.

Jack watches his eagle putt drop on the 15th hole in the last round of the 1986 Masters.

But asked once if there was a missed putt still stuck in his craw after all the years, Jack said, "Just one."

In the 1963 Bing Crosby, he was tied for the lead as he surveyed a 22-foot birdie putt above the hole on the 18th green at Pebble Beach. If he made it, he would take the lead. If he two-putted, he would be in a sudden-death playoff.

"I ran it by about four feet," he said, still annoyed more than four decades later. "Then I missed the four-footer."

On the four-footer, he misread where the Pacific Ocean was in relation to the green. He played the ball to break left toward Carmel Bay but he later realized that his putt went toward the ocean, which was straight ahead. His ball missed on the right edge. That three-putt green dropped him into a five-way tie for second, one stroke behind Billy Casper.

Jack celebrates his victory at the 1980 U.S. Open at Baltusrol.

Watson is jubilant after holing his wedge at the 17th green at Pebble Beach in the 1982 U.S. Open. That shot ended Jack's bid for a fifth Open title.

"I vowed never to do that again, and I never did," Jack recalled. "Never try to ram a 22-footer into the hole for a birdie and risk running it by, then missing that one."

But whenever he didn't win, he never griped, never had an alibi or an excuse. Usually because he had not lost the tournament so much as somebody else had won it.

When he thought he was assured of what would've been a record fifth U.S. Open at Pebble Beach in 1982 before Tom Watson snatched it by holing a wedge out of the rough alongside the 17th green, he just shook his head at his disappointment, smiled and put an arm around Watson near the scorer's tent. When his 66 in the final round of the 1972 British Open was a stroke short of forcing a playoff with Trevino, he turned what he has acknowledged as the "worst disappointment" of his career into thoughtful sympathy for a golf writer's disappointment. Had he won, he would have gone to the PGA Championship at Oakland Hills outside Detroit with a chance to complete the first pro Grand Slam. But as he settled into a chair on a platform in the press tent at Muirfield, none of the reporters knew how to break the silence until he did. Turning toward Norman Mair, the golf writer for *The Scotsman* in Edinburgh, he smiled.

"Well, Norman," he said softly, "I guess I cost you a trip to Detroit."

Nine years later, perhaps distracted by his 18-year-old son Steve flipping a car the night before on the Jack Nicklaus Freeway outside Columbus, he had the highest round in a major in his career, an opening 83 in the 1981 British Open at Royal St. George's. But that day he spoke to golf writers as easily as he had after his opening 63 had tied the U.S. Open record the year before at Baltusrol.

Despite his disappointment, Jack was quick to congratulate Watson at the 18th green at Pebble Beach.

"He fell asleep at the wheel," Jack said of his son. "He had a couple of beers and fell asleep."

Asked if Steve had been on his mind during the 83, he said, "Not really. I talked to him and he was fine. He just had a scratch on his leg. No excuses, thank you." And when there were no more questions about his 83 or his son Steve, he got up to leave and said, "I've an early starting time tomorrow." The next day, he shot 66 to make the cut.

"His mind," Paul Azinger once said, "is a cork jar full of positive thoughts."

His mind was always a silent factor in his success. Always positive thoughts, never negative thoughts. The day before the 1986 Masters began, he and four other winners at Augusta National were asked to name the toughest shot on the back nine on Sunday with the Masters at stake. Gary Player, Tom Watson and Seve Ballesteros agreed on the tee shot at the tricky 155-yard 12th hole. Arnold Palmer mentioned that if the wind forced you to lay up in front of the pond on the 500-yard 15th hole, then your delicate pitch to the green would be the toughest. But when Jack was asked for his choice, he politely refused.

> "No matter where you go in the golfing word," Bjorn said with a smile, "there's always a wall with Jack Nicklaus on it."

A final-round 65 propelled Jack to his sixth Masters win in 1986.

The 1926 U.S. Open was played at Scioto Country Club, Jack's home club in Columbus, Ohio.

"I don't want to be standing over a shot," he said calmly, "and thinking that I've said this is the toughest shot on the back nine."

No negative thoughts. Even at age 46 and not having won a PGA Tour event in nearly two years, Jack Nicklaus did not want negative thoughts sneaking into that cork jar of positive thoughts. Four strokes off the lead in the final round as he started the back nine after a birdie at the ninth hole, he birdied the 10th, 11th and 13th holes. After a big tee shot on the par-5 15th still left him more than 200 yards away, he had only a positive thought as he turned to his caddie, his oldest son Jackie, and said, "How far do you think a 3 will go here?" And he didn't mean a 3-iron.

"I think it will go a long way," Jackie said.

Moments later, everybody saw it, a solid 4-iron soaring high over the pond, thudding into the green and stopping slightly beyond and to the left of the flagstick, about 12 feet away. But to get the eagle 3 that he wanted and needed, he had to make the putt. He did. And after birdies at the 16th and 17th, he rolled a 50-foot putt to within inches on the 18th for a tap-in par. He had finished with an eagle, six birdies, two pars and a bogey (missing a six-foot par putt on the 12th) over the final 10 holes for 65 and his sixth green jacket. But for all the power and precision of the shots that set up that eagle and those six birdies, his putting had been the difference. If he had missed some of those putts, he would not have won the Masters at age 46.

Whenever he needed to, Jack Nicklaus always made the putt.

Not long after Jack's farewell putt at St. Andrews, Thomas Bjorn, the Danish pro, shot 63 at the 2005 PGA Championship at Baltusrol, tying the majors record shared by 19 others, including Jack, who had a 63 at Baltusrol while winning the 1980 U.S. Open. As Bjorn discussed his 63 that day, he mentioned

Bobby Jones (second from left) won the second of his four Opens at Scioto. Here he receives the trophy from USGA president William Fownes.

having noticed the framed scorecard of Jack's 63 and the larger-than-life photos of Jack on Baltusrol's walls.

"No matter where you go in the golfing word," Bjorn said with a smile, "there's always a wall with Jack Nicklaus on it."

In an earlier era, there was always a wall with Bobby Jones on it, especially at the Scioto Country Club in Columbus, Ohio where little Jack learned how Bobby Jones won the 1926 U.S. Open at Scioto.

"The members would talk about how Bobby Jones hit a 4-iron to the 18th," Jack recalled, "and how he never parred the ninth hole."

At that 1926 Open, Charlie Nicklaus, Jack's father, had trudged in the Jones gallery. The son of a railroad boilermaker, Charlie was a pharmacist who had worked his way through Ohio State and owned three drug stores in the Columbus area. Jack's mother, Helen, was the daughter of a railroad man. Charlie had earned 11 varsity letters in high

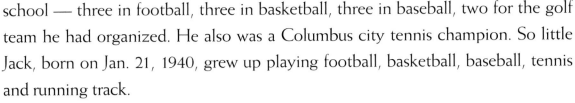

Jack's father, Charlie Nicklaus, was a pharmacist in Columbus and an avid golfer himself.

Helen and Charlie Nicklaus with their son, Jack, and daughter, Marilyn.

school — three in football, three in basketball, three in baseball, two for the golf team he had organized. He also was a Columbus city tennis champion. So little Jack, born on Jan. 21, 1940, grew up playing football, basketball, baseball, tennis and running track.

"If you're going to play football and basketball, you've got to be fast," his father told him. "You've got to learn to run on your toes."

In the seventh and eighth grades, Jack was the fastest kid in the school, running the 100, the 220, the relays and competing in the high jump. But at 10 he discovered golf. His father, to exercise a damaged ankle over 18 holes, had joined Scioto and one day Jack attended the junior clinic that Jack Grout, the Scioto pro, held Friday mornings for members' youngsters.

"He was just one of the kids, a chunky little kid with a crew haircut," Grout recalled years later. "The first thing I taught him was the grip. The first thing I told him was to hit the dickens out of it, but I didn't have to. He wanted it that way. He was a little kid and he wanted to fire that sucker. He had the instinct."

The little kid also had the ambition. Shooting 51 for the first nine holes he ever

Jack's first trophy, the 1950 Scioto Junior.

played, he found the game he would play for a living and for life. In the summer he would walk to nearby Scioto and be on the Scioto putting green before Grout opened the pro shop at 8 o'clock. He would play 36 or 54 holes, then hit balls and putt some more. He won Scioto's sub-juvenile title at 11, the first of his dozens of amateur trophies. And while playing with his father that year he learned about behavior in golf. With an 8-iron to the green of the 410-yard 15th hole, he flubbed it into a bunker and angrily flung his club.

Ten-year-old Jack (third from right) at his first golf class with Scioto pro Jack Grout, who became his teacher for the next 40 years.

"Go pick up your club, we're going to the clubhouse," his father barked. "That's the last time I'll see you do that or you'll never go to the golf course again."

Properly chastened, Jack never threw another club. And for all of Jack's success as a youngster, his father taught him how to act when he lost. "The other guy had to be pretty good to beat you," his father said, "so give him credit and mean it." His father also taught him that family obligations were important. Late one afternoon when Jack was 13, he shot 35 for nine holes and wanted to continue.

In 1955, Jack, then 15, shot 66 at Scioto, the amateur course record.

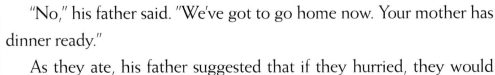

"No," his father said. "We've got to go home now. Your mother has dinner ready."

As they ate, his father suggested that if they hurried, they would have time to play the back nine. On the 502-yard 18th hole, near sunset, after having reached the green with a driver and a 2-iron, Jack holed a 35-foot putt for an eagle.

"That," he has often said, "was the first time I broke 70."

Another day that same year Jack felt a little stiff. His joints ached. He would lose about 15 pounds, and also lose his coordination. In a nine-

The Nicklaus swing, at age 13, shortly before Jack was diagnosed with polio.

hole exhibition with Patty Berg, a founder of the LPGA, he kept shanking his irons and shot 53, not a number expected of the Ohio state junior champion. He was diagnosed with polio. His 10-year-old sister, Marilyn, also contracted polio. She couldn't walk for a year before eventually regaining most of her movement, but Jack soon recovered.

"My immune system fought it off," he said. "About a year later, when the Salk vaccine was available, I got inoculated."

That same year, in his first U.S. Junior Amateur, at Southern Hills in Tulsa, Okla., Jack arrived at the first tee for his first match less than a minute before his scheduled starting time.

"Young man," said Joe Dey, the USGA executive director, "thirty more seconds and you would be going to the second tee 1 down."

> *. . . at 16 he won the Ohio Open, stunning the state's pros in a 72-hole event with 64-72 on the final day.*

Jack, who never cut a tee time that close again, won three matches in that U.S. Junior. In the next three, he lost in the second round, the quarterfinals and the semi-finals but at 16 he won the Ohio Open, stunning the state's pros in a 72-hole event with 64-72 on the final day. At 17 he qualified for his first U.S. Open at Inverness in Toledo, not far from Columbus.

"On the first hole, I drove with a 3-wood, hit a 9-iron to 35 feet and made the putt for a birdie," he has often said with a laugh. "After three holes I was on the leaderboard, then I made a double-bogey and I was gone. I shot 80-80 to miss the cut by 10 strokes."

That year he qualified for his first U.S. Amateur, at The Country Club outside Boston, but he lost in the fourth round. At 18, he finished 12th in his first PGA Tour event, the Rubber City Open in Akron, Ohio, and in the U.S. Amateur at Olympic near San Francisco he lost in the second round, 1 up, to Harvie Ward, Jr., the 1955 and 1956 champion. At 19, as a member of the 1959 Walker Cup team that would defeat Great Britain and Ireland at Muirfield in May (he would win both his foursomes and singles matches), he was invited to the 1959 Masters. Shooting 76-74, he missed the cut by a stroke, but he didn't miss any meals. Then a trencherman befitting his chubby physique, he was known to devour two or three steaks at a sitting. As an amateur staying with his pal Phil Rodgers in the Crow's Nest dorm in the Augusta National clubhouse, he was charged only a dollar a day for meals. At dinner, both he and Rodgers, another trencherman, had two or three steaks every evening until they were informed that they now would be charged a dollar for each extra steak.

"Neither of us complained," Jack said. "We still were allowed to order double shrimp cocktails."

All that steak and shrimp fortified him to win that year's North-South and Trans-Mississippi championships, go to the fourth round of the British Amateur and win his first of two U.S. Amateur titles, edging Charley Coe, an older Oklahoma oil man, 1 up, with an eight-foot putt on the final green of their 36-hole final at The Broadmoor in Colorado Springs.

"When I made that putt," Jack often said, "I told myself, 'Now I know I

At 13, Jack, here with Charlie Nicklaus, was the youngest player in the field of the 1953 U.S. Junior Amateur. He advanced to the fourth round of match play.

Longtime USGA executive director Joseph C. Dey Jr., later the first PGA Tour commissioner, taught young Jack a valuable lesson as a junior.

> "*I* played 36 holes today," Hogan said, "with a kid who should have won this thing by 10 strokes."

can do this, so let's do it again.'"

His accomplishments up to then were merely a prelude to his 1960 entrance into the consciousness of golf people every-where. After finishing a respectable 13th in the Masters, 11 strokes behind Arnold Palmer, the chubby 20-year-old amateur suddenly was leading the U.S. Open, at Cherry Hills outside Denver, on the back nine of the final round. Paired with 48-year-old Ben Hogan, the four-time Open champion, Jack was leading by a stroke as he surveyed a downhill 18-inch putt on the 13th green. Noticing a carelessly repaired ball mark in his line, he wondered if he could repair it. In retrospect, he could have fixed it, but he was too immature and too embarrassed to ask Hogan or a rules official. His putt veered off the ball mark, lipped the cup and spun out. Bogey.

He didn't always make the putt.

When he three-putted the 14th for another bogey, Palmer and Hogan shared the lead. At the 17th, Hogan's wedge spun back into the moat in front of the green and on the 18th, his tee shot hooked into the lake. Palmer went on to win, whirling his visor to the crowd after a 65, but Jack Nicklaus, second by only two strokes, had introduced himself to golf's elite.

"I played 36 holes today," Hogan said, "with a kid who should have won this thing by 10 strokes."

That kid soon was a married man. He had met Barbara Bash, the daughter of a Toledo, Ohio, school teacher, in 1957 during each's first week at Ohio State. Barbara would be the mother of their five children and the queen of his gallery wherever he played, the great woman behind the great man. "Without her," Jack has said, "I might have been just another golfer." And in planning their wedding, Barbara set the date around Jack's golf schedule.

"Jack was an amateur playing in some pro tournaments," Barbara has said, "but he couldn't play in the PGA Championship so that's the weekend we got married."

When they drove off on their honeymoon, Jack's golf clubs were in the trunk. In Hershey, Pa., he played with a former Scioto friend, then they went on to New York City and checked into the old Astor Hotel. Listening to jazz at Eddie Condon's that evening, they met somebody who arranged for Jack to play at Winged Foot, where he had missed the cut in the U.S. Open the year before.

"It was pouring down rain, nobody else was on the golf course," Jack said, "but Barbara walked all 18 holes in the rain with me."

After attending the Broadway play "Camelot" and having dinner at Sardi's restaurant, Barbara suggested they stop in Atlantic City, N.J., on the trip back to Columbus. That was fine with Jack.

Jack, the leading amateur in the country, playing in his second Masters, in 1960.

Jack played the final two rounds of the 1960 U.S. Open with Ben Hogan.

Barbara and Jack were married two months after his second-place finish at Cherry Hills.

Palmer, the 1960 U.S. Open champion, and runner-up Nicklaus.

Jack was unbeatable at the World Amateur at Merion.

"You know what's on the way to Atlantic City," he told her with a smile. "Clementon, New Jersey."

What was in Clementon, New Jersey, then and now, was Pine Valley, which many golf aficionados consider the world's best golf course. Jack didn't realize it was a strict male-only club that Barbara could not enter, but somebody sneaked her onto the fringes of the course where she could peek through the trees as Jack played. As the defending champion of that year's U.S. Amateur at the St. Louis Country Club, he lost in the fourth round to Charles Lewis, but at the World Amateur team matches at Merion outside Philadelphia, he shot 66-67-68-68, a dazzling 11-under-par 269. On the final green, a sudden gust of wind blew his cap off as he hunched over a four-foot putt, but he never seemed to notice. He made the putt. Merion's setup wasn't as difficult as it had been when Ben Hogan won the U.S. Open there in 1950 with a seven-over-par 287, or as it would be when Lee Trevino won the 1971 Open (in an 18-hole playoff with Jack), but in streaking to the individual title by 13 strokes, Jack had astounded the golf world, notably Dwight D. Eisenhower, then in the last months of his second term as President.

"Mr. Nicklaus," the President said upon meeting him shortly thereafter, "at Augusta National Golf Club, as you know, we build bridges to commemorate the records set by the top players in the Masters. The way you're going, perhaps we should stop building those bridges. You look like you'll beat all their marks."

Seldom has a President been so prescient. Instead of Augusta National later naming a bridge for Jack Nicklaus, as it had for Gene Sarazen, Ben Hogan and Byron Nelson, it honored its six-time winner in 1998 with a plaque affixed to a drinking fountain between the 16th and 17th holes. Still an amateur at the 1961 Masters, he tied for seventh, then tied for fourth in the U.S. Open at Oakland Hills, outside Detroit, before he routed Dudley Wysong, Jr., 8 and 6, in the 36-hole U.S. Amateur final at Pebble Beach. That was where Deane Beman taught him to walk off the yardage.

In 1998, Jack was honored with a commemorative plaque at the 16th hole at Augusta, just as Ike predicted.

In the final for 1961 U.S. Amateur, Jack defeated Dudley Wysong, 8-6.

"On the first hole," Jack recalled three decades later, "there was an oak tree, it's gone now, that was 156 to the front edge, 180 to the back. On the second, from the end of the bunkers on the right, it was 199 to the front, 222 to the back. On the third, from the big tree to the left of the fairway, it was 108 to the front, 124 to the back. I played by the yardage book. I never picked the wrong club. I was under par every round. I took it to the PGA Tour and I was the first guy on the Tour to walk yardage."

Having turned pro, Jack was at the 1962 Los Angeles Open with a sponsor's exemption. In those years before the PGA Tour had a Qualifying Tournament, if you made a tournament cut, you automatically qualified for the next tournament. Jack never missed a cut, so he never had to try to qualify on Monday for that week's event. But he had not turned pro for the money, After dropping out of Ohio

> *Whatever, the weather, Jack Nicklaus always kept trucking. And no matter what he shot, he always kept his poise.*

State two semesters short of a business degree, he had been earning about $30,000 a year, a solid salary at the time for a young husband with a wife and a baby son, Jackie. He sold insurance, worked for a slacks company and played customer golf as a slacks salesman. But he did not want to be an insurance man or a slacks salesman the rest of his life.

"The chance to make money," he has said, "was not a factor in my decision to turn pro, because I already had enough money. Heck, my first house cost only $22,000."

All he ever wanted to do was play tournament golf against the best players in the world. To do that, he had to turn pro and go on tour with the best players in the world.

The 1962 U.S. Open at Oakmont was Jack's first official win as a professional.

The week before the 1962 U.S. Open at Oakmont, 22-year-old Jack Nicklaus cashed his first big check as a rookie touring pro, $10,000 for finishing second to Arnold Palmer in the Thunderbird Classic at the Upper Montclair Country Club in Clifton, N.J. — not that he was completely satisfied with it.

"I'd rather have won $200," he said, "and finished first."

Finishing first is what Jack was all about as a little kid, a teenager, a Walker Cupper and two-time U.S. Amateur champion. And coming off that second-place finish in the Thunder-bird, he knew he was ready to win as a pro. He wasn't awed by the prestige of the U.S. Open, or the ogre of Oakmont outside Pittsburgh, or the hometown hero-worship for Arnold Palmer, who grew up in nearby Latrobe. He had finished second to Arnold in the Open two years earlier and in a tie for fourth to Gene Littler in the Open the previous year; his two-year Open total of 282 and 284 had been the lowest of any contestant. And he thought that Oakmont suited him despite its narrow fairways, thick rough, treacherous fairway bunkers known as "the church pews" and its slick sloping greens.

"You had to really keep the ball in play," he said. "Or be strong enough to play it out."

You also had to putt well, which he did. Over four rounds he had only one three-putt green while shooting 72-70-72-69 — 283, a formidable five under par. On the green of the 292-yard 17th hole, a tricky dogleg left, he rapped what he later called "an ultra-fast, double-breaking four-foot putt" into the hole to stay tied for the lead with Palmer down the stretch. He later got a note from Bobby Jones who had been watching the Open on television and understood both the difficulty and the risk of that putt.

"When I saw the ball dive into the hole," Jones wrote, "I almost jumped right out of my chair."

Turning the tables, Nicklaus defeated Palmer in an 18-hole playoff at Oakmont.

The playoff at Oakmont was the first of many times that Jack and Arnold would face off as professionals.

That par-saving putt at the 17th and a par at the 18th lifted him into an 18-hole playoff with, of all people, Palmer, the three-time Masters champion, the reigning British Open champion, the local hero of Arnie's Army, and the King, as his tour rivals had begun calling him. Not that Jack was intimidated. Paired with Arnold in the opening round, he birdied the first three holes and as he awaited the playoff, he knew that Arnold had needed 38 putts in Saturday morning's round and had missed a six-footer on the 18th green in the afternoon fourth round that would have won the Open. He realized that if Arnold were concerned about his putting, that was in his favor.

"As a young kid," he said later, "that's sometimes how you think."

Young or old, that's how Jack Nicklaus always thought, with a positive approach. Palmer wasn't so positive. Even though he had beaten Jack by three strokes when they were paired together during the first two rounds, he knew the big, beefy kid from Columbus could play.

Armed and victorious, in 1962 Jack hugged Barbara and the U.S. Open trophies.

"I wish it were someone else," Arnold said with a smile after Saturday's double round. "That big, strong dude. I thought I was through with him yesterday."

In the Sunday playoff Jack won the Open by three strokes, 71 to 74, and in a way Arnold was through with him. Arnold would win only two more majors, the 1962 British Open and the 1964 Masters, while losing two more U.S. Open playoffs. Not winning that Open at Oakmont at the peak of his career, especially after having led by three strokes with 10 holes to go in the fourth round, stung Arnold for the rest of his life.

"That loss," he has said, "was the most hurting of my career."

But that triumph launched Jack Nicklaus's career. He won two more tournaments as a rookie pro, the Seattle World's Fair Open and the Portland Open. After having won the Palm Springs Golf Classic early in 1963, he slipped his arms into his first Masters green jacket. With birdies at the 13th and 17th holes, he shot a final-round 72 for 286, but the day before, with what he called a "monsoon" soaking Augusta National, he learned not to surrender to bad weather. Paired that Saturday with Mike Souchak, the second-round leader, Jack was on the 13th fairway when both had to search for a lie that wasn't under casual water.

A year later, with help from Arnold, Jack donned the first of his six green jackets at the Masters.

"We asked for a ruling," he would tell reporters later, "and we were told to drop where there was the least amount of casual water."

Souchak, already annoyed at being six over par through 12 holes, wondered if they would be able to finish the round. He staggered to a 79 that dropped him out of contention. Jack was equally frustrated with the soggy conditions, but with his power of positive thinking, he told himself that the conditions were the same for all the golfers. His commendable two-over-par 74 grabbed a one-stroke lead. In ideal weather on Sunday, he won by one stroke over Tony Lema, who would win the 1964 British

"Jack is playing an entirely different game," Jones said at the presentation ceremony. *"A game I'm not even familiar with."*

Open, and by two over both 50-year-old Sam Snead, a three-time Masters winner, and 42-year-old Julius Boros, who would win his second U.S. Open two months later.

"After that," Jack has said, "anytime I wanted to give in to bad conditions, all I needed to keep me trucking was to think of that Saturday at Augusta."

Whatever the weather, Jack Nicklaus always kept trucking. And no matter what he shot, he always kept his poise. After winning the 1963 Masters, he arrived at that year's U.S. Open at The Country Club outside Boston not only as the defending champion but as the new big name in the game. He shot 76-77 to miss the cut, but when he was asked to go to the press tent to explain what happened, it never occurred to him to stalk off, as some 23-year-old golfers might have.

"My Dad always told me, 'You have to accept the bad with the good,'" he once explained. "You may not like it but you smile and keep a stiff upper lip. If I'm asked into the press room, I go in."

More than any other golfer, Jack appeared in the press room after *not* winning, but he always answered questions pleasantly and willingly. His record 19 second-place finishes in majors began with three in 1964 (to Palmer at the Masters, Lema at the British Open and Bobby Nichols at the PGA Championship). And as that year's PGA Tour wound down to its final tournament, he had to confront another possible second-place finish. He trailed Palmer by $318.87 as the leading money winner going into the Cajun Classic in Lafayette, La., a second-tier tournament each would ordinarily have skipped, but both arrived there to duel to the last putt for the last dollar.

"It's a matter of personal pride," Jack said, alluding to the money title. "It's a real measure of accomplishment, the next best thing to winning a major."

That year's money title also meant as much as $20,000 in bonuses in each of the Nicklaus and Palmer equipment contracts, but it was primarily a matter of personal pride. Palmer, still the people's choice, had been the leading money winner in four of the previous six years. Nicklaus was that big, strong dude with another opportunity to knock the King off his throne. But for all the pride and bonuses at stake, the money title would turn on Gay Brewer's 16-foot putt on the final green. If Brewer made it to finish second, Jack would be third and Palmer would be the leading money-winner. If Brewer missed, Jack would tie for second and lead by $81.13.

Brewer's putt stopped short. With $113,284.50 in PGA Tour earnings to Palmer's $113,203.37, Jack had earned his first of his eight money-winning titles. Palmer would

© BETTMANN/CORBIS

Returning the favor, Jack helped Arnold with his fourth green jacket at the 1964 Masters.

As agent Mark McCormack (back, left) looks on, Jack signs his first endorsement contract, for MacGregor golf equipment, to the obvious approval of company officials.

The Big Three--Player, Nicklaus and Palmer—Masters winners all, with Augusta National founders Jones (with cigarette holder) and Clifford Roberts, in 1965.

Nicklaus, circa 1966

never win another. And at the 1965 Masters those in the gallery who earlier had not accepted the big strong dude some called "Ohio Fats" began to appreciate him for what he was: the world's best golfer. When he shot 67-71-64-69 for a record 17-under-par 271 (nine strokes ahead of both Palmer and Gary Player), Palmer, as the previous year's winner, held another green jacket for him to slip his arms into and Bobby Jones realized that this big strong dude was somebody special.

"Jack is playing an entirely different game," Jones said at the presentation ceremony. "A game I'm not even familiar with."

The 64 on Saturday was a virtually perfect round. Ten pars, eight birdies. Three 2's, two 3's, thirteen 4's, no 5's. Thirty-four tee-to-green shots. Only two fairways missed, only one green missed. One chip, no pitch shots, no bunker or other recovery shots. Thirty putts, the longest from 25 feet. His longest club for a par-4 approach was a 6-iron, his longest to reach a par-5 was a 3-iron. All of this with the Augusta National galleries roaring for him as they never had before, and apparently inspiring him.

"It felt great to hear the crowds cheering me and it definitely helped my game," he said. "I'm not an outgoing person like Arnold and Gary and I guess some of the fans resented me for winning when I was so young. Maybe because I've matured, too."

After winning the 1965 Masters, Jack got a jacket assist from Arnold, the 1964 winner.

When he successfully defended his title in 1966, Jack had to go it alone, as Roberts stood by smiling.

That maturity was evident at the 1966 Masters after four of his Columbus friends were killed on the way to Augusta when their private plane crashed and burned on a Tennessee hillside. Despite a heavy heart, he opened with a 68 but then shot 76-72 and with five holes remaining, he was still three strokes off the lead. He birdied the 15th and 17th but drove into the gallery to the left of the 18th fairway. His approach flew 40 feet above the cup, but his delicate putt left him with a tap-in par that created an 18-hole playoff with Gay Brewer and Tommy Jacobs. With a 70 to Jacobs's 72 and Brewer's 78, he was the first to win the Masters in consecutive years, which prompted Bobby Jones to huddle with the Augusta National chairman, Cliff Roberts, over the green-jacket ceremony.

"At this point, Jack," Jones said, "you as defending champion are supposed to put the green jacket on the winner. Cliff and I have discussed the problem and have decided you will just have to put the coat on yourself."

At the British Open at Muirfield, Jack had another first — his first claret jug. At 26, he was the youngest golfer to complete a pro grand slam of the four majors, joining Gene Sarazen, Ben Hogan and Gary Player.

In remembering Muirfield's narrow fairways and how the Scottish wind off the Firth of Forth swayed the hip-high rough during his 1959 Walker Cup matches, he mostly used his 1-iron

Jack's first British Open win came at Muirfield, in 1966 (above and right).

or 3-iron off the tee. Of his 56 tee shots on the long holes over four rounds, he hit his driver only 17 times, his 3-wood only 10 times. After his 67 in the second round for a one-stroke lead, Pat Ward-Thomas, a high priest of British golf journalism, wrote in *The Guardian* that Jack would stroll to victory. But with a 75 in the third round, he lost the lead. Not that it shook him. Leaning out of a window of his room in the adjacent Greywalls Hotel, he noticed Ward-Thomas.

"Hey, Pat," he called with a big smile. "What's that you wrote about me not blowing the lead?"

Still smiling that evening, Jack predicted, "It's somebody else's turn to blow." As if he surely wouldn't shoot that high that again. He didn't. Tied for the lead on the 17th tee with Doug Sanders, who was about to finish, and Dave Thomas, who had finished, he took advantage of a helping wind, hitting a 3-iron short of the fairway bunkers and a 5-iron 238 yards to the green of the 528-yard par-5, then two-putting from 15 feet for a birdie. After a 1-iron off the tee on the 18th and a 3-iron into the wind to

22 feet, he two-putted for a one-under par 70 and 282, winning by one stroke.

Elated by that victory, when it came time to name the golf course he later designed outside Columbus, he baptized it "Muirfield Village."

The glow of the career grand slam soon disappeared. At the 1967 Masters, he missed the cut with a second-round 79, hooking his drives, hitting indifferent irons and putting worse than he could ever remember. But that embarrassment woke him up. He made some subtle changes in his swing and two days before the 1967 U.S. Open at Baltusrol, another touring pro, Gordon Jones, had a putting suggestion.

Among Jack's closest friends from Columbus, and instrumental in the founding of Muirfield Village Golf Club: (from left) Ivor Young, Jack, Bob Hoag, Pandel Savic.

"Go back to the way you used to putt," Jones told him. "Take it back a little shorter and hit it harder."

He also had a new putter. Fred Mueller, a friend of Deane Beman, handed him a center-shafted bullseye putter that had been dipped in white paint. White Fang, his wife, Barbara, dubbed it. And he also looked forward to Baltusrol's 7,015-yard Lower Course in leafy suburban New Jersey about 20 miles west of New York City, calling it "marvelously fair and yet exceptionally challenging, a perfect test of golf with a good balance between the opportunities for success and the chances of getting into trouble." After two rounds, he was only one stroke off the lead, held by Arnold Palmer, but many decibels behind.

Arnie's Army, New York division, was out in force. Since his playoff loss to "that big strong dude" in the 1962 U.S. Open, Palmer had lost two other

The 18th hole at Muirfield Village.

Jack's victory in the 1967 U.S. Open (above, and below with Barbara) was his seventh professional major.

Open playoffs, to Julius Boros and Jackie Cupit in 1963 at The Country Club near Boston, and to Billy Casper in 1966 at Olympic, outside San Francisco, after having blown a seven-shot lead with nine holes remaining in the fourth round.

All those soldiers in Arnie's Army wanted him to win his second U.S. Open and eighth major. As he strode onto the first tee for the third round, the cheers for him resounded across Balusrol's meadows; the applause for Jack was polite. It was that way all around. At the 542-yard 18th, the gallery roared when Arnold's 4-wood to the green hopped into the back rough. When Jack's 4-iron stopped 15 feet from the pin, polite applause. When Arnold wedged to 12 feet, another roar. When Jack two-putted for a birdie, polite applause. When Arnold missed his birdie, louder applause. And throughout the round, Jack heard some negative words, but ignored them.

"You have to develop selective ears that screen out the bad remarks," Jack would say years later. "I only hear the good things."

With a 72, Jack was at even-par 210 along with Arnold, who had shot 73, and Billy Casper, but the leader at 209, after a 69, was a virtually unknown amateur, Marty Fleckman, out of Port Arthur, Texas, who would tee off with Casper in Sunday's last pairing. In the next-to-last pairing were Jack and Arnold, together again.

After Jack and Arnold had hit their second shots Sunday on the first hole, Fleckman pushed his tee shot toward the trees to the right of the fairway. When he went to find his ball, for all practical purposes, he disappeared into those trees. He would shoot 80 and Casper would struggle to a 72, while Jack put together a 3-2-3 birdie streak at the third, fourth and fifth, but he bogeyed the sixth, narrowing his lead to one stroke. At the 470-yard seventh, Arnold drilled a 1-iron to within 12 feet for a makeable birdie putt. Jack was 22 feet away. When Jack's downhill birdie putt with White Fang plunked into the cup, Arnold grimaced, then missed his putt. Jack's lead was now two strokes.

Palmer and Nicklaus played the final round together at Baltusrol.

"That putt you made at the seventh absolutely crushed me," Arnold told him later.

At the 365-yard eighth, Arnold blocked his tee shot into the rough and bogeyed. Jack's birdie there opened his lead to four strokes. With two more birdies on the back nine, he arrived at the 542-yard 18th needing another birdie to break the U.S. Open record of 276 that Ben Hogan had set at Riviera in 1948. After a 1-iron off the tee faded into the right rough, Jack slashed an 8-iron into the fairway, striped a 1-iron 230 yards uphill to within 22 feet of the cup, then holed the birdie putt for 65 and the record 275.

But after having won seven majors over his first six years as a pro, Jack didn't win another for more than three years. During that empty span he won several tour events —three more in 1967, two plus the Australian Open in 1968, and three in 1969 when, as a Ryder Cup rookie, he graced the matches at Royal Birkdale in Southport, England, with a memorable gesture of sportsmanship.

After having been prevented from qualifying for previous Ryder Cup teams by the

> *"I knew you would make it," he told Jacklin, "but I didn't want you to miss it."*

PGA's old five-year rule after turning pro, Jack holed a four-footer for par on the 18th green in the final singles to ensure the United States' victory, but Great Britain's Tony Jacklin still had a two-footer to halve the match. If Jacklin missed, the United States would win outright, 16½-15½. If Jacklin made it for a 16-16 tie, the Americans would still retain the cup. But to the surprise of everyone there, Nicklaus conceded Jacklin's putt.

"I knew you would make it," he told Jacklin, "but I didn't want you to miss it."

Over his six Ryder Cup matches through 1981, all won by the United States team, Jack Nicklaus had a 17-8-3 won-lost-halved record — 4-4-2 in singles, 5-3-1 in four-ball and 8-1-0 in alternate-shot foursomes. But when his father, Charlie, died of cancer early in 1970, he felt guilty over not having won a major since the 1967 U.S. Open at Baltusrol. Had he worked harder at his game, maybe he would have won one or two more majors. His father would have enjoyed another major or two. And as the 1970 British Open at St. Andrews wound down, it appeared his streak of 12 winless majors would continue. After three-putting three of the last five holes in the final round for 73 to fall one stroke behind, Jack thought he had wasted an opportunity for another major as Doug Sanders measured a three-foot par putt on the final green. Over near the Royal & Ancient clubhouse, Jack's wife, Barbara, was standing next to Gerald Micklem, an R.&A. official.

"That is a very difficult putt for Sanders," Micklem told her. "It looks straight but it breaks to the right. You cannot read it."

Sanders's putt never touched the hole. In their playoff the next day, Jack, bundled in two sweaters against the chill, was ahead by one as they walked onto the tee of the 348-yard 18th hole. With the honor, Sanders slugged a long drive into the fairway near the Valley of Sin, the severe swale in front of the green. Jack debated between his driver and his 3-wood, and decided on the driver. Before addressing his ball, he put down his driver and took off one sweater. "It was hot," he later explained. Swinging freely, he smashed his tee shot high and far above all those weathered Scots looking on from Rusacks Hotel and the shops to the right and from the grandstand behind the adjacent first fairway to the left. His ball bounced onto the green, but scooted beyond it into heavy grass next to the gray stone wall in front of the grandstand.

The consummate competitor, Jack's concession of Tony Jacklin's putt at the 1969 Ryder Cup is still considered one of the finest sporting gestures ever.

Sanders bumped a 4-iron to five feet, Jack nudged a sand wedge to eight feet. His putt was on the same line as the putt that Sanders had missed the day before. Remembering what Barbara had told him about Micklem's assessment, he putted carefully. His ball, breaking slightly, caught the right side of the hole and dropped in. Birdie, British Open,

claret jug. To celebrate, he tossed his putter 40 feet into the Scottish air.

Early in 1971, he added his ninth major, the PGA Championship, which had been switched to February at PGA National in Palm Beach Gardens, Fla., and at the U.S. Open at Merion he appeared about to add another until Lee Trevino forced an 18-hole playoff. As Jack walked onto the tee, Trevino, ever playful, pulled a small rubber snake out of his golf bag and tossed it at Jack, who jumped away but laughed. When Trevino won the playoff, 68 to 71, some observers thought that he had psyched Jack with the snake. Hardly. Jack took a quick lead with a par at the 355-yard dogleg right first hole when Trevino bogeyed. What cost Jack that Open was his wedge game: two bunker shots he left in the sand at the 535-yard, uphill second for a bogey 6, and at the 183-yard third for a double-bogey 5, and a chunked wedge in front of the 10th green for a bogey 5.

Jack nearly beaned Sanders (above) when he tossed his putter in the air at St. Andrews on his way to a playoff victory at the 1970 British Open (at right, with Barbara and the claret jug).

"I guess I hit them all fat and I lost by three," he said. "Those three."

The disappointment of losing that U.S. Open did not diminish his determination to do in 1972 what no professional golfer ever had: Win all four majors in the same calendar year for a Grand Slam.

"I'm convinced," Jack wrote in *Sports Illustrated*, "that with the right set of golf courses, a little luck and a great deal of preparation, the Grand Slam can be won."

The four courses appeared to be the right set for him: The Masters as always at Augusta National, where he had won three green jackets; the U.S. Open at Pebble Beach, where he had won the 1961 U.S. Amateur; the British Open at Muirfield, where he had won the claret jug in 1966; and the PGA Championship, at Oakland Hills outside Detroit, where he had tied for fourth as an amateur in the 1961 U.S. Open.

"I am also convinced," he wrote, "that as each leg fell, the next leg, contrary to what you might think, would be that much easier to capture."

As a 28-year-old amateur, Bobby Jones put together a Grand Slam in 1930 (U.S. Open, U.S. Amateur, British Open, British Amateur) and Ben Hogan won three majors in 1953 (Masters, U.S. Open, British Open). Hogan never considered entering that year's PGA Championship, a possible grueling match-play event that would be too demanding on his aching legs which had been shattered in a 1949 automobile accident; the PGA also conflicted that year with the British Open.

Jack found himself on the losing side of this playoff with Trevino at the 1971 U.S. Open at Merion.

Nobody had ever won the Masters, the U.S. Open, the British Open and the PGA Championship in the same year, but Jack Nicklaus knew he had a chance.

At the Masters, he won wire-to-wire with a two-under-par 286, three strokes ahead of Australia's Bruce Crampton, Tom Weiskopf and Bobby Mitchell. Asked that Sunday night about the Slam, he said, "This is the Masters, I want to savor

After winning the first two legs of the Grand Slam, the British Amateur and British Open, Bob Jones is feted with a triumphant parade up New York City's Broadway.

In 1972 Jack won the Masters (above) and U.S. Open at Pebble Beach (right).

the Masters." Questions persisted. "The odds now, they're down from 100,000 to 1, to 1,000 to 1," but seriously, he recalled that when he assessed the 1972 sites of the four majors, "I thought I had a good chance to win all four, but to put them together in the same year is something else."

At the U.S. Open at Pebble Beach, where as a pro he had won the 1967 Bing Crosby National Pro-Am, he had a four-stroke lead going to the 10th tee but a double-bogey there cut it in half. When he glanced at the leaderboard near the 12th hole, he only wanted to see the scores, or so he said later, adding that the names never interested him.

Maybe not, but one of the names that interested everybody else was most familiar — Arnold Palmer, suddenly only one stroke back. At the short 12th, Jack walloped a 3-iron into the thick grass behind the green, chopped it out, chipped poorly and was confronted with an eight-foot putt for bogey. Up ahead at the 14th, Arnold was measuring a birdie putt. If Jack missed and Arnold made, Arnold suddenly would lead by one, but Jack wasn't about to let that happen.

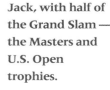

"I told myself," he said later, "'Look, you just made one double bogey, you're not going to make another one.'"

He didn't. He made his bogey putt. Arnold missed his birdie putt. By the time Jack arrived at the tee of the 17th hole, with its treacherous green out there against the horizon of Carmel Bay, he had opened a two-stroke lead, but he was somewhat spooked by Pebble Beach's last two holes. That morning, after waking up around 7 o'clock, he kept trying to play the 218-yard 17th and the 540-yard 18th over and over in his mind.

"I can't play them," he told Barbara that morning. "I don't know what I'm going to do if I ever get there today with a three- or four-shot lead."

What Jack did at the 17th a few hours later is considered by many as the single most memorable shot of his career. With the cup cut at the front of the left tongue of the wide but shallow green, his 1-iron into the wind landed a few feet short of the flagstick, glanced off it and spun to a stop inches away. Tap-in birdie. Even with a bogey at the 18th for a 74 and a two-over-par 290, he won by three over Crampton and by four over Palmer. The Grand Slam was alive. He had led or shared the lead in every round of both the Masters and the U.S. Open. And to prepare for Muirfield, where at the time he could use the slightly smaller British golf ball rather than the slightly larger American ball, he went to Great Harbour Bay in the Bahamas to hit a batch of those smaller balls with the English clubs he was under contract to use in tournaments outside the United States.

"I've never used the big ball in a small-ball tournament," he explained. "If you really get the small ball going, you can shoot nothing. By using the American ball, you're giving away too much to the rest of the field. You don't stop the ball with spin on those greens, you stop it with

Jack, with half of the Grand Slam — the Masters and U.S. Open trophies.

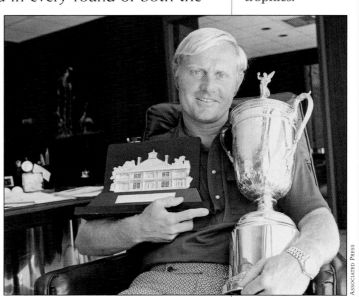

wind. The British ball is about 1/16th smaller, but it weighs the same. It slices less, doesn't fly as high, doesn't hook as much, doesn't spin as much, but it does go farther. The English clubs are the exact same weight as my American clubs with the same balance and loft, but the heads are shaped a bit differently."

At Muirfield, along the southern coast of the Firth of Forth not far from Edinburgh, the Scots, in their tweeds and turtlenecks, were waiting for the golfer who had won the British Open there six years earlier and who now was

> *"I was there and I let it get away," he told Barbara, hugging her on his way to press tent.*

going for the Grand Slam. During one of Jack's practice rounds, when his long iron bored through the breeze to within 15 feet on the 14th green, a gray-haired Scot mumbled, "Aye, he's something to beat." But when Jack had awakened in his room at Greywalls, the small stone hotel near the ninth green, he had felt a crick in his neck. He told Barbara about it, but she was not to tell anybody and he would not tell anybody else. If he didn't win, he didn't want anybody to think he was copping an excuse.

"My neck wasn't very good," he would say years later, "until halfway through the third round."

With even par 70-72-71 through three rounds, Jack was six strokes off the lead held by Lee Trevino, who had won their U.S. Open playoff the year before and was the defending British Open champion. During three rounds, with the narrow fairways and hip-high rough, Jack had been cautious off the tee, seldom using his driver, a strategy that had helped him win in 1966 at Muirfield, but wasn't helping him now. Six strokes behind as he teed off, he was desperate. He felt he needed a 65 in the final round to have a chance, and to shoot 65, he decided he had to hit his driver more often. On the 349-yard second hole, where he had hit his 3-wood in each of the previous three rounds, his drive rolled to the fringe of the green. After a pitch to six feet, he made the putt. Birdie. At the 379-yard third, his wedge stopped six feet away. Birdie. At the 558-yard fifth, a drive, a 3-wood to the green and two putts produced another birdie. At the 493-yard ninth, his chip to three feet set up another birdie for 32, four under for the day. Walking toward the 10th tee, he searched the gallery for Barbara.

"Ask Barbara to stop after nine and get me a cold lemonade," he had asked a friend on the seventh hole. "Tell her no lime juice. It's dry enough out here without any lime juice."

After he drank the lemonade, a four-foot putt on the 473-yard 10th disappeared for another birdie. Five under. With the cheers of his gallery rumbling across Muirfield's moors, he had caught and passed both Trevino and Tony Jacklin, the English pro who had won the 1969 British Open at Royal Lytham & St. Annes and the 1970 U.S.

As the man to beat, Jack was also the fans' favorite at Muirfield in 1972.

ASSOCIATED PRESS

Open at Hazeltine near Minneapolis. On the 11th green, Jack was hunched over a five-foot birdie putt when a roar erupted back at the ninth green. Trevino had rolled in an 18-footer for an eagle to go six under. Distracted, Jack stepped away, then settled again over his putt. Another roar. Jacklin had holed a 10-footer for an eagle to go five under. Hearing the second roar, Jack had straightened, smiled and stepped away. He hunched over his ball again, then stroked it. Birdie. Another roar. Back on the 10th tee, Trevino turned to Jacklin.

Coming so close to having a chance for the Slam only increased Jack's obsession to do it. But he never came close again.

"I think the man just gave us something to think about," Trevino said.

At six under, Jack had to par in for the 65 he thought he needed. None of his next four birdie putts from 12, 15, 20 and eight feet dropped, but as he stood on the tee of the short 16th hole, he remembered how he had finished par 3, birdie 4, par 4 to win at Muirfield six years earlier. The difference was that in 1966 the 188-yard 16th and the 542-yard 17th were downwind. On this sunny Saturday in 1972 they were into the wind. Perhaps too conscious of the wind, he pulled a 4-iron into the light rough to the left of the green. After pitching to about eight feet above the hole, he thought his downhill putt would break slightly from right to left. Stroking it gently, he watched it slide past the cup. Bogey. Five under. Into the wind again on the 17th, he couldn't get home in two. Par. Another par at the 18th completed a 66 for 279, but it wouldn't be enough, although for a few minutes it seemed like it might be. Back on the 17th hole Trevino was about to lose a stroke, if not two or three.

Distracted by a cameraman with a tripod and by another with cans of film, Trevino had hooked his tee shot into a deep fairway bunker. After blasting out sideways onto the fairway, he pulled a 3-wood into the rough short of the green, then his 7-iron chip hurried across the green into heavy grass on the back slope. There in four, he would be lucky to salvage a bogey.

Near the R&A shed behind the 18th green Jack Nicklaus was checking his scorecard when somebody watching television yelled, "Trevino's blown!"

Before Jack faulted in the homestretch at Muirfield, Trevino had built a six stroke lead after three rounds.

THE PHIL SHELDON GOLF PICTURE LIBRARY

Trevino would admit later that as he stabbed his 9-iron into the heavy grass on the back slope, "I might have given up. My heart wasn't really in that chip shot." His ball hopped onto the green and appeared on the way to hurrying well past the cup when it clunked into the flagstick and disappeared. Another roar, the loudest of the day. And as Jack emerged from the scorer's shed, his caddie, Jimmy Dickinson, flung down his yellow caddie vest in disgust.

"He holed a chip shot for a 5," Dickinson yelled.

"He what?" Jack said, his voice shrill in shock.

Trevino remained one stroke ahead, but if Jacklin, on the green in three, could hole his 16-foot birdie putt, he suddenly would be the leader. Instead, he three-putted for a bogey, missing a 30-inch par putt that would have tied him with Trevino. By now Nicklaus was watching television in an R&A trailer. His arms folded, his legs crossed, he saw Trevino's tee shot on the 447-yard finishing hole bounce into the fairway.

"Hit a long drive, didn't he?" Jack said.

Long enough for Trevino to float an 8-iron to seven feet behind the cup as Henry Longhurst, the BBC announcer, intoned, "At long last, we have seen the shot that has won the Open." The shot that ended Jack Nicklaus's bid for a Grand Slam.

"I was there and I let it get away," he told Barbara, hugging her on his way to the press tent. "I felt a 65 would do it. I had a 65 and let it get away."

Minutes later, Jack told the writers, "I'll always believe I played the course the right way, " alluding to his caution the first three rounds, "and just didn't play well." But in quiet moments much later, he acknowledged that he had been "over-influenced by my conservative winning strategy" at Muirfield in 1966, that he had played too cautiously in the first three rounds. He also acknowledged that not winning that British Open was "the No. 1 heart-breaker" of his career.

"What caused it," he said, "was living in the past instead of the here and now. Muirfield in 1972 called for a different strategy than 1966, but I was either not smart enough or too stubborn to see that I'd backed myself into a corner. Use your past experience, but never let it blind you to present conditions."

And never use an alibi. He never mentioned the crick in his neck that had bothered him until halfway through the third round. Instead, he always talked about his mental mistake in playing too cautiously and the basic difficulty of having to beat all the other golfers in all four majors in the same year. "That's what you're fighting, that somebody will beat you," he said. "For 16 rounds, to put it together, that's difficult." He never copped an excuse about his neck, but years later, in recalling the disappointment of that British Open at Muirfield, he alluded to it.

"That's why the Slam is so tough," he said. "You've got to win those four tournaments over a span of four months. When you wake up every day, you never know how you're going to feel."

Years later, Jack recalled that after that 1972 British Open he developed an infection in his right forefinger after a manicure. He had to play the PGA Championship a month later with that finger off the club and tied for 13th. Then again, if he had won at Muirfield, maybe he would not have had a manicure. Coming so close to having a chance for the Slam only increased Jack's obsession to do it. But he never came close again. At the 1973 Masters another 66 in the final round lifted him into a tie for third but couldn't overcome his 77 in the second round as Tommy Aaron won by three strokes. At the PGA Championship at Canterbury in Cleveland four months later, he arrived with alternate plans. If he didn't win, he would play some tournaments in November; if he won, he would hunt elk in New Mexico that month. When he led

Trevino was the spoiler at Muirfield when he holed a miracle chip to win the 1972 British Open by a stroke.

© Hulton-Deutsch Collection/CORBIS

> *"Records were never really that important to me until it was too late to go back . . . To me, my record is 18 professional majors, five kids, 46 years of marriage, 19 grandkids and a successful business."*

by one stroke Saturday night, even with Sunday's round still to play, he made his decision. "Book the hunt," he told a friend.

With a two-under-par 69 the next day, Jack added his 12th major, winning by four over Bruce Crampton. Counting Jack's two U.S. Amateurs, it was his 14th major, surpassing Bobby Jones's total of four U.S. Opens, five U.S. Amateurs, three British Opens and one British Amateur.

"Once I got past that record, I didn't have the big push to do much else," he told the *Sunday Times of London* in 2006. "I didn't know I had Tiger pushing me. I would have probably worked harder and maybe won more if I had. I can't say I prepared for every major the way I should have."

In retrospect, that 1973 PGA was Jack's 12th as a pro, two-thirds of the way to his eventual record 18 that Tiger Woods has chased.

"I can't say I didn't give away opportunities," Jack said. "Records were never really that important to me until it was too late to go back and go for them. Never in my life did I add up how many I had won. Tiger has been adding them up from day one. He has grown up that way and the more he does it, the more he is reminded of it. He doesn't know anything else. To me, my record is 18 professional majors, five kids, 46 years of marriage, 19 grandkids and a successful business.

Winning the 1973 PGA was some consolation after losing the British Open in 1972.

ASSOCIATED PRESS

"I have other friends, I have enjoyed what I've done, and I have been able to smell the flowers along the way. Those are the things that are important to me, not the 18 majors.

"The 18 majors," he said, "are not my life, they are part of it. If I had been really serious about building a record that nobody was going to touch, I wouldn't have been able to do a lot of things I have enjoyed. I have had a very balanced life. I spent time with my kids, I have grown up knowing them, and if golf had been the only thing I did, that wouldn't have happened. I could have won 20 or 25 majors, but I think I would have been a miserable person."

Golden Bear and cubs: Jack and Barbara, holding Gary, along with Nan, Jackie and Steve. Michael was born in 1973.

Go Buckeyes! Jack and longtime friend Pandel Savic, a former Ohio State quarterback.

When Jack might have won another major, he showed, quite simply, that he was human. At the 1974 Masters he was one stroke off the lead with a tap-in birdie on the 15th after having submerged his right foot into the pond in front of the green and splashed a sand wedge from a chunk of watery soil. But at the 170-yard 16th he pushed his 6-iron "a tad heavy" into a bunker. Bogey. At the 420-yard 14th a bogey had wasted a 33-foot eagle putt on the 13th green.

"Instead of getting better on the last few holes, I got worse," he said later. "That's not like me. That's stupid. That's the thing some of those other guys do."

Jack seldom put down other golfers, but in that flash of ego, he had put down some with that remark. In his anger at himself for those two bogeys that dropped him into a tie for fourth, three strokes behind Gary Player, he revealed his obsession with the Grand Slam.

"I'm always more disappointed when I don't win at Augusta," he said. "I'm 34 now. I'm not 24 anymore. Every year you don't win the first one, you can count the years you don't have a chance to win all four."

The next year, Jack won the first one, but not easily. His 68-67 start opened a five-stroke lead but on Saturday, as often happened whenever he was paired with Arnold Palmer, both played poorly. Instead of competing against the course as a golfer must in a medal-play tournament, they seemed to be competing against each other as if it were match play. In a way, neither won. Jack shot a one-over-par 73, Palmer 75, hardly the stuff of legends.

Early on, Jack and Arnold enjoyed an intense rivalry and later, a close friendship.

"It seems like every time we play together, neither of us plays well," Arnold said. "I can't recall either of us ever having a good round. We've discussed it and neither one can put a finger on it but there is an outside factor. The people want Jack to beat me, or me to beat Jack, and the galleries are always big."

At the beginning of their rivalry, Arnie's Army often was hostile toward Jack, who was younger, stronger and quickly showed he was better. As Jack kept winning majors while Arnold stopped winning them after his 1964 Masters victory, he earned grudging respect from Arnie's Army, although Arnold's popularity never dwindled. But that Saturday afternoon, they were startled by another golfer's name and numbers on the leaderboard. With a Masters record six consecutive birdies from the second through the seventh holes, Johnny Miller's cumulative score had gone from two over par at the start of the round, signified by a green 2, to four under, signified by a red 4 at the seventh. Soon they realized that Miller shot 30 on the front nine, another Masters record.

"That was a good nine," Jack said.

"It wasn't bad, was it?" Arnold replied with a straight face.

Jack's final-round 66 secured a fifth Masters title in 1975.

"Nobody ever did it before," Jack said.

Miller would shoot 65 and jump into third place at five under par after three rounds, as Tom Weiskopf, with a 66 for nine under, snatched the lead from Jack, who was eight under. On Sunday, with Weiskopf and Miller paired in the last group behind Jack and Tom Watson, the leaders traded birdies on the front nine. As they started the back nine, Jack and Weiskopf were tied for the lead, Miller was two behind. When Jack arrived at his

> *In retrospect, 1975 was the last time a Masters victory allowed Jack Nicklaus to realistically consider the possibility of a Grand Slam.*

260-yard drive at the 500-yard 15th, he trailed Weiskopf by one. Needing a birdie, he hit what he later described as "the best pressure shot of my life" — a 240-yard 1-iron that soared high over the pond and settled 15 feet from the cup. Two-putt birdie, tied for lead. On the 16th, he holed a 40-foot birdie putt. He leaped and danced, his left hand holding his putter high in the air. Back on the 16th tee, Miller shook his head.

"I saw the Bear tracks," Miller would say.

With a flimsy tee shot and a worse chip, Weiskopf bogeyed. Up ahead, Jack finished with a 66 but as Weiskopf and Miller surveyed their birdie putts on the 405-yard 18th, each had a chance to force a playoff. Miller's 20-footer curled away to the left.

This time, in 1975, Player presented the Masters jacket.

Weiskopf's eight-footer somehow stayed above the hole. Jack Nicklaus had a record fifth green jacket, one more than Arnold Palmer.

"To be out there in the middle of something like that is fun," he said that Sunday evening. "You're inspired, you're eager, you're excited. You almost want to break into a dead run when you hit a good shot. It's what you've prepared yourself for, what you wait a year for. To know that you can look back some day and know you were a part of something like it, that's just great."

When he tied for seventh in the U.S. Open at Medinah, outside Chicago, his chance of a Grand Slam evaporated, but at that year's PGA Championship, he earned his 14th major, winning by two over Bruce Crampton at Firestone in Akron, Ohio.

In retrospect, 1975 was the last time a Masters victory allowed Jack Nicklaus to realistically consider the possibility of a Grand Slam. The next year he tied for third with six-under 272 as Raymond Floyd's 17-under 271 equaled Jack's record score. In 1977 his 66 in the final round for 10-under 278 was second to Tom Watson by two strokes in a back-nine duel. In the press center later, Watson waited nearby as Jack was asked about Ben Crenshaw's comment the day before that while the young pros still respected Jack "as the best," their attitude was, "if they have their day, they're going to beat him." Before Jack could reply, Watson spoke up, saying, "I'll answer that. I'm always afraid of this man,"

"No, he's not," Jack said. "He's not afraid of anybody. That's why he won."

At that year's British Open at Turnberry, with its tall lighthouse in Ayrshire on Scotland's west coast where the Ailsa Craig protrudes from

At the hard-fought 1977 British Open, at Turnberry, Watson edged Jack by a single stroke (above, and below left).

With the prized claret jug in 1978.

the sea, Jack learned the painful truth of his tribute to Watson's heart. During the third round Watson rallied from two strokes back to share the lead with Jack as each shot 65. During the final round Watson twice came from behind to tie, once from three strokes back and again from two back.

"I just couldn't shake him," Jack would say later.

On the 15th hole, Watson's tee shot missed the green but, using a putter off hardpan, he holed a downhill 60-footer that bumped the flagstick and clunked into the cup. Birdie and a share of the lead again. As they waited on the 16th tee for the gallery to clear the fairway, Watson turned to Jack and said with a smile, "This is what it's all about."

"You bet it is," Jack said.

After pars at the 16th maintained the tie, Watson whistled a 3-iron to within 20 feet on the 500-yard 17th but Jack's 4-iron missed the green. He chipped up to four feet but after Watson's two-putt birdie, he missed his birdie putt to fall one behind. At the 18th, Watson hit a 1-iron into the heart of the fairway while Jack pushed his tee shot into tangled rough near a bush. Watson spun a 7-iron to two feet. Jack's recovery barely made the green, some 40 feet from the cup. But as if to prove the point he made in the Augusta National press room, Watson feared what Jack would do now.

"He's going to make that putt," Watson told his caddie.

Jack did make that putt for a birdie, then Watson quickly stepped up and knocked in his two-footer for a birdie and another 65. Jack's 66 was a stroke short. After shaking hands, they walked off the 18th green together, arm in arm.

"I gave you my best shot," Jack said, "but it wasn't enough."

At St. Andrews the next year, Jack won the British Open for the third time. One stroke behind Watson and Peter Oosterhuis after three rounds, he had his caddie, Jimmy Dickinson, up at six o'clock to check where the R&A officials cut the pin positions on each green for what would be his duel with little-known Simon Owen of New Zealand.

"I felt I knew the course better than Simon did," Jack said later. "You have to know what club to play and where to play it."

At the 16th green, Owen pitched long, his ball running to the 17th tee. Using his putter, he failed to get through the swale and bogeyed as Jack holed an eight-foot birdie putt for a one-stroke lead. At the 17th another bogey dropped Owen two back as Jack went on to shoot 69 for seven-under 281, the first golfer to win each of the four majors at least three times.

"St. Andrews, to me, is the home of golf and where it all began," he said later, wearing the blue diamond sweater, the replica of which he would wear there early in the final round of his 2005 farewell. "It is my favorite place and where I most want to win."

But in 1979 he didn't win anywhere. His best finish in a major was a tie for second at the British Open at Royal Lytham & St. Annes, three strokes behind Seve Ballesteros. On the PGA Tour, his best was third at the Philadelphia Classic; in 12 events, he had only

The next year it was Jack's turn again, here hugging his caddie, Jimmy Dickinson, after winning at St. Andrews.

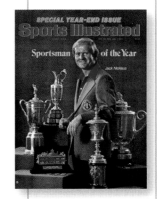

In 1978 *Sports Illustrated* honored Nicklaus as its Sportsman of the Year.

... when he arrived at Baltusrol for the 1980 U.S. Open he had not won a PGA Tour event that year.

three top-10s, only six top-25s, only $59,434 in prize money that ranked an embarrassing 71st down there with some of those other guys. At the U.S. Open at Inverness in Toledo, Ohio, he didn't seem to care that he barely made the cut with a 74-77 start.

"I guess I've got to go out and play tomorrow," he said with a shrug.

He closed with 72-68 that tied for ninth, but Jack Nicklaus suddenly was no longer Jack Nicklaus and he knew why. By reducing his tournament schedule and cutting his practice time, he knew he had not worked as hard at golf as he had in the past. He knew that he wished he was designing golf courses instead of having to play them. He also knew what to do: Visit his original teacher, Jack Grout. And when he did, he heard, in no uncertain terms, what to do.

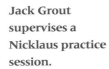

"Stop dragging the putter through the ball, stop blocking the hit," Grout barked. "Take the thing back inside and release it. *Hit* the damn ball."

Jack also worked on his short game under the tutelage of Phil Rodgers, a savant of the sand wedge. But when he arrived at Baltusrol for the 1980 U.S. Open he had not won a PGA Tour event that year. He had tied for 33rd in the Masters, his worst 72-hole finish there. The week before the U.S. Open, he missed the 36-hole cut at the Atlanta Classic when a 67 couldn't overcome a 78 in the first round. When he bogeyed the second hole at Baltusrol, he wondered if this would be another woeful week. But then he birdied the third, fifth, sixth, 11th, 12th, 13th, 15th and the 630-yard 17th to go to seven under. With a par 5 at the 542-yard 18th, he would match Tom Weiskopf's 63 nearly an hour earlier that had tied the U.S. Open record set by Johnny Miller in 1973 at

Jack Grout supervises a Nicklaus practice session.

Woeful putting added to Jack's frustration in early 1980.

Jack turned his game around in time for the 1980 U.S. Open.

Oakmont. And if he made a three-foot birdie putt on the final green for 62, he would set a record for the lowest score not only for the U.S. Open but also for any of the four majors.

He missed. The golfer who always made the putt, missed. "I babied it," he confessed.

At Baltusrol, Jack was officially back, winning his fourth Open title (above, and left).

But with a 63 that shared the lead, Jack Nicklaus was Jack Nicklaus again, the golfer to beat on the same Lower Course at Baltusrol where he had won the 1967 U.S. Open. Not that a Japanese stranger, Isao Aoki, was intimidated. With three consecutive 68s while paired with Jack, Aoki used his inimitable touch, gently striking the ball with the heel of his putter as if it were a feather-duster, to climb into a share of the lead after three rounds. Paired again in the final round, Jack held a two-stroke lead as they surveyed their birdie putts at the 17th, but Jack was 20 feet away, Aoki only five feet.

"I just knew Isao would make his putt," Jack said later. "I knew I had to make mine to keep that two-stroke lead going to 18. It was a putt I had been making for 15 years when I needed it, but it was the kind I hadn't made for nearly two years."

Somewhat ghostly, that eerie element of doubt had crept into his psyche as he hunched over the putt. But when the ball plunked into the cup for the birdie he felt he had to have for breathing room on the 542-yard finishing hole, Jack Nicklaus was really Jack Nicklaus again. Not that Aoki faltered. He drained his birdie putt. Aoki almost chipped in for eagle at the 18th, but Jack's 10-foot birdie putt assured his two-stroke triumph to the roar of thousands, including some who had trampled through the bunkers to the left of the green to get closer to him.

"Jack Is Back" announced the impromptu sign on the nearby leaderboard.

Two months later, Jack was back again. His fifth PGA Championship tied Walter Hagen's record total as his seven-stroke victory at Oak Hill, outside Rochester, N.Y., was the largest winning margin since the tournament switched to stroke play in 1958. At the 1982 U.S. Open at Pebble Beach, he appeared about to make even more history on what he has often called his favorite course. Having shot 69 for four-under 284 and the clubhouse lead as Tom Watson's tee shot on the 17th hole disappeared into the rough, Jack stood outside the scorer's tent with television announcer Jack Whitaker, who was waiting to congratulate him on his record fifth U.S. Open.

Jack closed out 1980 with a fifth PGA title at Oak Hill.

"It's been an honor," Whitaker started to say, "to be a part of your time…"

Just then a roar erupted back near the 17th green. "Whoops — not quite yet," Jack said. Turning to watch the television set in the scorer's tent, he and Whitaker saw a replay of Watson's sand wedge out of the rough dive into the cup for a birdie 2 and a one-stroke lead. When

Jack receives the Wanamaker trophy from (from left) Joe Black, Frank Cardi and Mark Kizziar of the PGA of America.

> *Another birdie, a one-stroke lead and maybe the loudest roar in Masters history rumbling through the pines. At 46, Jack Nicklaus was Jack Nicklaus again.*

Watson also birdied the 18th, he won by two and as Watson walked off the green towards the scorer's tent, Jack was waiting for him.

"You little s.o.b," Jack said with a smile. "You did it again."

Always the gracious loser on the outside, Jack was crushed inside. He would acknowledge later that having a record fifth Open snatched away was now the most disappointing loss of his career. And for nearly four years after Watson's heist at Pebble Beach it appeared that Jack's last chance for an 18th major had been snatched away. As the 1986 Masters approached, he was aging fast. He couldn't make the short putts anymore. He wouldn't wear contact lenses. He didn't compete in enough tournaments and when he did, he often missed the cut. He was too busy designing courses instead of playing them. He was too concerned with his Golden Bear, Inc. finances that cost him what he later described as "a lot of money." He asked Jack Grout to check his swing. He adopted Chi Chi Rodriguez's short-game tips to his oldest son Jackie. Quite simply, at 46 he appeared too old to win.

"Nicklaus is gone, done," wrote Tom McCollister of the *Atlanta Journal-Constitution* in his Sunday preview of the 1986 Masters. "He just doesn't have the game anymore. It's rusted from lack of use. He's 46, and nobody that old wins the Masters."

To motivate Jack, a longtime family friend, John Montgomery, taped a clipping of McCollister's words to the refrigerator door in the Augusta home that Jack rented. Not that Jack needed motivation. Annoyed at not having won since the 1984 Memorial, he was determined to play well at the Masters. And as he strode toward the back nine on

It was longtime friend John Montgomery (below right), pictured here with another friend, John Hines (center), who posted the now famous clipping on the Augusta refrigerator in 1986.

Twelve feet and in for the birdie at the 17th hole that provided the one-stroke edge to win Jack's sixth Masters (facing and following pages).

HISTORIC GOLF PHOTOS/THE RON WATTS COLLECTION

Jack's caddie for the 1986 Masters was son Jackie, here helping his dad read his birdie putt on 17.

Sunday, paired with Sandy Lyle, he was thinking only positive thoughts. With his son Jackie, in a white caddie's coverall, reminding him to "keep your head still" as they surveyed an 11-foot birdie putt on the slippery ninth green, two roars erupted from near the green of the 535-yard eighth hole. Tom Kite had holed a wedge from 81 yards for an eagle, then Seve Ballesteros holed a wedge from 40 yards for an eagle. Hearing the roars, Jack grinned.

"Let's see," he said loud enough for some in his gallery to hear, "if we can get a roar up here."

When he holed that 11-foot putt with the new Response ZT putter that Clay Long had designed for MacGregor, he heard his first roar for his first birdie and a one-under-par 35 on the front nine. When he also birdied both the 485-yard 10th with a 4-iron to 25 feet and the 455-yard 11th with an 8-iron to 22 feet, he was only two strokes off Ballesteros's lead.

"Suddenly," he said later, "I just believed I could putt again."

At the 155-yard 12th over Rae's Creek, he pulled his 7-iron onto the back fringe of the shallow green. His chip left him six feet away. "There was a spike mark right in front of my ball, a big one," he would say. "I hit a good putt, but the spike mark made it veer to the right. That made me mad. The hole in general made me mad." Angry at the bogey, Jack turned aggressive. At the 465-yard dogleg-left 13th, he wisely used a 3-wood off the tee because he didn't want to force a driver, but as his ball drew toward the towering pines on the left, it narrowly missed a high branch before landing in the fairway. "Dad," said his son Jackie, "that's not good on a 24-year-old's heart."

"What about me?" Jack said, smiling. "I'm 46."

After a 3-iron to 30 feet, he two-putted for another birdie and another roar. At the 405-yard 14th, his approach bounced to the back fringe, then his sand wedge pitch-and-

HISTORIC GOLF PHOTOS/THE RON WATTS COLLECTION

> *"All my professional life, my priority has been family first, golf second and business third, but that's changed," he said late in 1991. "It's now family first, business second and golf third.*

run crawled to within a foot to save par. At the 500-yard 15th he "absolutely nailed" his driver and from 212 yard to the pin, his 4-iron soared high to within 12 feet. Surveying the line, he remembered a similar putt in 1975 that he left short because he didn't hit it firm enough. When this eagle putt disappeared, the gallery roar raised the hair on Sandy Lyle's arms.

"I'd never heard a roar like that," Lyle said later. "Jack was so focused. He kept the same rhythm and the same pace all day."

Jack now was tied for second with Kite, who was seven under through 14 holes, and both were only two behind Ballesteros, the 1980 and 1983 Masters winner who was nine under through 14 holes. Tom Watson was three back through 15 holes, Greg Norman four back through 13 holes. At the par-3 16th, Jack's 5-iron floated high toward the flagstick.

"Be the right club," Jackie pleaded.

Without looking, Jack said, "It is."

After landing, the ball spun and rolled slowly past the cup, inches from a hole-in-one, stopping a little over three feet away. Another birdie, another roar. As he strode toward the 17th tee, the people in the gallery were yelling, screaming. "You had to semi-protect yourself," he would say. "I thought I might get hurt." He had climbed to within one stroke of Ballesteros, who heard the roar for Jack's birdie as he waited in the 15th fairway for Watson and Tommy Nakajima to putt out. The Spaniard decided on a 5-iron, but he switched to a 4-iron that he wanted to hit softly. He hit it too softly, too fat actually. His ball splashed into the pond in front of the green. Over on the tee of the 400-yard 17th hole, Jack was about to hit his driver.

"I heard the noise, a loud roar with a deep groan underneath it." Jack would say. "I knew exactly what had happened."

After Ballesteros's bogey and Kite's two-putt birdie, Jack was in a three-way tie at eight under. Norman, who had birdied the 14th, and Watson each were at six under. But after a wayward drive into the trees on the left, Jack slashed a pitching wedge under the pine branches to within 12 feet on the 17th green.

"I think it'll break a little to the right," Jackie said.

"No, Rae's Creek will keep it to the left," Jack said.

Just as Jack thought, the ball started to slide to the right, but straightened out and plunked into the cup. Another birdie, a one-stroke lead and maybe the loudest roar in Masters history rumbling through the pines. At 46, Jack Nicklaus was Jack Nicklaus again. But he still had the 405-yard, uphill dogleg-right 18th to play. After a careful 3-wood off the tee, he had 179 yards to the hole. Choosing a 5-iron, he knew he needed to get the ball to the top level of the green. He hit it solidly, but as the ball rose against a sudden slight breeze, it landed on the lower tier, about 50 feet below the cup. As he marched toward the green, he was engulfed in cheers.

"Walking up the fairways on the last few holes, I had tears in my eyes," he said later. "But then I told myself, 'Hey, you've got golf to play.'"

And a 50-foot putt to stroke. "The speed," he thought, "was crucial." The speed would also be perfect, the ball stopping inches below the cup for a tap-in par, a six-under 30 on the back nine and a seven-under-par 65 for 279, nine under. Surrounded by another roar, Jack hugged Jackie and disappeared into the green scorer's shack to sign his scorecard, then walked to the Jones Cabin to wait and watch television. He sipped a glass of water, did a few exercises to loosen his back, paced back and forth. When Ballesteros three-

Arm in arm: father and son, Masters champion and caddie.

HISTORIC GOLF PHOTOS/THE RON WATTS COLLECTION

putted the 17th to fall two strokes behind, he was done. But now Kite and Norman were coming up the 18th in the last two pairings, Kite needing a birdie to tie, Norman needing a par to tie and a birdie to win. Kite had a 12-footer for that tying birdie, but his ball slid to the left. Norman had holed a 12-footer at the 17th for his fourth consecutive birdie, but his 4-iron to the 18th green sailed into the gallery on the right. His chip stopped 10 feet above the hole, then he missed the par putt to the left.

Jack shares this victory with his mother, Helen (left), and sister, Marilyn.

Jack Nicklaus had won his sixth Masters and his 18th major, at age 46.

As relieved as he was joyous, in the Jones Cabin he hugged Jackie again and kissed Barbara, who left a small smudge of lipstick on the collar of his yellow shirt. He hugged his mother, Helen, who had not been to Augusta since Jack's first Masters as an amateur in 1959, and his sister, Marilyn Hutchinson. After the green jacket ceremonies, he was whisked to the interview area of the press center.

"Where's Tom McCollister?" he asked with a smile.

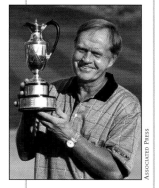

A triumphant Nicklaus acknowledges the cheers after the green jacket presentation from 1985 Masters winner Bernhard Langer.

The golf writer who had buried Jack as "gone, done, too old" was pounding his computer in the working area of the press center but minutes later, having finished his early-edition story, he arrived in the interview area where Jack was still answering questions. Seeing him, Jack grinned and said, "Thanks, Tom."

"Glad I could help," Tom said.

Jack Nicklaus would never win another PGA Tour event, much less a major, but he accepted it with a smile. The day before the 1992 Masters, he told the story about the guy who brought his dog into a bar where Jack Nicklaus was playing in a golf tournament on television. When Jack made a long birdie putt, the dog did a flip. When Jack hit a long straight drive off the next tee, the dog ran up and down the bar. When Jack made another long birdie putt, the dog did another flip.

"And," Jack said, "the bartender says, 'That dog must be a real Nicklaus fan. What's he do when Nicklaus wins a tournament?' And the guy says, 'I don't know. I've only had the dog for six years.'"

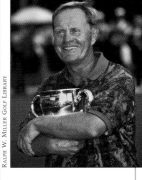

Jack's second U.S. Senior Open win came at Cherry Hills in 1993.

The story was good for a laugh and, as a senior golfer, his golf was still good. Beginning in 1990 when he turned 50, Jack had been winning tournaments on the Senior PGA Tour (now the Champions Tour). Winning a record eight senior majors, including the 1991 U.S. Senior Open at Oakland Hills outside Detroit and the 1993 U.S. Senior Open at Cherry Hills outside Denver, was better than not winning them but to him, it wasn't golf as he, more than anyone else, knew it. But golf was no longer what drove him.

"All my professional life, my priority has been family first, golf second and business third, but that's changed," he said late in 1991. "It's now family first, business second and golf third. I'm being very practical doing it this way. I don't make a living playing golf anymore and I haven't for some time."

Jack didn't always trust the business world. "In golf when somebody beats you," he

Jack after winning the 1996 Tradition, one of the majors on the Senior PGA Tour.

VICTORIES IN THE SENIOR MAJORS

Year	Championship	Course	Score
1990	The Tradition	Desert Mountain (Cochise Course)	206*
	Senior Tournament Players	Dearborn Country Club	289
1991	The Tradition	Desert Mountain (Cochise Course)	288
	PGA Seniors	PGA National Golf Club	271
	U.S. Senior Open	Oakland Hill Country Club	278
1993	U.S. Senior Open**	Cherry Hills Country Club	278
1995	The Tradition	Desert Mountain (Cochise Course)	276
1996	The Tradition	Desert Mountain (Cochise Course)	272

* Played over three rounds.   ** Won in playoff over Chi Chi Rodriguez, 65-69.

once said, "you know it was fair and square. In business, you don't always feel that way." But he felt life as a golf-course architect was fair and square. At last count, Nicklaus Design had designed, co-designed, re-designed or had under design more than 300 courses in more than 30 countries, including those developed by his sons Jackie, Steve, Gary and Michael along with Bill O'Leary, his daughter Nan's husband.

Designing golf courses is now the business of golf's first family: Jack and Barbara, their five grown children and their spouses, and their 19 (and counting) grandchildren. Another grandchild, 17-month-old Jake, drowned in Steve's family hot tub early in 2005.

"You never get over it," Jack has often said.

In the middle of the latest Nicklaus family Christmas card, a photo of Jake is there with the rest of the family that is lined up in a sports team picture. At their North Palm Beach, Fla., home is the painting of Jake that the American golfers at the 2005 Presidents

The Nicklaus family, 2006.

Jack is quick to credit his success to Barbara, who was officially honored as the PGA First Lady of Golf in 1998 (below).

Cup presented to Jack, their captain, and Barbara, once canonized by *Golf World* magazine as "Saint Barbara."

"She'll always do something for somebody else before she'll do something for herself," Jack often said. "She always put my career first and everything else second. As a result, I was free to do what I had to do, which was play golf, and she did what she had to do."

Even when playing in tournaments, Jack made sure to get home to attend his kids' games and school events whenever possible. Barbara remembers him flying back between rounds in Mexico to see Jackie and Steve play in a state championship football game. But what Barbara had to do, meanwhile, was everything but play golf. After trying it once, she declared it a "dumb game." But as the queen of Jack's galleries, usually with a small gold Golden Bear around her neck and with their kids tagging along, she never forgot somebody's name, much less a face.

Whether coaching Little League, as above, or watching high school football, Jack was always on the sidelines for his kids' games.

Her two most endearing moments were watching Jack hug his caddie Jackie on the 18th green at Augusta National in the 1986 Masters and hug his caddie Steve after his farewell birdie putt on the 18th green at St. Andrews in the 2005 British Open.

In helping to raise more than $12 million for charities, Barbara was the first winner of the First Lady of Golf Award from the PGA of America and the first winner of the Winnie Palmer Award from the Metropolitan Golf Writers Association. She chaired both the Nicklaus Children's Hospital at St. Mary's Medical Center in West Palm Beach, Fla., and the Children's Health Charity that sponsored the nearby Honda Classic on the Champions Course that Jack redesigned.

"My golf game can only go on so long," Jack said during his twilight years of competition, "but what I have learned can be put into a piece of ground and that will last beyond me."

Even in those twilight years, Jack Nicklaus was always a golfer at heart, a competitor, a champion who didn't want to finish far down the list in majors, or worse, miss the cut.

"To me, competition is not walking down the 18th fairway at noon on Sunday," he said in 1998 when the Masters unveiled the Nicklaus plaque for the water fountain between the 16th green and the 17th tee. "To me, competing is walking down the 18th fairway at 6 o'clock on Sunday."

And around 6 o'clock the following Sunday as he walked down Augusta National's 15th fairway at age 58, he thought he was 38, or maybe 46.

Only three strokes off the lead, he turned to his son Steve, his Masters caddie that year, and said, "If I can get an eagle and two birdies, that's what I need to win. I know I've done it before." But at 58 he couldn't quite do it again. He missed his eagle putt, then he missed two birdie putts. With a 68 for 283, he tied for sixth, four strokes behind Mark O'Meara, a remarkable performance that prompted a question: Was what he did at 58 a greater accomplishment than winning the Masters at 46?

"There's no greater accomplishment," he said, "than winning."

Put those words on his tombstone. Winning is what Jack Nicklaus was all about. Just showing up for the applause wasn't him. At the 2000 Masters, after undergoing ceramic-hip replacement surgery early the year before, he was grouped with Arnold Palmer and Gary Player for the first two rounds — the Big Three, together again. And when Arnold and Gary each missed the 36-hole cut while he made it with 74-70, he was the Big One again. But when asked if it had been like old times to be out there on Augusta National "with all that nostalgia," he frowned.

"There's no greater accomplishment," he said, "than winning." . . . Winning is what Jack Nicklaus was all about.

"I don't pay much attention to that nostalgia stuff. It was very nice, the gallery was very nice, but I'm a funny duck," he said firmly. "I come here to play golf."

To play golf. To shoot a score. To be competitive. To win. As he had six times at Augusta National in the past. At 60 that year Jack Nicklaus had come to the Masters "to play golf" but he did not play golf the way he wanted to play golf. It would be the last time he made the cut in a major, but to him, a tie for 54th after an 81-78 finish wasn't playing golf. At 60, he knew he had to start saying goodbye to the majors, which he did that year at both the U.S. Open at Pebble Beach and the PGA Championship at Valhalla in Louisville, Ky., and in 2005 at both the Masters and the British Open where, with the golf world watching, he lined up that 15-foot putt on the 18th green at St. Andrews.

"I hadn't holed a putt all day," he said later, "but I had no doubt I would make that putt."

Of course Jack Nicklaus had no doubt he would make that putt.

He always made the putt.

Jack and Arnie at Laurel Valley, 1965.

TAKING PRECAUTIONS

By
Dan Jenkins

Your basic owner of this byline covered 16 of Jack Nicklaus's 20 triumphs in major championships, 16 of his 19 runner-up finishes in the majors, and numerous heroics in lesser events, so let me confess right now that observing the Golden Bear romping through all that golf history ranks pretty close to the top on my journalism pleasure meter.

In all the stuff Jack accomplished, he set the bar higher than a '60s hippie for anyone who might follow. This included his weight loss and discovery of fluff-dry hair, two primary things that made him more popular with the public and enabled him to overcome his image as, well, "The Man Who Shot Arnold Palmer."

Today it's accepted that a fellow named Tiger Woods has a legitimate chance in the coming years to surpass Nicklaus's 20 wins in the majors, but Jack's particular feat of grabbing 19 silver medals in majors represents a record that will, in this humble opinion, require a set of Tiger Woods twins to equal or erase. More about that in a moment.

First, it needs to be pointed out that Jack was not only the greatest winner the game has seen, he proved to be the most gracious loser golf has known — and he was certainly the greatest natural interview in the whole wide world of sports. And it should come as no surprise that the incredibly thoughtful Barbara Nicklaus was the all-time Tour wife.

Yeah, characters like a Muhammad Ali and Jimmy Demaret and Lee Trevino were always good for sound bites, and Sam Snead and Babe Didrikson Zaharias could tell jokes and stories forever, some of which were even printable, and certain football personalities could give you humor mixed with insight. I specifically speak of such folklore heroes as Bear Bryant, Darrell Royal, Bobby Layne, Sonny Jurgensen and Dandy Don Meredith. But nobody loaded you down with information the way Jack W. Nicklaus did.

Whether Jack had won or lost a tournament, he could tell you how and why in such detail that when he'd get around to the poa annua part, a lesser man's eyes might slowly close and his chin might make an audible thump on his chest.

If you wanted to know why this golf course was wonderful or that golf course was overrated, Jack could tell you about it, blade of grass by blade of grass, with pinches of bunker sand thrown in. Mix and stir.

If you cared to have the golf game of one of his rivals appraised, Jack could turn into a swing-tip guru before your very eyes, painting with words all those curved arrows and dotted lines you come across in a magazine's instruction article.

Even if you wanted to track down the rumor that Gary Player liked to pour catsup over everything he ate, Jack was your source.

Which prompts the mind to retreat back to a Saturday morning in February of 1971, to the Jack Nicklaus-Gary Player Show in the locker room at the PGA National Golf Club. This was during the PGA Championship, a major that had bizarrely been scheduled that winter so the PGA of America could show off its own golf course.

Nicklaus shares insights with Jenkins, circa 1975, at the Lodge at Pebble Beach during the Bing Crosby Pro-Am.

Nicklaus didn't live far from the course, and Gary was Jack's houseguest for the week. As they sat down in the locker room that morning, Jack humorously said to a group of loitering sportswriters, "Gary will answer any of my questions."

Some laughter among the writers. Then someone asked Gary what he'd had for breakfast in the Nicklaus household.

"It doesn't matter," Jack said, butting in. "He puts catsup on everything he eats. Barbara's getting a complex. She gives him a cheese omelet, he pours catsup all over it. She cooks him a steak, he pours catsup all over it. A couple of fried eggs…catsup all over it."

More laughter.

Player said, "So would you if you had a catsup contract."

Greater laughter.

"I didn't know you had a catsup endorsement," Jack said.

Gary said, "I will when these fellows get through writing about it."

Room-filling laughter from us writer fellows.

That was the time Nicklaus won his 11th major. Two years later, when he was winning his 14th to break the record of Bobby Jones, there was very little comedy — he was all business at Canterbury Country Club in Cleveland that week.

In truly uncharacteristic fashion he refused to do a network TV interview one day at Canterbury — they wanted him to talk about the upcoming Ryder Cup. But he was taking dead aim at Bobby Jones, struggling to clear that historical hurdle, and said to the network folks, "I don't want to talk about anything this week that doesn't concern itself with this championship."

It was after he'd cleared the Jones hurdle and was finished with the winner's interview that I spoke to him outside the Canterbury press center. As jovially as possible I reminded him that while he had finally topped Bobby Jones, he was still two short of Walter Hagen.

"What are you talking about?" he said.

I said, "Hagen is credited with 11 majors but he really has 16. He won the Western Open five times in the days when the Western was definitely considered a major. You're two short."

"Let me up, will you?" he said with a smile.

Another two years later, in August of 1975, we were at Firestone Country Club in Akron, Ohio, and Jack had won the PGA again. It was his 16th major — he had tied Walter Hagen.

Funny thing was, he did it in an unusual way for him. He finished the championship with a double bogey on the last hole, but he was far enough ahead of Tom Weiskopf and Bruce Crampton that it didn't matter.

Crampton paid Nicklaus a high compliment afterward. Bruce said, "We all suffer from human deficiencies. Jack Nicklaus just suffers from fewer of them. He wouldn't have made a six at the last hole if he'd needed something better."

Jack was asked if that were true, what Crampton had said.

"I wouldn't have," he said, winking.

Later that evening in the press center I found myself gazing at a blank piece of paper in the typewriter. I was on deadline for *Sports Illustrated* and waiting for the muse. Cussing the muse for being late.

No prize-winning thoughts ever came to mind, so I wound up with a lead that appeared in *SI* as follows: "He is a known Communist. He kidnapped the Lindbergh baby. He attacked

Pearl Harbor. He peddles dope and he — what? Oh, sorry. We were all just sitting around out here in Akron trying to think up something new to say about Jack Nicklaus."

Actually, I do have something new to say about Jack Nicklaus now. While he was winning those 20 majors — six Masters tournaments, five PGAs, four U. S. Opens, three British Opens, two U. S. Amateurs — he took precautions. In as much as majors were his goals.

He took the precaution of winning the Western Open twice — in 1967 at Beverly Country Club and in 1968 at Olympia Fields — in case history allowed the Western to reclaim the major status it enjoyed from 1899 until, by my judgment, the middle 1950s, which was when the Masters went on national TV and the Western didn't.

He took the precaution of winning The Players Championship three times — in 1974 at Atlanta Country Club, in 1976 at Inverrary Country Club in Fort Lauderdale, and in 1978 at Sawgrass — in case at some future date the press would ordain the TPC a major.

Jack also took the precaution of winning the World Series of Golf in Akron in 1976, the first year that it became a 72-hole event, in case it, too, might someday become a major.

For my money, his 19 silver medals in majors are as intriguing as anything he ever did. Let me walk you through them again.

JACK'S SECOND-PLACE FINISHES IN THE MAJORS

The Masters:

1964 – 6 behind Arnold Palmer	1977 – 2 behind Tom Watson
1971 – 2 behind Charles Coody	1981 – 2 behind Tom Watson, again

The U.S. Open:

1960 – 2 behind Arnold Palmer at Cherry Hills	1971 – lost playoff to Lee Trevino at Merion
1968 – 4 behind Lee Trevino at Oak Hill	1982 – 2 behind Tom Watson at Pebble Beach

The PGA:

1964 – 3 behind Bobby Nichols at Columbus CC	1974 – 1 behind Lee Trevino at Tanglewood
1965 – 2 behind Dave Marr at Laurel Valley	1983 – 1 behind Hal Sutton at Riviera

The British Open:

1964 – 5 behind Tony Lema at St. Andrews	1976 – 6 behind Johnny Miller at Royal Birkdale
1967 – 2 behind Robert de Vicenzo at Hoylake	1977 – 1 behind Tom Watson at Turnberry
1968 – 2 behind Gary Player at Carnoustie	1979 – 3 behind Seve Ballesteros at
1972 – 1 behind Lee Trevino at Muirfield	Royal Lytham and St. Annes

What that means is that Jack was first or second in 39 major championships. Think about that for moment. How many more majors he might have won.

Now think about this. He finished third in nine other majors, and in 20 more he finished in the top 10. That's a grand total of 68 out of the 100 majors he played from 1960 through 1986, the year of his last victory in Augusta, which can be marked as the proper end of his career.

I repeat: 68 top 10 finishes out of 100 major championships.

That's a hell of a lot of leaderboards, folks.

Small wonder there was a group of us in the press rooms during these years who had a saying. It became a habit that every time the Nicklaus name would go up on the leaderboard at this or that major, one of us poets would stroll past a fellow typist, who might be hunched over his writing machine, and casually remark:

"Jack Nicklaus, comma..."

The first four players to win all four of golf's professional major championships, pictured here at Westchester Country Club, (from left to right) Gene Sarazen, Ben Hogan, Gary Player and Jack Nicklaus.

ALWAYS A PRESENCE

*By
Jack Whitaker*

e was always a presence. Even before we had seen him in person. Nicklaus was someone to whom you had to pay attention. He overflowed every newspaper account of his exploits. He dominated every AP wire photo that came into TV newsrooms. He was a big, burly fullback type of golfer who could not be ignored. When he left the world of amateur golf in 1961, he was already a clubhouse-hold name. He had won almost everything there was to win, including two national championships and had finished second to Arnold Palmer in the U.S. Open in 1960.

Later that same year at the World Amateur Team Championship at the Merion Golf Club, his four sub-70 rounds merely added to the presence. Not since Bob Jones had an amateur golfer commanded so much attention. So pervasive was the coverage of Nicklaus turning professional that one weathered tour veteran said, with more than a little sarcasm, "Well, if he is so good, let him come out here and try us." He did.

I first saw Jack Nicklaus in person at that World Amateur Team Championship at Merion. On an overcast Friday morning I stood on the 14th tee and watched him tee up. His heavy build made him look older than his 20 years. The massive force of his swing was unlike anything I had seen before. It was power you could clearly see and hear, and in that swing was the universal desire of every golfer. To hit the ball as far as possible. His tee shot exploded into the autumn mist as the gallery gasped.

The next time I saw Jack Nicklaus was at the PGA Championship in 1962. This time I observed him from a television tower, from which I would look at the golfing world for the next 35 years. That year the PGA was held at Aronomink Golf Club, just a few miles away from Merion where I had first seen Nicklaus, and the presence had gotten bigger. Earlier that year he had beaten Palmer in a playoff to win the U.S. Open. This prompted Palmer to remark, "Now that the big guy's out of the cage, everybody better run for cover."

And they were beginning to. Several players stayed and faced the challenge Nicklaus posed and gave us the most memorable golfing experiences over the next 25 years. But in 1962 the feeling was that in any tournament, Nicklaus was the one to beat. He finished third in that PGA Championship behind Gary Player and Bob Goalby, but we all knew he was there. In 1963, the momentum increased and it began in the spring at Augusta.

The Masters Tournament has been flourishing since the end of World War II but it was in 1958 that it had a second birth. That was the year Arnold Palmer, television and golf all came together in one serendipitous meeting. Arnold looked into the camera, hitched his pants and won the tournament. He won again in 1960, and for a third time in 1962. He was the big name at Augusta and in golf. Then in 1963, Nicklaus stuck his head in the door and won his first green jacket. No one seemed to sense any drastic change, since Arnold came back and won his fourth title in 1964. Jack finished second. Then Nicklaus won the next year, by nine strokes, and again the following year in a Monday

Emmy-award winning broadcaster Jack Whitaker with Jack Nicklaus at a Metropolitan Golf Writers Association dinner in the early 1970s.

playoff. From 1963-66 he had won three out of the four and finished second. Now there was a different feeling among the azaleas and dogwoods. Aside from the hard statistics, there were subtle changes. From the second-floor veranda of the handsome clubhouse we could hear the gallery cheers when someone birdied or hit a great shot. We could tell by the tenor and the volume of the cheer whether it was Palmer who had done the deed, or someone else. Palmer's cheers were special. Then in the mid-1960's there was another sort of gallery response, different from Palmer's. It was perhaps not as exuberant as the Palmer cheer, but it was strong and deep. It was for a Nicklaus birdie and those cheers became more and more frequent, and louder.

> *"He had a way of knowing just how good he was and he never let that self-confidence, and often stubbornness, melt into arrogance."*

As we entered the 1970s, Nicklaus's presence was as large as ever, but he was not. Gone was the hefty, crew-cut youngster. The hair has grown longer and the weight had diminished. The weight loss was not done for cosmetic reasons. Health and the increase of stamina were the motivating forces behind the change, but the result was a new-looking Nicklaus. And his game had changed, too. It had also slimmed down. The power was still very much there, but it was more controlled, and course management became one of his major tools.

Through those years there were many unforgettable shots struck at important times. The 1-iron to the 18th at Balustrol to clinch the 1967 Open; the 1-iron at the 17th at Pebble Beach that nailed the 1972 Open; and the 1-iron at the 15th hole in the 1975 Masters. Dear members of the gallery, we are talking about a 1-iron, the most difficult club in the bag to hit, a club that most of today's players consider a museum piece and something to be avoided, like early tee times. And then there was the putting. Was there ever anyone better under pressure? I think not.

Through those brilliant years of the '60s and '70s, Jack was not unmolested on the mountaintop. Someone was always trying to push him off. In 1975, two of the game's best tried to thwart him. That year's Masters Tournament produced one of golf's most dramatic championships: Tom Weiskopf, Johnny Miller and Jack Nicklaus all firing away on a Sunday afternoon at Augusta. All these years later, when I think of Nicklaus holing that 40-foot putt at 16 with Weiskopf and Miller looking on from the tee, I know that golf and the theater were never more closely aligned. Jack won that one for his fifth Masters title.

He didn't always win the big ones. His 19 second-place finishes in major championships is a record that seems unbreakable. No one remembers who finishes second in a golf tournament? If he is Jack Nicklaus we do. Some of those second-place finishes hurt. In 1972 Lee Trevino holed out from off the green at the 71st hole for a par to edge him by one stroke in the British Open. Then again at the British in 1977, in a breathtaking performance by Tom Watson and Nicklaus, Tom sank a 60-foot putt at the 70th hole to win by a stroke at Turnberry. And then there was Pebble Beach in 1982. Watson again.

Nicklaus had shot a 69 in the final round of that U.S. Open. He was four under par and tied with Watson, who was playing two groups behind. I was waiting to interview Nicklaus and we both watched a TV monitor lying on the ground as Watson hit his tee shot at 17 into the left rough. As Tom was walking to his ball, I interviewed Jack. His eyes were bright and the adrenalin was pouring out of him. I was as excited as he was and almost conceded him his fifth U.S. Open title.

"Not yet," he said, "I'll settle for a playoff."

We ended the interview and both of us looked down at the monitor as Tom made the shot that became instant lore, immediately immortal. Jack sagged for a moment, as if he had been hit by a tremendous body punch. Then very softly, almost wistfully and with no malice, said, "That's the second time that son of a bitch has done that to me."

That, of course, was a reference to the British Open at Turnberry. I don't know which of those 19 runner-up finishes hurt Nicklaus the most, but I know that 'disappointment' does not describe Pebble Beach in 1982. That one, as Duke Ellington used to say, was beyond category.

Yes, there were disappointing moments in Nicklaus's career, but the successes far outweighed them. He had a way of knowing just how good he was and he never let that self-confidence, and often stubbornness, melt into arrogance. He seldom blamed anyone other than himself for his defeats. At Turnberry in 1977, he told Watson, "I played my best, you played better." And at Pebble Beach in 1982, again to Watson, he said, "I'm proud of you." And as the years went by, the public began to appreciate more and more the man and his ethics. Two of the most moving displays of respect and affection I've seen were extended to Nicklaus.

The first, and to me the most impressive, was on a cool gray day at St. Andrews in 1978 as he approached the home green to claim his third British Open title. As he neared Granny Clarks Wynd, the path that runs across the first and 18th holes, the applause began to deepen markedly. It swelled up into the evening air and floated over the old town. The thousands in the grandstand stood and the crowds on the roofs of the buildings along Banks Road joined in. There was little yelling or cheering, just a deep, steady applause, stately and dignified, that seemed to go back to the beginnings of the game. The Scots tribute to the best of his time.

The second accolade occurred at the same 18th hole 27 years later, on a bright summer afternoon. It was the second round of the 2005 British Open. Golfing galleries have changed over the years and, of course, this was a different occasion. This was Jack's farewell appearance in a major golf tournament. The acknowledgment was still one of deep affection and respect, but now those feelings were wrapped around memories. There was cheering and whistling as loud as this seaside has ever heard. Nicklaus paused with his playing partners, Tom Watson and Luke Donald, on the King William IV bridge and waved as the cheering grew. Jack beamed back at the crowd, his face as bright as the sun that shone on it.

Those memorable moments of his career that touched four decades are endless and his longevity will be a major factor in determining his place in the game. That longevity was supported by the manner in which he led his life; family first, golf second, business third. Since that Friday morning at Merion when I watched that hefty 20-year-old drive off the 14th tee, to the 65-year-old elder statesmen at St. Andrews in 2005, Jack Nicklaus has always been a presence, an inspiring presence that changed and lifted the game.

Jack with long-time caddie Angelo Argea.

Principle Number One: Keep the head still

Morrison believed that the head is the balance center of the swing. If it shifts during the swing, bad things happen: Overall balance changes, as does the swing arc, timing and sequence of movements throughout the swing. Therefore, **the imperative of keeping the head still is paramount**.

Grout taught that at address, the head should be set behind the ball and stay there both on the backswing and the downswing. He emphasized that the head should stay behind the ball, not in one immobile rigid position, but behind the ball throughout the entire swing.

When Jack was 11 years old, Grout taught this by having his assistant, Larry Glosser, stand in front of him at address and grab hold of his hair with his hand as Jack made a swing. Grout felt this was the only way he could get Jack to stop his head from bobbing up and down throughout his swing. While it was painful if he moved his head, Jack soon learned to swing without moving his head no matter how hard he swung at the ball.

This head position was one of the hallmarks of Jack's swing throughout his entire career.

IF YOU SUSPECT A MOVING HEAD IS COSTING YOU SHOTS, HAVE SOMEONE GRAB A FISTFUL OF YOUR HAIR WHILE STANDING IN FRONT OF YOU AS YOU SWING, AS JACK GROUT DID WITH ME IN MY LEARNING DAYS.

IT COULD BE PAINFULLY REVEALING!

by King Features Syndicate, Inc. World rights reser

Head Position

Note the position of the head and eyes just past the point of strike: Bobby Jones (above), Jack (right) and Ben Hogan (inset right).

Jack Grout's Swing Fundamentals

by Martin Davis

*T*he story of how Jack Nicklaus came to golf is an interesting one.

When Charlie Nicklaus, Jack's father, required an operation on his ankle, the doctor recommended walking on soft ground as rehabilitation. Joining Scioto Golf Club, in Columbus, Ohio, Charlie was only able to play a few holes at a time before he had to take a rest. As a result, he took his 10-year-old son, Jack, to play along with him.

Charlie Nicklaus's bad ankle resulted in the greatest competitive record in golf.

At about this time a new head pro came to Scioto, one Jack Grout, who had had some success on the fledgling golf circuit, winning the Oklahoma State Open and placing well in several other events. In addition to playing golf with his father, young Jack Nicklaus took part in a weekly golf clinic for the youngsters at the club and also took a private lesson every two weeks.

Grout began his golf career in 1930 as an assistant professional under his brother Dick, the head professional at Glen Garden Club,

Grout in an early session at Scioto with Jack.

Jack Grout played golf with Ben Hogan (left) and Byron Nelson (right) while an assistant pro at Glen Garden Club in Fort Worth, Texas.

in Fort Worth, Texas. While there, he learned a good deal about the golf swing from his brother, and also by watching and playing with two former Glen Garden caddies — Ben Hogan and Byron Nelson, then just under 20 years old but fine players, who had playing privileges at the club. Grout had also worked with Henry Picard, the winner of the 1938 Masters and the 1939 PGA Championship, at Hershey Country Club, and Picard's philosophy of the golf swing had a profound effect in shaping Grout's instructional methods.

The person who did the most to influence Picard's ideas about the golf swing was Alex Morrison, one of the first golf-swing gurus. In 1935, about a month before the Ryder Cup Matches, Picard began a lifelong relationship with Alex Morrison and took eight days to learn the "Morrison" system, hitting more than 500 balls a day. Morrison's theories on the golf swing were quite advanced, and somewhat controversial, too. For example, one of his bedrock principles involved the use of the feet in the swing.

You might say that Alex Morrison's teaching philosophy begat that of Henry Picard's, which, in turn, heavily influenced Jack Grout.

Thus, three of the greatest players of all time — Bob Jones, Ben Hogan and Jack Nicklaus — shared a common philosophy and somewhat interrelated or "connected"

Jack Grout with his star pupil Jack Nicklaus.

teachers — Stewart Maiden, Henry Picard and Jack Grout, each of whom in turn, had his foundation swing philosophy in the teachings of Alex Morrison. Picard emphasized these "teaching fundamentals" with Grout and he further honed and refined them into his own teaching philosophy.

Grout distilled them into three essential fundamentals: 1. Keep the head still; 2. Proper foot action; and 3. Develop as full an arc as possible.

In addition to being an early innovator in golf instruction, Alex Morrison was a trick shot artist. Here he attempts to hit a golf ball off of the watch of Miss Atlantic City in the mid-1920s. Note the split grip and the beginning of the rolling of his left ankle.

Jack Grout's Swing Fundamentals

"(Jack) Grout was a teacher with some firm convictions, one of which,
however, was that every golfer is an individual. "

— Alistair Cooke, 1972

Principle Number Three: Develop as full an arc as possible.

For his young students **Grout encouraged as big a backswing as possible** so as to hit the ball as far and as hard as they could. His thought process was that by developing the widest arc possible, the muscles would be stretched and extended early in his career. Control would come later.

Grout felt that the key to distance was "a longer arc of the swing on the backswing, and the more acute the angle between the club shaft and the left arm as the hands come down and go ahead of the ball, the better."

Additional Swing Keys

GRIP

Grout encouraged the overlapping grip, the one popularized by Harry Vardon, but because Jack had smallish hands, he felt from the very beginning that his right hand would slip off the club either in the backswing or the downswing.

Eventually, after much trial and error, Jack went to the less popular interlocking grip, which he used throughout his entire career.

HIT ON THE UPSWING

Jack Grout taught hitting the ball on the upswing with both the driver and the putter in order to get the most out of each club.

SQUARE STANCE

Although Jack Grout emphasized a square stance for most of his students, he allowed Jack to adopt a slightly open stance. He believed that a heavy-set golfer could pivot through with a modified open stance better from a somewhat open position. Off the tee, Jack would aim towards the left side of the fairway and gently fade the ball about 10 yards towards the center of the fairway.

Principle Number Two: Balance through proper footwork.

Grout believed that all great players possessed exceptional foot action that permitted them to move swiftly and freely on the downswing. And the key to foot action, he believed, is balance.

Bobby Jones, who was strongly influenced by the Morrison philosophy, possessed incredible foot action in the era of hickory shafts. Although Jones's foot action was somewhat exaggerated in comparison to the modern swing, the wooden shafts he used required longer swings due to the inherent torque in the hickory shafts. (Jones was known to have said that golf is played "between the knees and on the inside of your feet" and J.H. Taylor urged one to "play beneath himself.")

And **the key to good foot action**, Grout taught, **is based on rolling the ankles**.

As Jack described the proper motion in his book *The Greatest Game of All*, written with Herbert Warren Wind, on the backswing as "… the left ankle rolls in laterally, toward the right foot, the right ankle braces against this motion. On the downswing, as the left ankle rolls back to the left and into a firm bracing position, the right ankle rolls in toward the left. This enables the golfer to turn properly going back and to move forward properly into the ball — and to avoid a hundred and one faulty motions."

To teach the proper foot action, Grout had his pupils keep their heels on the ground at all times during the swing, thereby having them feel a combined rolling of the feet and ankles. Jack believed that in addition to teaching one to roll the entire foot, it also encourages a keen sense of balance, a good arm swing and promotes the suppleness to make a full shoulder turn.

Incredibly, Jack claimed that it was three or four years before Grout permitted him to raise his heels during the swing.

On the backswing note how Jack's left ankle rolls laterally against the brace of the right ankle, thus permitting a proper turn back and subsequently a move forward into the ball. The major reason for the use of the rolling of the ankles was to quiet the body during the swing and to allow the arms to fully release the clubhead through impact.

by *Jim Flick* with *Roger Schiffman*

The Evolution of the Nicklaus Swing

The late and great golf writer Peter Dobereiner contended that every golfer has a swing that stays with you for life, like a fingerprint. Once you develop that basic motion, it is distinctive to you and doesn't really change. Jack Nicklaus is an exception to that rule. His golf swing evolved, rather dramatically, over time.

True, the basic principles that he learned as a youngster from Jack Grout, such as "reach for the sky" stayed with him throughout his career, but a comparison of his muscular swing during his amateur and early professional years shows a much different look from his classic swing that evolved as he grew older. That's because Jack's genius for making adjustments, as well as major swing changes, fed his competitive instinct throughout his career.

Jack learned as a 13-year-old that he didn't want to hook his golf ball. Distance was not a problem for him, and a fade gave him control. Grout showed the junior Nicklaus one of the best exercises you could ever give a young golfer. He had him hit balls for hours thinking only of rolling his feet and ankles. This promoted feel and rhythm (a consistent sequence of motion to a beat), a wide vertical arc, a stable lower body and a centered, steady head. Grout taught Nicklaus to replicate his address position and full release away from the course without a club. Starting with his hands a foot apart, Jack was instructed to swing his arms back and through, turning his right arm over his left, and feel how his feet would respond. This basic feeling stayed with him for life.

As a youth, Jack met with early success, which set the stage for Jack's mind. He loved the learning process and problem solving, and this resulted in a swing that changed over time.

Jack's muscular swing was built to hit the ball very high and overpower golf courses. He set up well behind the ball and drove his massively strong legs through impact. He was not yet a good wind player. As he got older and couldn't drive his legs as dynamically, he started setting up more on top of the ball. He was able to hit the ball lower when he wanted and became better in the wind and a more effective shotmaker. He learned to control the distance of his medium and short irons — his 7-iron became his 150-yard club, though he could still hit it 185 if needed. As a result, he stayed competitive and continued to play with even fewer mental and course-decision mistakes. As his swing developed, he played to stop the ball with trajectory, not spin.

Alex Morrison once wrote the following: "Once you have mastered the correct swing, the excellence of your game will depend upon the extent to which your mind takes charge and the nicety with which your body responds to its commands." No one has fulfilled that description more consistently over more years than Jack William Nicklaus.

"Muscular Jack"

"Classic Jack"

"Young Jack"

The Swingaway

Note how wide Jack is swinging the club while still maintaining a stable lower body.
Jack felt as if he were swinging the club back with his right forearm,
which is why his backswing looked different from other players' at the time.

The higher right elbow at this stage of the swing closes the clubface slightly,
however, the shaft is swung more vertically, which puts the clubface square at the top.

Into the Hitting Zone

Jack's chin is staying back — an Alex Morrison principle — and keeps the shoulders
from overworking, allowing the arms to swing freely toward impact.
Note how his left hip is over his left heel, which helps eliminate the left side of the golf course.

The chest is facing the ball at impact and the left forearm
is bowed, the right heel is barely off the ground and the feet are rolling.
His left hip is starting to rotate around him.

Address

*Look at how Jack's left arm and shaft form a line from
his left shoulder to the clubhead. He has a very wide stance, with his right toe turned out,
which will enable him to turn more easily.*

Initial Swingaway

*Jack is left-eye dominant, which allowed him to turn his chin to the right,
setting up the conditions for an incredible shoulder turn.*

Halfway Down

*Jack's arms are swinging and his shoulders are reacting
as his hands come close to his legs. The shaft is fairly vertical and in line with the ball.*

*The hands and wrists are staying hinged, setting up the tremendous
centrifugal force of the clubhead to be used as late as possible. The right knee is moving inward
and supporting the right side toward the impact position.*

Jack's Muscular Swing

"Jack has a sound swing,
constructed along classic lines,
and majestic in its power;
yet he is capable of a deftness
in the strokes around the green
that is astonishing in such
a strong player.

— **Bobby Jones,** *1969*

Starting Down

The left foot, knee and thigh are moving laterally to support
the swinging of his arms and club. Such a vertical swing required this kind
of lateral support, rather than rotating the hips.

The shaft is vertical, therefore the clubhead feels very light, allowing
the arms to swing freely away from the shoulders. The arm swing controls the shoulders.
The left knee and thigh continue to move laterally, controlling the hips.

Finish

Jack's chin, head, chest and hips are reacting to the swinging
of the arms and club, supported by the feet and legs.

Despite Jack's massive clubhead speed, his head and body finish
in perfect balance equally placed over his legs. Don't you feel sorry for that ball!

ck

Observe how the swinging motion of his arms is putting
his upper body in a position so that his left shoulder is over his right knee,
and he's fully loaded over his right leg.

Jack starts a lateral move with his left foot and knee while his arms and
club are reacting to this dynamic movement. This creates a slight downcock of his wrists at the
transition into the downswing, due to the weight of the club and his relaxed arms.

Jack's spine angle is tilting backward, in response to the club being swung
slightly upward through impact. The left forearm is still bowed and stabilizing the clubface.
His chin is still pointing well back, keeping the right shoulder from interfering.

The upper left arm is staying close to his chest while his forearm rotates
and fully releases the clubhead in harmony with the rotation of the left thigh and hip.
The right foot is rolling inward and the right heel is still close to the ground.

MORE
Muscular Jack

Jack rehearsed the shots he needed for the conditions he was about to face. Here he is practicing knockdown shots in preparation for a round at the British Open. Notice how he keeps his weight left through the entire swing with this medium iron. He allows his arms to separate from his shoulders on the backswing, while he keeps his head very steady.

Jack kept the trajectory of the shot low not by getting his upper body out front. Instead, he hit the ball down by holding the grip end of the club ahead of the clubhead through impact. Look how stable the clubhead is. Even though his chin is well back — his trademark look at impact — his arms extend through the strike, and his right heel is barely off the ground. As Alex Morrison taught, Jack's bowed left forearm stabilized the clubhead well through impact and into the follow-through.

The Swingaway

Jack's body lines are slightly open to play a fade. Jack Grout encouraged Nicklaus to be 30½" from his toes to the ball with a 43" driver.

Jack's arms are swinging and his shoulders are reacting as his hands come close to his legs, the clubhead remaining outside the hands.

Halfway Back

Jack's lower body is starting to react to the swinging of his arms.

The shaft is swinging slightly vertically with the shoulders continuing to react to the swinging of the arms and the club.

Control Your Pace

Jack believed you should swing the club at a pace you can control. Grout taught him to swing the club back and apply the head of the club at a speed that allowed him to control his shots. While different players describe impact in different ways, Nicklaus used the words "applying the clubhead to the ball." Jack's swing was built for control, necessary for winning on major championship courses. His higher follow-through was a safety factor for eliminating the left side of the golf course. His swing was more upright to hit the ball higher. He never worried about coming over the top because Jack Grout taught him to "get collected" behind the ball (his left shoulder well to the right of the ball).

"Jack allowed his body to respond to the swinging of the club. However, his swing was very upright. Due to his tremendous influence, the golf swing became much more of a vertical motion..."

Perfect setup with the left hip slightly higher than the right, creates a slight tilt of the spine angle away from the target resulting in a high ball-flight.

A free arm swing away from the ball with minimal upper-body tension.

Note the swinging of Jack's arms and club with the body reacting. His tilted chin, established at address, allows for a fuller shoulder turn.

Jack's hips are staying level, keeping the desired spine tilt.

Ball Position

Jack played all of his shots from one ball position — off his left heel — but because he then narrowed his stance as the club got shorter, and put more weight on his left side, he, in fect, had 13 slightly different ball positions.

By playing the driver opposite his left heel, and keeping his weight toward his right side, he created a level to slightly upward blow with that club. He was simply letting his setup body position react to the design and usage of the club. With a middle iron, his weight was more centered and his stance narrower. This created a very slightly descending blow, resulting in a shallow divot. Jack never took deep divots, which is one reason he played so well in damp or muddy conditions, common in the fall and spring in Ohio.

But Jack's most distinctive feature, to my eye, was the way he remained on top of the ball throughout the swing while keeping his upper body behind the ball at impact. This is why he was able to hit the ball so high, especially with his irons. He was the straightest, longest driver in the history of the game. And due to his upright motion, he was able to hit towering iron shots from the rough. From the fairway, he took very little divot, which is one reason his distance control was so precise with his short and medium irons. Jack took a lot of pride in hitting the ball not only a long way, but the right yardage.

In fact, he was consumed with playing shots the correct dis-

> *"I practiced mechanics, but played by feel."*
> — *Jack Nicklaus*

tances. Jack was ahead of his time in figuring out how to play a golf course. Extremely conservative on the course, he rarely if ever hit a shot too far into a bunker or other hazard. He told me he practiced mechanics, but played by feel. He would create pictures in his mind of the ball landing on the green and rolling to the hole. He called it "going to the movies." Jack had that special knack of enjoying pressure, relishing the excitement of getting in the hunt.

When the heat was on, he played more deliberately and gave more consideration for his shot and club selection. I don't

Jack and Jim discuss the swing philosophy used in the Nicklaus-Flick Schools from 1991-2002.

advocate that for everybody, but it worked for Jack.

Many kids today don't understand their swings. They just want a teacher to tell them what to do without explaining the "why." Not Jack. He enjoyed finding answers for himself. He was constantly asking Jack Grout questions, and he has done the same with me. He routinely changed his swing keys and made adjustments, even from day to day during a tournament.

One of the most intriguing aspects about Jack's approach to golf is that as he aged his concept for the game evolved. For example, he didn't always practice his trademark spot-lining at address. He told me that he started spot-lining at the 1970 British Open at St. Andrews. Because there are so many blind shots on the Old Course, Jack discovered that he could establish his target line by looking from behind his ball, down the line through his ball, to a distant target like a church steeple, pick out a spot on the ground in front of his ball along that line, then simply aim his clubface at that spot, build his stance

and swing. It worked so well at St. Andrews, where he defeated Doug Sanders in an 18-hole playoff, that he decided to continue spot-lining for all of his shots, and he has done so to this day.

In 1980, feeling he needed to convert his standard shot from a fade to a draw to regain some distance at age 40, he worked with Jack Grout to make his swing "deeper," that is, less upright on the backswing. At the same time, he enlisted short-game guru Phil Rodgers to help with his chipping, pitching and sand game, always Jack's nemeses. These two improved parts of his game propelled Jack to winning both the U.S. Open at Baltusrol and the PGA Championship at Oak Hill that year.

Jack's swing was built to win major championships. His higher follow-through was a safety factor. He bent from the hips, putting his weight on the balls of his feet, making his swing more upright for a higher ball flight. He never worried about coming over the top because his left shoulder was so far behind the ball at the top of the backswing.

What people today fail to realize is Jack's work ethic. Yes he took time off from the game, and

Jack and Phil Rodgers have been competitors and friends since their amateur days. Phil helped Jack rework his pitching, chipping and bunker game in 1980.

didn't play as many tournaments as other professionals, but as a youngster he hit countless practice balls, and no one prepared for major championships like Jack. He never wanted to begin a tournament feeling he was unprepared. And no one ever made a greater number of important putts—putts he had to have — than Jack in his prime. His putting style was very different from all the other players' styles. I discuss Jack's putting technique, and why it was so effective, on pages 114-117.

There has never been a better, more complete, more gifted golfer than Jack Nicklaus. He left nothing to chance. For years, his equipment was built for high, soft, left-to-right, controlled shots. His irons were ½ inch short, more upright, with two degrees more loft.

In 1986, when he won his last of 20 majors, the Masters at age 46, he again tweaked his swing during the tournament, using his legs more aggressively through impact. Before winning the first of two U.S. Senior Opens, in 1991, he took a putting lesson from his son, Jackie. Jack never stops looking for a better way to do things.

The Classic Nicklaus Swing

The year was 1990, and it was Jack's first senior event, The Tradition at Desert Mountain, in Scottsdale, Arizona. At the time I was Desert Mountain's Director of Instruction and made a point of watching all the senior tour players as they practiced. I had followed Jack for several holes in a practice round with Chi Chi Rodriguez, Paul Runyan and the founder of Desert Mountain, Lyle Anderson. I could tell Jack was struggling with his game. He'd hit one ball left, the next one right, then shrug in frustration.

On the 13th hole, Jack noticed that I was observing from a distance. His teacher since boyhood, Jack Grout, had passed the previous year, and Nicklaus was clearly floundering. I watched him for a few more holes and when he finished, he asked me to work with him on the range. I watched Jack hit some balls, and it was the same story. His body and club were not in sync — his body was outracing the club. Finally, I said, "I don't see Jack Nicklaus." In other words, Jack had ventured away from the things that had made him such a phenomenal ball-striker and player. I had remembered a more dynamic swinger of the club, someone who played golf with the head of the golf club, allowing it to swing freely, hitting the ball long, high and under control. We worked together the rest of the tournament, which Jack went on to win, and we've been working together ever since.

To this day, I am fortunate to help Jack with his game whenever he calls on me, and I have learned untold amounts about golf from the man I consider the greatest player of all time. Not only has he given me tremendous insight into his own game and the games of others, but this insight has influenced my teaching immeasurably. I have studied his swing for years and have spent countless hours on the practice tee not only coaching him with Grout's principles, but absorbing his wisdom.

Jack allowed his body to react to the swinging of the club. However, his swing was very upright. Due to his tremendous influence, the golf swing became much more of a vertical motion, though it has returned to more of a rotary motion today due to such changes in equipment as big-headed drivers and lighter yet stronger shafts. Such players as Tom Weiskopf, Greg Norman and Payne Stewart exemplified Jack's "swingaway" that put his hands high at the top. This lateral, not rotary, motion helped Jack eliminate the left side of the golf course. He was able to achieve a full release of the clubhead, controlled by bowing his left forearm through the strike, for his desired trajectory and precise distance. He was the best I've ever seen at controlling the clubhead through impact.

Impact

Jack is creating an efficient impact position with the right arm under the left, releasing and squaring the clubface with his arms.

Release

Jack's body is reacting in synchronization with the arms swinging and the clubhead freely and fully releasing.

Halfway Through

The momentum of applying the clubhead to the ball pulls Jack's body around and into a full and free finish.

Finish

This high finish eliminates the left side of the golf course.

Face the Ball at Impact

Look at Jack at impact and you will always see that his shoulders are square while his hips are slightly open. His key thought here was to have the placket of his shirt pointing at or slightly to the right of the ball at impact (*below*). This thought alone assured a free release of the club, with the shoulders never interfering and the arms coming into impact from slightly inside the target line.

> "Jack's swing was built to win major championships. His higher follow-through was a safety factor for creating the desired ball flight."

Jack's synchronizing his arms, clubhead and legs allows his left forearm to become bowed to stabilize and control the clubhead.

His chest still faces the tee well past impact, which leads to consistency and power. Note the rolling of his left foot.

Jack is still in balance and well behind the ball, with his left thigh starting to create a rotary motion of his body.

Body perfectly in balance in response to applying the clubhead.

> "Jack was influenced by Alex Morrison, who advocated a dominant left side. Jack was able to achieve a full release of the clubhead, which was controlled by bowing his left forearm through the strike."

Completing the Backswing

Starting Down

Halfway Down

...e shaft swinging between the arms creates a light feeling of the clubhead.

Jack's body is "collected." His hands are under and supporting the shaft with the face square to slightly open.

The legs are moving laterally, holding the right hip and shoulder back, allowing room for the arms to swing from the inside.

The right arm swinging in front of the right hip and underneath the left arm allows the clubhead to remain slightly open, which eliminates a hook.

Club Support

...upports the club well at the top of the swing with his hands, the toe of the club ...ng down, evidence of a square to slightly open clubface at the top. He used the club ...t identically to Byron Nelson. This allowed Jack to release the club fully and natu- ...hrough impact without fear of hooking the ball. He wanted to eliminate one side of ...olf course, and that was usually the left side. The toe-down clubface position is also ...ason he was able to hit the ball so high.

Keep Shaft between Arms

At address, halfway back and at the top of the swing, you'll see that Jack's clubshaft remains between his arms. This is a simple yet effective way to swing the club.

> *"He never worried about coming over the top because he was so far behind the ball."*

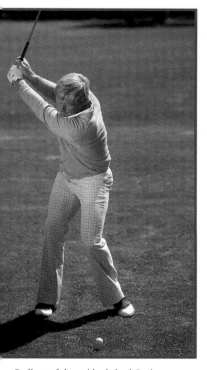

Rolling of the ankles helped Jack stay "on top" of the ball.

The swinging of the arms and club fully loads the body over the right leg, with the left shoulder well behind the ball.

A lateral movement of the left knee and thigh controls the hips and shoulders, with the left hip moving toward and over the left heel.

Jack's right arm is into his side and under his left arm. The lateral movement of his legs has allowed him to maintain the width of his arms.

Swing Arms to the Sky

...ertainly learned this at an early age from Jack Grout, and it is the main reason he ...ch an upright swing and full arc. This enabled him to drive the ball prodigious ...ces and hit high long-irons.

Head Steady

Swinging around a steady head is a bedrock principle for Jack. The head should neither move laterally nor up and down. Jack felt the body should swivel around this steady head for stability and consistency.

Swing Analysis

Muscular Jack vs Classic Jack:
A Comparison

From my discussions with Jack Nicklaus and my observations of his game, I've determined that there are clear principles that influenced the way he played golf. Whether Jack was playing with his muscular swing earlier in his career or his classic swing as he grew older, these eight tenets helped frame his golf game and kept his mind clear so he could produce the shots he needed no matter the conditions or the situation.

1. APPLYING THE CLUBHEAD is the term he often uses for describing his philosophy of getting the club to strike the ball. That is a subtle way of identifying his priority to control the ball into the target area and then make a score. He did not think so much about what his body might be doing because the ball only knows what the clubhead tells it to do. Jack felt that when playing under pressure it was easier and more effective to make adjustments to hit the desired shot, not with his body, but with how he was using, or applying, the clubhead. I have found similar opinions from Sam Snead and many other fine players.

2. JACK FELT HIS ADVERSARY WAS THE GOLF COURSE, not the other players. He could only control himself, so in that way he was not concerned with other competitors on the course. This led to great course strategy, shot management and sound decisions. That's why he loved the pressure of the last nine holes of major championships when he was in contention.

3. HE WAS ALWAYS PREPARED. There was no excuse for not being ready for the course or the tournament. Jack would start

Muscular Setup

Circa 1962

In his muscular swing, Jack's ball position is slightly more forward, opposite his left heel. His left foot is flared dramatically and his stance is very wide. Note that the outside of his left hip is in line with the ball and shoulder. In the classic swing (opposite page) Jack's hip is well outside that line. In the muscular swing, Jack is in a more dynamic position, his chin turned to his right, with his body more behind the ball, which will create a shallower angle at impact, resulting in a higher ball flight. This required a more lateral motion with his legs to get his body back to the ball at impact.

preparing for majors and the courses they were played on months ahead. Often while playing regular tour events he would hit shots he would need for the next major. For example, he practiced hitting knockdown shots in the tournaments preceding the British Open, even if the situation didn't call for them.

Key

■ Elements in red indicate a DIFFERENCE between Jack's muscular swing and his classic swing.

■ Elements in blue indicate a SIMILARITY between Jack's muscular swing and his classic swing.

4. JACK PRACTICED MECHANICALLY BUT PLAYED BY FEEL. He visualized the shot before playing. Jack always had a complete understanding of what he was trying to do with his club and body to hit the shot he pictured in his mind. He was a master at making adjustments to he always checked his aim — as if he were on the course. He hit every practice shot to a target with a committed ball flight.

6. SWING THE CLUB WIDE AND HIGH. From the very beginning "Mr. J. Grout," as Jack affectionately referred to his

Classic Setup

In his classic swing, Jack is set up more on top of the ball. He stated that as he got older, his body was not able to make as strong a lateral move to the impact position. His chin is still slightly turned to his right, allowing him to make a greater shoulder turn, and he played left-eye dominant. He liked a starting position that has a straight line going from his left shoulder through his left arm to the clubhead. In both the muscular and the classic swings, he set up slightly open to encourage a slightly more upright swing so as to help eliminate the left side of the golf course.

Circa 1978

keep improving as the week went along. That gave him more confidence so he would peak on the weekends and get into contention for the final nine.

5. JACK LEFT NOTHING TO CHANCE. Being a perfectionist, he was very detailed about his grip, hand and arm tension, setup and alignment. Even in practice, teacher, coach and mentor, taught him a very simple but complete approach for playing golf. Grout gave the young Nicklaus a very special exercise: Swing his arms and club wide and high to the sky while rolling his ankles and feet, but keeping the inside of his heels on the ground, even at the finish of the swing. The shoulders and body reacted to the free swinging of his arms both on the backswing and forward swing. His feet rolled and controlled his legs and hips while the clubhead was being fully released in harmony with the movement of his body. His feet controlled his rhythm, and his arms and hands "applied the clubhead." Great distance and feel was the result. This exercise put the clubface square to open at the top of the swing with his hands and arms under the shaft. This also put the shaft between his arms as he was swinging the club. His swing path was not in to out, but very much on the target line through impact. This created no need for manipulation but allowed a full release of the clubhead.

7. KEEP THE HEAD STEADY. Jack's upper body was quiet through the strike. This created consistency and the ability to repeat his motion, and it resulted in creating the bottom of the arc where he wanted it to be for solid contact. The swinging of the arms to control the shoulders with the feet and legs controlling the hips allowed him to "face the ball at impact." That made his swing feel as if it were controlled by his arms and legs, not his hips and shoulders. He said he "armed" the ball through impact. That gave him a feeling for controlling distance and the trajectory of the ball.

8. USE THE EYES. For all truly great athletes, the eyes are most productive and profound. Jack's eyes missed nothing! The information and pictures they sent to his mind created a marvelous blueprint — his eyes committed his mind and body to the target, so his hands and arms felt and swung the club in sync with his feet and legs. Sometimes even good and playable shots happened because his mind was so positive and strong. The state of a completely focused mind is a trademark of a champion. Only a few possess "that look."

The Swingaway

Jack's muscular setup allowed him to swing his arms and clubhead away from the ball in a slightly wider arc. On both swings his legs are very stable, supporting the swinging of the arms. His hips have not yet started turning. The wider the arc, the later the right shoulder starts turning. In fact, in both swings, his shoulders are reacting to the swinging of the arms.

Transition

Notice how Jack's head and body are much farther behind the ball in the muscular swing. In the classic swing, he's more on top of the ball, with his right leg angled inward. Jack always wanted his chest and shoulders to react to the swinging of the arms and club during the transition. Note how he replants his left heel toward the target, which kept his left hip from opening too soon.

Impact

Release

In the muscular swing, slightly prior to impact, his chest is facing the ball, one of Jack's key principles. His chin is still tilted to the right, which helps keep his right shoulder back and his right arm close to his body. In the classic swing, just past impact, his chest still faces the ball. In both swings, his right heel is barely off the ground.

Jack's forearms are rotating to release the clubhead fully, and his left upper arm stays close to his chest. No chicken wing here. Because of the ball being teed, the clubhead is being swung upward through impact, resulting in a slightly more tilted spine angle. Note his head has moved even farther behind the ball as a result.

Putting

Everybody thinks of Jack as making those key putts to win major titles, like the snake he holed on the 16th hole for birdie to win the 1975 Masters, or the putts he made on 17 and 18 to win the 1980 U.S. Open at Baltusrol. But the real secret to Jack's putting prowess was how he prided himself on never three-putting the last hole to lose a tournament, after he did so early in his career at Pebble Beach to lose to Billy Casper. Jack would play as many as three or four tournaments in a row without a three-putt. He was a remarkable lag putter. He had a style that was very unusual, and in fact has never been copied by any other great player. Jack putted as he played golf. He felt and used the head of the club to control the ball. Here are the other points that set Jack's stroke apart from all the others:

"The Stare"

Reading Greens

Jack believed reading the greens was done a lot with his feet. He felt the changes in the terrain through his shoes.

He tended to look at putts as a golf course architect, in other words — where's the drainage?

He used his feet to reinforce what his eyes told him.

Setup

Head set up behind ball

Shaft tilted forward

JACK'S PUTTER

George Low, a golf professional renowned both for his putting ability and crafting fine putters, gave Jack one of his Model 600 Wizard putters at a pro-am in Tucson in 1964. Employing an undersized leather grip and three degrees of loft, Jack won 15 of his 18 professional majors with this putter. Jack felt that the smallish grip gave him better feel of the putterhead so as to apply it to the ball.

In setting up to the putt, Jack's first goal was to get behind the ball.

Note that Jack's putting posture was similar to his driving posture — his right shoulder was lower than his left. He felt these were the only two shots that you wanted to hit up on.

Jack held the putter very softly with an absence of tension in his forearms.

Jack had great distance control. He tried to roll the ball gently over the front edge of the hole, which, in effect, made the hole larger. He loved fast greens.

On shorter putts, Jack felt that his right eye looked at the ball and his left eye at the hole. To do this, he set his eyes well behind the ball on the target line. He wanted his eyes directly over the target line. Sometimes Jack's tendency was to get his eyes too far outside the line, something he checked for constantly.

Feet open to intended line

Starting Back

Backswing

Low

Completed B

As in his full swing, Jack tended to aim his body slightly left, and push the ball into the hole. He wanted the ball to roll with minimal backspin off the putter.

He accomplished this by tilting the shaft slightly toward the hole, and because of his setup behind the ball, he struck the ball on the upswing.

Jack used his left arm to stabilize the putterhead at impact, but his right arm acted like a piston to control the speed of the stroke for distance control.

His right eye looked at the ball and his left eye at the hole.

From inside ten feet, he felt he could see the ball and the hole at the same time.

However, while Jack swung at his full shots using a dominant left eye, he putted with a dominant right eye, partially because he was set up so far behind the ball at address.

Jack had such a strong w he refused to take the putter ba the ball going i

Jack held the putter very s of tension in his

Jack putted with his ha not his shoulders. As he got o and more fo

Just as in his full swing, Ja the putterhead

Backswing | Impact | Follow-Through

High

to hole the putt,
k until he had visualized
the hole.

tly with an absence
orearms.

ds and forearms,
er, he used less hands
arms.

s goal was to apply
the ball.

One of Jack's keys to putting well was to hit the ball
on the upswing.

His putter shaft was tilted forward at point of the strike.

Jack did not enjoy practicing putting,
and therefore practiced in short intervals.
He was always adjusting his stance in practice,
then often using the new position
on the course to maximum effect.

Because Jack had such incredible touch, he really
concentrated on hitting the ball solidly.

Jack always wanted his right
elbow and arm to rest against
his side when he putted. He
set his feet open, so he could
see the line better. Jack had a
slight pop in his stroke, with
the follow-through often
shorter than the backswing.

The head of Jack's putter
worked low to high, not high
to low. It was taken care of by
the way he set up to the ball.

At the 1986 British Open, after winning the Masters for the sixth time earlier in the year.

Bobby Jones

Although Jack met Bob Jones at his first U.S. Amateur, the 1955 event at the Country Club of Virginia, he had been regaled about Jones's exploits at the 1926 U.S. Open at his home course of Scioto, by both his father, Charlie, and his teacher, Jack Grout. In fact, Jack knew about Bob Jones's record better than any other golfer. Clearly, Jones was Jack's hero.

As Jack was finishing up his last practice round on the eve of the tournament, Jones sat behind the green of the hilly 460-yard, par 4 in a golf cart. In the time Jones was watching, Jack was the only competitor to reach the putting surface in two. He asked who this young player was, and finding out that he was only 15 years old, asked to meet him. That initial meeting lasted about 20 minutes and thrilled not only Jack, but his father, a Scioto regular, as well. Jack remembers Jones saying, "Young man, I heard that you're a very fine golfer. I'm coming out and watch you play a few holes tomorow."

Although Jack lost in the first round to Robert Gardner, the meeting with Bob Jones was the first of many to come. One time at the Amateur Dinner at the Masters, Jones laughingly told him that during the 1926 Open his caddie put down his golf bag in the very high rough on the eighth hole to help their playing competitor look for his ball and almost couldn't find his golf bag when play resumed.

Bob Jones and Jack became friends over the years, as Jack won the Masters three times before Jones passed away in 1971.

After Jack's second win at Augusta in 1965, Bob famously remarked, "Jack Nicklaus is playing an entirely different game — a game I'm not even familiar with." It was a sentiment, coming from his boyhood hero, that Jack always felt humbled by.

The mutual admiration between Jones and Nicklaus is evident at the 1957 U.S. Amateur.

"I really felt he could accomplish anything in golf after that victory."

— Charlie Nicklaus

1956 Ohio Open

Marietta Golf Club
Marietta, Ohio

Winning Score 76-70-64-72—282

*I*n a portent of golf events to come, Jack won the 1956 Ohio Open against both pros and amateurs over the lush fairways of Marietta Country Club in Marietta, Ohio, by eight strokes, at the ripe old age of 16. The 1956 Ohio Open was played over 72 holes, with 36 holes played on the third and final day. Included in the field was Frank Stranahan, a player on the PGA Tour who finished second in the British Open twice and once in the Masters.

Jack — referred to as Jackie in the press accounts — opened with a 76 on the first day and added a 70 on the second day. With a 64 in the morning round on the third day, Jack broke open the tournament, as he added a 72 in the afternoon to win.

Years later Jack attributed his sharpness on the last day to playing in an exhibition match with Sam Snead at Urbana Country Cub on the afternoon of the second day of the Ohio Open. Bob Kepler, who ran the Ohio Open that year — later he was Jack's golf coach at Ohio State — arranged for Jack to play his second round early in the morning so he could play the exhibition match in the afternoon. After he completed the second round, Jack was flown to Urbana in a small private plane — by Warren Grimes, who had organized the exhibition and who worked for an aviation instrument manufacturer — and then back to Marietta that evening. Jack later recalled both he and Snead drove the ball about the same distance but, interestingly, Sam putted better as he shot a 68 to Jack's 72. However, the one thing about the exhibition that he wasn't happy about was that Sam kept calling him "Junior." Jack claimed that Snead's incredible rhythm rubbed off on him, as he swung on the last day with a wonderful sense of rhythm and timing, just like Snead's metronomic swing.

Several years later, Snead played a practice round with a young Nicklaus at Augusta. After hitting their drives into the fairway on the par-5 13th, Sam told Jack that when he was Jack's age, he would hit his drive over the tall Georgia pines on the left side of the hole where the fairway doglegs to the left, thus shortening the second shot considerably. As the story goes, Jack teed up a second ball, hit it with a mighty wallop, but it hit only two-thirds of the way up the tree. Thinking if Snead could do it, he could, too, Jack teed up another ball, but again hit it only two-thirds of the way up the tree. Walking off the tee and laughing hard with his Cheshire-cat smile, Sam turned to Jack and said, "But when I was your age, Jack, the trees were much shorter!" True or not, Snead loved retelling that story through the years.

Still only 16, Jack wins the Ohio Open after playing an exhibition match with Sam Snead, while Earl Christiansen, 45, finishes as low professional.

THE 1959 WALKER CUP

	United States		Great Britain & Ireland	
Captains:	Charley Coe		Gerald Micklem	
Foursomes:				
Harvie Ward and Frank Taylor (1 up)		1	Reid Jack and Doug Sewell	0
Bill Hyndman and Tommy Aaron (1 up)		1	Joe Carr and Guy Wolstenholme	0
Billy Joe Patton and Charley Coe (9 and 8)		1	Michael Bonallack and Arthur Perowne	0
Ward Wettlaufer and Jack Nicklaus (2 and 1)		1	Michael Lunt and Alec Shepperson	0
Day One Total		**4**		**0**
Singles:				
Charley Coe		0	Joe Carr (2 and 1)	1
Harvie Ward (9 and 8)		1	Guy Wolstenholme	0
Billy Joe Patton		0	Reid Jack (5 and 3)	1
Bill Hyndman (4 and 3)		1	Doug Sewell	0
Tommy Aaron		0	Alec Shepperson (2 and 1)	1
Deane Beman (2 up)		1	Michael Bonallack	0
Ward Wettlaufer (6 and 5)		1	Michael Lunt	0
Jack Nicklaus (5 and 4)		1	Dickson Smith	0
Day Two Total		**5**		**3**
TOTAL		**9**		**3**

The 1959 Walker Cup

The Honourable Company of Edinburgh Golfers
Muirfield, Gullane, Scotland
May 15-16, 1959

6,806 Yards   Par-72

*T*he United States Golf Association selected what playing Captain Charley Coe called "one of the youngest and strongest" teams ever assembled to compete against an eight-member British squad in the biennial Walker Cup matches to be contested at storied Muirfield.

The youngest member of the U.S. team was a 19-year-old Ohio State sophomore majoring in pharmacy, one Jack Nicklaus. Among other accomplishments, Jack was selected for his win at the Ohio Open, which included professional golfers and amateurs as well, at age 16, and his victory in the 1959 North-South Amateur at Pinehurst.

Also selected for the team were Walker Cup newcomers Deane Beman, a 21-year-old University of Maryland junior, Tommy Aaron, a 22-year-old senior at the University of Florida, and Ward Wettlaufer, 23, a senior at Hamilton College. Rounding out the team were veterans Harvey Ward, Bill Hyndman, Billy Joe Patton and Frank Taylor.

Because of the conditions expected at Muirfield — constant wind and possibly rain — Captain Coe decided on using the smaller British golf ball. At the end of the first day — foursomes play — the point total was U.S.–4, GBI–0, as the U.S. side swept all four matches.

In the 36-hole singles matches the next day, Jack Nicklaus — playing in a light mist that enveloped the course all morning — shot 33 on the back nine to go 5 up at the break. Winning the first four holes in the afternoon, Jack closed out Dickson Smith, his British competitor, 5 and 4 for the win.

In a match that pitted the future Commissioner of the PGA Tour against the future Secretary of the R&A, Deane Beman had a much tougher time as he was paired against Michael Bonallack who was at the top of his game, shooting a strong 69 in the morning. Beman needed a 12-foot birdie putt on the 18th hole to stay three back after the first 18. With a burst of superlative play, Beman squared the match with Bonallack on the 27th hole. All even at the 34th hole, Beman went on to win the final two holes in perhaps the best match of the 1959 Walker Cup matches. It was the 16th time out of the 17 matches played that the American squad had prevailed.

Significantly, Jack was introduced to Muirfield, a course and a name that would have great significance later in his career.

ABOVE: **The 1959 U.S. Walker Cup team at practice.**

LEFT: **Standing, left to right: Tommy Aaron, Jack Nicklaus, Ward Wettlaufer, Bill Hyndman. Seated, left to right: Harvie Ward, Deane Beman, Charley Coe (Captain), Billy Joe Patton, Frank Taylor.**

"...Jack Nicklaus will surely be a major force in American golf for many years to come. ... he has the poise of a veteran ... He is a very exciting player to watch. He bashes his tee shots with everything he has, plays his irons with great boldness right at the stick and, especially for so burly a youngster, has an unusually sensitive touch on the greens... "

— Herbert Warren Wind
Sports Illustrated, September 28, 1959

The 1959 Amateur

The Broadmoor (East Course)
Colorado Springs, Colorado
September 14 - 19, 1959

7,010 Yards   Par-71   1,696 Entries   200 Players

*N*ow a 19-year-old junior at Ohio State, Jack qualified for the Amateur at the Broadmoor in Colorado Springs, Colorado.

Jack had played in the Amateur since he was 15 years old, but never went past the fourth round. Interestingly, Jack defeated Robert T. Jones, III, the son of Bobby Jones, 7 and 6, in the first round.

In the semi-final against 46-year-old Gene Andrews, of Whittier, California, Jack needed to hole a tricky 25-foot downhill putt over a ridge on the 35th hole to save his 1-up advantage. Both had fives on the 36th hole, as Jack gained the final against the reigning Amateur champ Charley Coe.

After firing three consecutive birdies on the first three holes, Coe only picked up one hole as the much younger player hung in. Coe was 2 up after shooting a fine 69 in the light Colorado morning air to Jack's 71. By the 32nd hole Jack went 1 up to lead the match for the first time. With halves on the next two holes, Jack, admitting to some nervousness on the 17th tee, closed the face of his driver on the downswing and hit his ball far off-line into the pine trees. Coe, playing cautiously, made his par 5, which Jack was unable to equal — making the match all-square with one hole to play.

Jack played with a bold and courageous power game, even when cautious play seemed appropriate.

Coe had a chip for birdie as his shot to the last green ended behind the green. His chip went straight for the cup but stopped just one turn of the ball short.

With an eight-foot birdie putt for a 1-up victory, Jack won the first of his 20 major championship titles in spectacular fashion.

Jack, thus, became the second-youngest winner of the U.S. Amateur.

ABOVE: Because of the elevation in Colorado, Broadmoor's East Course played closer to 6,700 yards, considerably shorter than its listed length at 7,010 yards.

LEFT: Jack's 1-up victory over Charley Coe in the 36-hole final earns him his first major championship.

"This was, to put it mildly, the wildest Open yet."

— Herbert Warren Wind
Sports Illustrated

1960 U.S. Open

Cherry Hills Country Club
Englewood, Colorado
June 16 - 18, 1960

7,004 Yards   Par-71   2,453 Entries;   150 Starters
55 Players made the cut at five over par

If Jules Verne had invented an honest-to-goodness time machine, golf aficionados would likely line up to be transported back to 1960 and the U.S. Open at Cherry Hills, just outside of Denver.

For in the 1960 Open three eras of golf came together for perhaps the only time as Ben Hogan, Arnold Palmer and Jack Nicklaus simultaneously challenged for the National Championship right up to the 17th hole of the final round.

It was the past — in the form of the 47-year-old, four-time Open winner Ben Hogan, sharing the lead with two holes to play — playing with the future — in the form of the 20-year-old U.S. Amateur titleholder Jack Nicklaus — contending nip-and-tuck with the current hero — 30-year-old Arnold Palmer, who would go on to win his one and only Open. It was a three-dimensional inflection point, if you will, with each battling over the last few holes on the last day for the most significant prize in golf.

The Cherry Hills course was a good one, with four very good short holes and five difficult finishing holes, but seven of the par-4s played essentially as drive-and-pitch holes. Granted, the course did play tough — small, hard greens with plenty of bunkers and many water hazards — but overall, it was just a little too short for the U.S. Open, especially in the thin air of mile-high Denver.

Given the relatively shorter length of the layout, seven Open records were broken on

Jack practices at Cherry Hills with his 1959 Walker Cup teammate Deane Beman.

the first day. The 36-hole cut score of 147 was one shot lower than the record 148 set at Riviera in 1948 when Hogan won his first official U.S. Open.

Still, this 1960 U.S. Open at Cherry Hills was one of the most significant tournaments in American golf history.

Through the first two rounds, Mike Souchak, the third-place finisher in the 1959 Open, led by two at seven under, with scores of 68-67–135. Finishing up the first of his two rounds on Saturday, he ran into some trouble on the 18th tee, as he was upset by a photographer taking a picture while he was in the middle of his swing, and hit his drive out of bounds. With a double-bogey six for a 73, he still had a two-stroke lead starting his final round over his closest competitor, and a full nine-stroke lead over Palmer.

Walking the Final 36 with Ben and Jack

"In 1960 I missed the cut at Cherry Hills by one shot after shooting 74-74–148. When I decided to stay and watch the last day of the Open, Joe Dey, then the Executive Director of the USGA and later the first Commissioner of the PGA Tour, asked if I'd like to walk with him — under the ropes — and follow Ben and Jack who were paired together for the double round on the last day. I enthusiastically accepted.

What I saw amazed me.

In all the rounds I had been privileged to play with Ben (in 1959 I had been paired with Ben in the Open at Winged Foot), I never saw him watch another player swing or do anything but fully focus on his own game. (The only exception was on a par 3 where he would watch, not the player's swing, but the flight of the ball as he wanted to see if there was any wind.)

For the first time, I noticed that Ben was watching — even studying — the way Jack hit the ball at places where he had no interest. Usually Ben had a completely neutral look on his face when he played a round. But the look on Ben's face was telling — his expression seemed to be saying "This is something very, very special." The look on his face was the same look of awe that I observed when people watched Ben hit the ball.

Those 36 holes were something special to behold."

— DEANE BEMAN

Playing the final 36 holes with Jack, Hogan finished four strokes back in ninth place.

"If I were a kid named Nicklaus,
I'd feel worse than I do. I watched him lose
this Open by six strokes through inexperience."

— **Ben Hogan,**
*just after the final round
of the 1960 Open*

In the afternoon Souchak got off to a bad start with a double bogey on the first hole and never regained his fine play of the previous rounds, playing himself out of the tournament.

Palmer, embellishing his reputation for playing aggressively, drove the first green and two-putted for birdie. It was wonderful start, as he made five more birdies and one bogey on the front side en route to a record 30 on the first nine.

Palmer played steady golf, as his main rivals playing ahead of him fell by the wayside. Nicklaus three-putted the 13th and 14th holes on his way to a 71 and second place; 1955 Open champion Jack Fleck had problems on the greens and ended up with a 283, tied for third; two-time Open winner Julius Boros was bunkered on the 14th and 18th holes and missed a three-foot putt on 17 to finish three back; and hard-luck Mike Souchak just couldn't get a putt to drop and also finished tied for third at 283.

An exuberant Palmer (top and left) celebrates after coming from a seven-stroke deficit to win his only U.S. Open championship.

But most significantly, it was Hogan who was tied with Palmer at four under with just two holes to play and had hit 34 consecutive greens in regulation or better but made a six on the par-5 17th hole after hitting into the water-filled moat fronting the green. He then made a triple-bogey seven on 18, after once again hitting into the water before the begining of the 18th fairway. It was Hogan's last legitimate run at the one tournament with which he had become synonomous. Sadly, for many golf fans, he finished with 284, four back, in a tie for ninth.

Jack's score of 282, just two strokes behind Arnold, was the lowest score ever by an amateur in the Open, including all four of Bob Jones's victories in the Open.

Playing cautious, steady golf on the back nine, Palmer went on to win his only U.S. Open against a very strong and determined field.

TOP: **Hogan removes his shoes on the bank of the 17th hole, the 71st hole of the Open, in order to hit his ball out of the shallow water.**

RIGHT: **Sizing up his new rival, Arnold gives Jack a playful rub on the head for being runner-up. (Inset) Hogan pitches to the 17th green from the edge of the lake.**

1960 U.S. OPEN	
1. Arnold Palmer	72 – 71 – 72 – 65 – 280
2. Jack Nicklaus*	71 – 71 – 69 – 71 – 282
3. "Dutch" Harrison	74 – 70 – 70 – 69 – 283
Julius Boros	73 – 69 – 68 – 73 – 283
Mike Souchak	68 – 67 – 73 – 75 – 283
Ted Kroll	72 – 69 – 75 – 67 – 283
Jack Fleck	70 – 70 – 72 – 71 – 283
Dow Finsterwald	71 – 69 – 70 – 73 – 283
9. Ben Hogan	75 – 67 – 69 – 73 – 284
Jerry Barber	69 – 71 – 70 – 74 – 284
Don Cherry*	70 – 71 – 71 – 72 – 284
*Amateur	

1960
OPEN CHAMPIONSHIP
CHERRY HILLS
COUNTRY CLUB
ENGLEWOOD, COLORADO
LOW AMATEUR SCORER

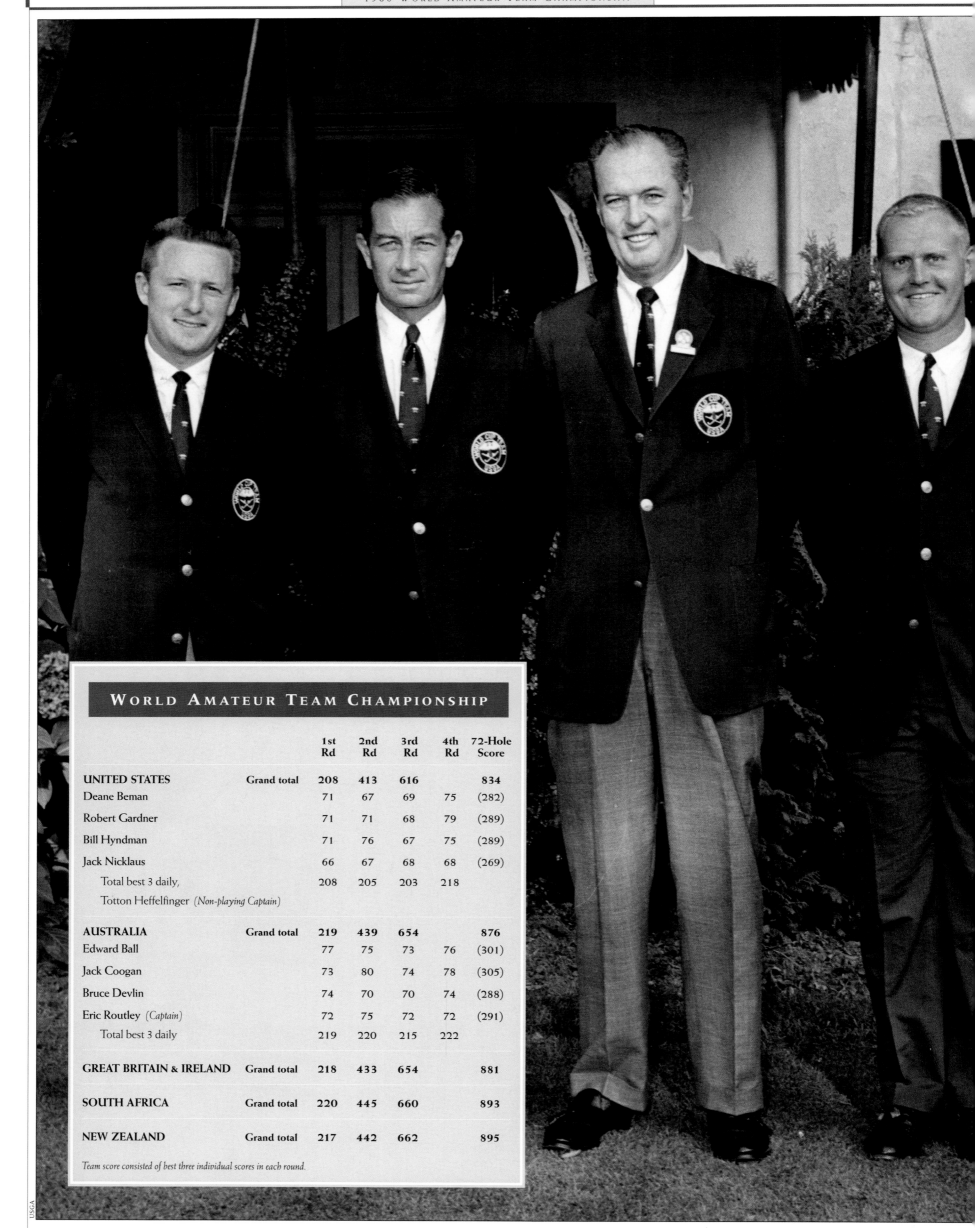

WORLD AMATEUR TEAM CHAMPIONSHIP

		1st Rd	2nd Rd	3rd Rd	4th Rd	72-Hole Score
UNITED STATES	Grand total	208	413	616		834
Deane Beman		71	67	69	75	(282)
Robert Gardner		71	71	68	79	(289)
Bill Hyndman		71	76	67	75	(289)
Jack Nicklaus		66	67	68	68	(269)
Total best 3 daily,		208	205	203	218	
Totton Heffelfinger *(Non-playing Captain)*						
AUSTRALIA	Grand total	219	439	654		876
Edward Ball		77	75	73	76	(301)
Jack Coogan		73	80	74	78	(305)
Bruce Devlin		74	70	70	74	(288)
Eric Routley *(Captain)*		72	75	72	72	(291)
Total best 3 daily		219	220	215	222	
GREAT BRITAIN & IRELAND	Grand total	218	433	654		881
SOUTH AFRICA	Grand total	220	445	660		893
NEW ZEALAND	Grand total	217	442	662		895

Team score consisted of best three individual scores in each round.

The 1960 World Amateur Team Championship

Merion Golf Club (East Course)
Ardmore, Pennsylvania
September 28 - October 1, 1960

6,694 Yards   Par-70   32 Team Entries;   126 Players

"No one had ever seen anyone play Merion like this."
— Deane Beman

"…the most exciting and memorable formance by an amateur golfer since Bobby Jones's Grand Slam in 1930."
— Gwilym Brown
Sports Illustrated, October 10, 1960

The initial World Amateur Team Championship for the Eisenhower Trophy was played in 1958 at the home of golf. The American team was captained by Robert Tyre Jones, Jr. — the much beloved "Wee Bobby" to the citizens of his adopted hometown of St. Andrews. It was during the inaugural event that Bob Jones gave one of the most memorable speeches in sport when he was made an Honorary Burgher of St. Andrews for his exploits in the ancient game and for the way he comported himself. In his speech to a packed Younger Hall at St. Andrews University, Jones said, "If I took everything out of my life except the time I spent in St. Andrews, I would still have lived a full rich life."

It was against this glorious beginning that 126 players from 32 teams came to historic Merion Golf Club in Ardmore, Pennsylvania. Merion, where some of the greatest events in golf history took place — the Merion of Jones completing his Grand Slam on the 11th hole against Gene Homans in 1930, and the Merion of Ben Hogan hitting a 1-iron to the 18th hole in the fourth round to force a playoff of the 1950 U.S. Open, where he capped perhaps the greatest comeback in golf history. Merion is a grand stage, fitting for great golf and great feats.

The American team of Deane Beman, Robert Gardner, Bill Hyndman and Jack Nicklaus did not disappoint. Playing a format of the three best scores of each four-man team over four rounds, the American team won by a whopping 42 strokes over the second-place Australian team. Moreover, the youngest member of the American team, Ohio State University's Jack Nicklaus, shot a four-round total of 269 — an amazing 18 strokes below Hogan's winning score over the same ground as in the 1950 Open.

Jack's scoring in that second World Amateur Team was indeed a great feat in a marvelous and historic setting.

LEFT: The American World Amateur Team (l to r): Deane Beman, Robert Gardner, Bill Hyndman, Jack Nicklaus and Totton Heffelfinger, the non-playing captain.

UPPER RIGHT: Jack, somewhat incredulous after his record-setting total of 269, 11 under par and 18 strokes lower than Hogan's Open record.

LOWER RIGHT: Pitching back to one of Merion's greens with its signature basket-topped flagstick.

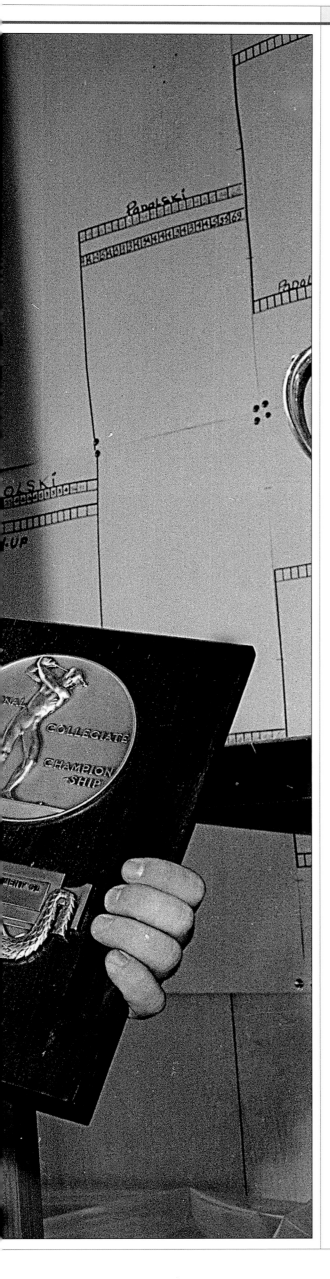

The 1961 NCAA Championship

Purdue University
Lafayette, Indiana
June 19 - 24, 1961

*A*lthough not generally considered a major, the NCAA, the championship for collegiate golfers, is every bit the national championship for the college set and, if not generally considered a major, it is on a rung just slightly below that of the U.S. Amateur. In addition to the individual winner, there is also a team award for the best scoring team in the tournament.

Playing on the waterlogged Purdue University North Course in Lafayette, Indiana, the week after the U.S. Open, where he finished as low amateur in fourth place, Jack was the qualifying medalist, with rounds of 70-70–140 to edge Mark Darnell of Purdue by one stroke, and enter the 64-man championship flight for individual honors. Significant additional qualifiers were Homero Blancas of Houston, Dave Stockton of USC, Frank Beard of Florida and Labron Harris, Jr. of Oklahoma State.

In an all-Ohio State final, Jack bested OSU teammate Mike Podolski, 5 and 3 over 33 holes. Jack's eight birdies and 23 pars won 10 holes to Podolski's six birdies and 21 pars.

Five down after 27 holes, Podolski ran in a 40-foot putt on the 28th hole for birdie, lost the next with a poor chip, and won the 30th when Jack three-putted before birdieing the next hole. Despite winning three of the last six holes, Podolski lost the match on the 32nd hole when he chipped too hard and conceded Jack a six-foot birdie putt for the win and the 1961 NCAA Championship.

It was Jack's second "national" championship.

ABOVE: Jack (standing, right) with his Ohio State teammates and Coach Bob Kepler (standing, left).

LEFT: Jack Nicklaus, 1961 NCAA Champion.

1961 U.S. Amateur

Del Monte Golf & Country Club (Qualifying Rounds)
Pebble Beach Golf Links
Pebble Beach, California
September 11 - 16, 1961

6,747 Yards   Par-72   1,995 Entries   200 Starters

The 61st U.S. Amateur was scheduled for Pebble Beach for the first time since 1947, when Skee Riegel won the Havermeyer Trophy and quickly turned professional. But the first Amateur ever held at Pebble Beach was perhaps best known not for who won, but who lost in the first round. In 1929 Bob Jones traveled across the country via train to play in the Amateur. In the very first round he was beaten by Johnny Goodman, who went on to win the U.S. Open in 1933 — the last amateur to do so.

With his dominating record as an amateur, Jack was the co-favorite with the defending U.S. Amateur champ Deane Beman.

In the 36-hole final against Dudley Wysong, of McKinney, Texas, Jack won 8 and 6 on a day that alternately featured fog, rain and sunshine. In the morning 18, Jack gave an exhibi-

GOLF DIGEST

ABOVE: Jack and Deane Beman pacing off the course and making notes prior to the Amateur.

INSET: Jack's yardage card used in the '61 Amateur.

RIGHT: Dudley Wysong watches as Jack drives from the ninth tee.

tion of power off the tee in the fog and rain, shooting a 69 to lead, 4 up, at the lunch break. In the afternoon the sun came out, but it was all over on the 13th hole. Such was Jack's strong play that Wysong won only four holes over the 30 played.

Interestingly, Jack's caddie for the week was 58-year-old Al Gonzales, who had carried the bag of Harrison Johnson when he won the Amateur at Pebble in 1929.

TOP: **Dudley Wysong and Jack prior to the start of the final round of the 1961 U.S. Amateur Championship.**

BOTTOM: **Jack, S.F.B. Morse, John Glock and Dudley Wysong at the award ceremony.**

LEFT: **Jack drives from the tee in the final round. Note long-time USGA official P.J. Boatwright on the seat stick on the back left of the tee.**

The 1961 Walker Cup

Seattle Golf Club
Seattle, Washington
September 1-2, 1961

6,713 Yards   Par-71

*N*amed to his second Walker Cup team, Jack was joined by Deane Beman, Charley Coe, Bill Hyndman and Dr. Frank Taylor from the winning 1959 U.S. team at Muirfield. Also named to play at the 6,713-yard, par-71 Seattle Golf Club, overlooking Puget Sound, were Gene Andrews, Don Cherry, Robert Cochran and Charles Smith.

Jack was clearly the leading amateur in the country, having won the Amateur in 1959, finishing second in the 1960 U.S. Open, tying for fourth in this year's Open and winning the NCAA title earlier in the year.

The American team routed the British, 11 matches to 1, with Jack defeating Ireland's Joe Carr in the singles and teaming with Beman in the foursomes on the first day to defeat James Walker and Brian Chapman.

THE 1961 WALKER CUP

United States		Great Britain & Ireland	
Non-Playing Captains: Jack Westland		C.D. Lawrie	
Foursomes:			
Deane Beman and Jack Nicklaus (6 and 5)	1	James Walker and Brian Chapman	0
Charley Coe and Don Cherry (1 up)	1	David Blair and Martin Christmas	0
Bill Hyndman and Robert Gardner (4 and 3)	1	Joe Carr and Gordon Huddy	0
Robert Cochran and Eugene Andrews (4 and 3)	1	Michael Bonallack and Ronald Shade	0
Day One Total	**4**		**0**
Singles:			
Deane Beman (3 and 2)	1	Michael Bonallack	0
Charley Coe (5 and 4)	1	Michael Lunt	0
Frank Taylor (3 and 2)	1	James Walker	0
Bill Hyndman (7 and 6)	1	David Frame	0
Jack Nicklaus (6 and 4)	1	Joe Carr	0
Charles Smith	0	Martin Christmas (3 and 2)	1
Robert Gardner (1 up)	1	Ronald Shade	0
Don Cherry (5 and 4)	1	David Blair	0
Day Two Total	**7**		**1**
TOTAL	**11**		**1**

LEFT: The 1961 Walker Cup team.

1962 U.S. Open

Oakmont Country Club
Pittsburgh, Pennsylvania
June 14 - 17, 1962

6,894 Yards   Par-71   2,475 Entries;   150 Starters
51 Players made the cut at eight over par

The 1962 U.S. Open was scheduled for big, tough Oakmont Country Club on the outskirts of Pittsburgh, Pennsylvania, just 35 miles from Latrobe, the hometown of local icon Arnold Palmer.

Oakmont was one of the most famous of all of the Open courses, having hosted the Open previously in 1927 (won by Tommy Armour), 1935 (Sam Parks) and 1953 (Ben Hogan). It was a course that featured length, narrow firm fairways, penal rough, quick greens and numerous punishing bunkers, including the famous furrowed "Church Pews." It was a test truly worthy of the National Championship.

The first-round leader was Gene Littler, the defending champion with one of the best

ABOVE: **Teeing off in the first round at Oakmont, Jack takes aim at his first win as a professional.**

RIGHT: **Jack reacts with a dance step on the sixth green as he makes his putt during first round of U.S. Open.**

swings in all of golf, with a two-under 69.

Littler fashioned his two-under-par total on the strength of a spectacular eagle 3 on the up-hill 480-yard, par-5 ninth hole when he pitched in from 35 yards on his third shot, while Bob Rosburg and Bobby Nichols came in with one-under-par 70s.

The crowd favorite, Arnold Palmer, was two off the lead with a 71. Paired with 22-year-old Jack Nicklaus, who had just turned professional seven months earlier, Arnold drove the ball beautifully, making three birdies and four bogeys. Jack was one back with a one-over-par 72.

In the second round, Arnold continued his good play as he shot a three-under-par 68 to tie Rosburg, who had a 69, for the lead. Jack carded a 70 to lie three back, while Player scored his second consecutive 70. Jack and Arnie played together in the first two rounds.

In the Saturday double-round final, before the largest gallery in the history of the Open — some 24,492 spectators — Arnold shot 73-71—144 to tie Jack's 72-69—141, playing just

ABOVE: Arnold Palmer and Jack Nicklaus before the playoff.

LEFT: With Arnie's Army loyally cheering their hometown hero, Jack watches Palmer hit first in their 18-hole playoff. Jack still insists he heard nothing negative from the gallery.

ASSOCIATED PRESS

one hole ahead, for a four-round total of 283. Long drives and deft putting characterized Jack's play. In the fourth round, every time Arnold made a putt or hit a good shot, the highly partisan crowd was loud and enthusiastic for the hometown hero. Clearly, Nicklaus was the fly in the ointment, as far as the fans were concerned.

On the final hole in the fourth round, both players had straightforward birdie putts but missed. Arnold had played exceptionally well, missing only four fairways all week and hitting 63 greens in regulation, but his putting proved to be his Achilles heel. Interestingly, Jack had only one three-putt green over the first 72 holes of the Championship, to Arnold's 10. Yet Arnold had shot 283, to equal Ben Hogan's winning score at Oakmont nine years earlier.

There are usually a few "if only I had's" in each Open. This year it was Jack's pal Phil

©BETTMANN/CORBIS

Throughout the week Arnold and Jack crossed paths at Oakmont before meeting in the Monday playoff.

Rodgers who sang that refrain. On the short par-4 17th, he made an eight in the first round after driving into a small evergreen and taking four blows to get it out; in the second round he four-putted the 10th for a double-bogey six. Despite throwing away six shots on these two holes, he finished in third place, just two shots out of the playoff.

An 18-hole playoff was set for Sunday.

In the playoff Arnold continued to putt poorly, as Jack took a four-stroke lead. Arnold came on with a rush, birdieing nine, 11, and 12 to get within one stroke of Jack, but bogeyed the 13th with yet another three-putt. From there in, Jack held on to win his first U.S. Open in a playoff by three over Arnold.

When it was all over, Arnold famously remarked, "I'll tell you one thing. Now that the big boy's out of the cage, everybody better run for cover."

It was to become one of the greatest rivalries in all of sport.

1962 U.S. OPEN	
1. Jack Nicklaus*	72 – 70 – 72 – 69 – 283
2. Arnold Palmer*	71 – 68 – 73 – 71 – 283
3. Phil Rodgers	74 – 70 – 69 – 72 – 285
Bobby Nichols	70 – 72 – 70 – 73 – 285
5. Gay Brewer	73 – 72 – 73 – 69 – 287

*Playoff: Nicklaus, 71; Palmer, 74.

Their rivalry now established, Arnold congratulates Jack on his playoff victory, and his first U.S. Open Championship.

1963 Masters Tournament

Augusta National Golf Club
Augusta, Georgia
April 4 - 7, 1963

6,925 Yards   Par-72   84 Invitees
50 Players made the cut at eight over par

*M*ike Souchak and Bo Wininger shared the first-round lead in the Masters Tournament, at 69, while defending champion Arnold Palmer was five strokes back along with Jack Nicklaus, who played an indifferent round of 74.

In the second round, Jack moved within a stroke of the lead behind Souchak with a spectacular 66. After a long drive on the first hole, Jack had just a wedge from the fairway. In what appeared to be a replay of his so-so play of the day before, the reigning U.S. Open champion missed the green, but made his par four. But for the next 17 holes, Jack hit every green in regulation en route to his six-under-par round. Based on his superb shotmaking that day, his round was called one of the finest ever over the Augusta National course.

In the cold rain that plagued the third round, there were puddles on the fairways and the greens were saturated, so much so that the course was almost declared unplayable. But in the end, play continued as Jack gained a one-stroke lead with a 74, for 214. Just behind were former U.S. Open champions Ed Furgol at 215 and Julius Boros at 216. Sam Snead and Tony Lema, who was making his first appearance at Augusta, were three back at 217. Arnold, playing with 61-year-old Gene Sarazen, went out in 35, but stumbled on shorts putts coming in, shot 73 and was six back at 220. Interestingly, it was so wet that Jack had used five golf gloves by the 11th hole in an effort to keep dry.

In winning the rain-plagued 1963 Masters at 23, Jack becomes the youngest champion, staving off strong challenges from Lema, Boros and a senior Snead.

Despite all the bad weather on Saturday, by the time the leaders teed off on Sunday, there was bright sunshine with very fast greens — ideal conditions for final-round play in the Masters.

Jack parred the first seven holes, but bogeyed the long uphill par-5 eighth. After pars on the next two holes, Jack was on the fringe of the 11th green lining up his putt as shouts erupted from the nearby 14th green — 50-year-old Sam Snead, winner of three green jackets, made birdie and was now tied with Jack for the lead. Standing on the 12th tee, with the pin on the front of the green, the easiest pin placement on one of the most challenging holes in golf, Jack came off his 7-iron just a bit, and the ball went right and ended up buried in the wet sand of the front bunker. Luckily he was allowed to drop out of the casual water in the bunker and hit his sand wedge to between six and seven feet, but the ball kept rolling on the slick green and ended up 25 feet beyond the hole location. Inexplicably he hit his putt for par too hard and the ball rolled well past the hole. Now faced with making a tough breaking nine-footer for bogey on the fast green, Jack firmly and confidently stroked the putt into the back of the cup. His unhurried stroke changed the complexion of the tournament — just at the time it looked like the young Nicklaus would collapse under the pressure. It was one of the most significant shots of Jack's golf career and perhaps the best bogey he ever made.

Jack birdied the beautiful par-5 13th and parred the 14th. On the 520-yard, par-5 15th, the site of Gene Sarazen's double eagle in 1935, Jack hit a big drive, leaving a shot of barely 200 yards over water to the green. He badly hooked a 3-wood as his shot rolled quickly down the back slope of the green — heading towards the pond fronting the 16th green — but luckily stopped on a soft patch of mud just before the water hazard. Jack hit a good chip back to the putting surface but missed the birdie putt.

The second par 3 on the back, the 16th, proved to be equally determinative to

the '63 Masters as the 12th, as Jack made a birdie two. Tony Lema, playing three holes ahead, made a 25-foot birdie on the 18th to move one behind Jack.

With pars on the last two holes Jack became the youngest winner in Masters history with a four-round total of 286.

ASSOCIATED PRESS

ABOVE: **Jack gets a bear hug from his proud papa, Charlie Nicklaus.**

RIGHT: **With Masters founders Bobby Jones (left) and Clifford Roberts (far right) looking on, Nicklaus accepts the winner's trophy and green jacket, ceremonially passed from 1962 winner Palmer (inset).**

Herald Tribune

MONDAY, APRIL 8, 1963

VIEWS OF SPORT

By RED SMITH

It Ain't No Game

Mr. Thomas Bolt, the gentle philosopher who can throw a putter as far as he can drive, has stated it as his considered judgment that this accursed game of golf has to make a blankety blank indelicate adjectival idiot out of anybody.

That goes for the man who plays it and it also goes for those who stand and watch, as the desperadoes of the pastures demonstrated yesterday in a crazy, clamoring, headlong rush to the finish of the wet but wonderful Masters Championship.

Only the breeze remained cool as the pack went baying and snapping across these moist hills in pursuit of Jack Nicklaus, and bug-eyed galleries scrambled and whooped with the excitement of the chase.

It was a manhunt that Alfred Hitchcock might have hesitated to present as fiction, an implausible thriller that confirmed the dictum of another philosopher—the old curmudgeon of the baseball dugouts, Burt Shotton.

"Any game," said Shotton, who despised all sports except his own, "where a man 50 years old can whip a man 25, ain't no game."

THE DOGFIGHT

It ain't either, not when they play as they played yesterday's fourth and final round over the Augusta National Club's squishy turf. Then it's a dogfight among preposterously ill-matched dogs. Here was the unlikely cast in this battle royal:

On the front end, 23-year-old Jack Nicklaus, the strong, silent type who must be the least emotional red head who ever beat a ball with a stick.

Clamoring after him, running him down, chewing away his lead and in some cases passing him, then falling back as the United States champion put on a finishing burst—gimpy old Sam Snead with a wart on his foot, dapper little Gary Player, slender Tony Lema, lean Dow Finsterwald, and 42-year-old Julius Boros, who was National Open Champion when Nicklaus was 12.

They couldn't keep the kid from Ohio State down, the narrowness of his escape would have

driven Burt Shotton to drink. If Samuel Jackson Snead were four years younger, he'd be twice as old as Nicklaus.

DOWN THE STRETCH

After two nights and a day of heavy rain, Georgia's skies were beginning to clear when the troops set out, and there was little indication of what was to follow. Two under par for 54 holes, Nicklaus led Ed Furgol by a stroke, Boros by two, Snead and Lema by three, and Player by five.

Boring along methodically, Nicklaus added seven straight pars to the 11 in a row which had closed out Saturday's round, and although virtually all his closest pursuers gained a stroke or so in the early holes, it appeared unlikely that any would catch him unless he left the door open.

On the par-5 eighth it happened. Using a four-iron instead of chipping, Nicklaus slammed his third shot into the slope leading up to the green. He took a bogie 6.

Snead had birdied the second, seventh, and eighth, and now to join him on the 12th. At this point Boros drew into a three-way tie. Snead birdied the 14th and 15th for a one-stroke lead and Player pulled up even with Nicklaus, Boros having dropped a shot back.

THE GREEN JACKET

Snead was in front for only one hole, however. On the par-3 16th, he took a four and Nicklaus had a deuce. This brought Jack up to where he had started, two under par for the tournament, and he held that position. After Snead bogied the 18th Lema birdied it and slipped into second place ahead of Sam, who finished in a tie with Boros for third.

The winner's 72-hole total of 286 was the highest in seven years, but first rate over a course which many players considered unplayable during Saturday's rain. The winner's purse was $20,000, a bagatelle to the golden, boy, but nice. He also gets a sports jacket of hunter green, which becomes a redhead.

A rare golf column by the legendary writer Red Smith extols the new Masters champion (right).

1963 MASTERS

1.	Jack Nicklaus	74 – 66 – 74 – 72 – 286
2.	Tony Lema	74 – 69 – 74 – 70 – 287
3.	Julius Boros	76 – 69 – 71 – 72 – 288
	Sam Snead	70 – 73 – 74 – 71 – 288
5.	Dow Finsterwald	74 – 73 – 73 – 69 – 289
	Ed Furgol	70 – 71 – 74 – 74 – 289
	Gary Player	71 – 74 – 74 – 70 – 289

1963 PGA Championship

Dallas Athletic Club
Dallas, Texas
July 18 - 21, 1963

7,046 Yards   Par-71   Field: 165   82 Players made the cut at nine over par

*J*ack didn't have much cause for optimism entering his second PGA Championship. After all, he had missed the cut defending his U.S. Open in June, had played a bad final round in the Cleveland Open to finish seventh, and felt that he'd thrown away the British Open on the final two holes the week before the PGA. He was also tired, still jet-lagged from the seven-hour time difference between England and Dallas, as the British Open ended only five days before the start of the PGA Championship. To add more confusion to the mix, Jack played the small ball in the British Open in 50-degree weather, and then had to switch to the larger American ball for the PGA in much hotter weather.

But it was his mother-in-law, Helen Bash, who emphatically told Jack, "You only lost by two strokes at Cleveland and one stroke in England. So I just know you're going to win the PGA."

And she was right.

Shooting a five-under-par 66 in the final round over the long course of the Dallas Athletic Club, Jack defeated the third-round leader, Bruce Crampton, who finished in third place after a disappointing fourth-round 74. Second place went to Dave Ragan, who had a fine 69 in the last round. Jack won the first-place prize of $13,000, out of a total purse of $80,900, and the first of his five PGA Championships.

With his victory at the 45th playing of the PGA in oppressive 110-degree heat, 23-year-old Jack Nicklaus joined Gene Sarazen, Byron Nelson and Ben Hogan in winning the Masters, the U.S. Open and the PGA during their careers. But Jack did it in only his second year on tour.

At 7,046 yards, the course was considered exceptionally long and featured tight fairways, deep rough and large greens that could leave the player putts of 80-100 feet. It was reported that Jack hit several drives of around 350 yards during the week — immense distance for the time given the predominant balata-covered wound balls and persimmon-headed drivers.

The key hole was the 15th, where Jack firmly rapped in a 30-foot putt for birdie. Although safely ahead by two on the 18th tee, Jack almost stumbled. Realizing that he could make bogey and still win, he chose a 3-iron. Not knowing quite how hard to hit it, he hooked it into the right rough and then had to play safely from the rough short of the pond, about 140 yards to the green. Hitting a strong 9-iron right at the pin, he knew he had won his first PGA by the crowd reaction as he ended up just three feet from the hole.

In a strange happenstance, Tony Lema, after posting a final-round 69 for a 287 total and a tie for 13th place, was picked up by the Texas Highway Patrol on a

Jack, on the first tee at Dallas Athletic Club, demonstrates his power game.

year-and-a-half old speeding ticket which cost him $115 to settle.

After the tournament, Jack commented that because golf was becoming a more international sport, the world's leading ruling bodies (and he included Australia in this) should get together and coordinate both the dates for their major championships and the rules as well.

Jack went on to win 105 tournaments around the world, including six Australian Opens — the most national championships of any that he played.

1963 PGA CHAMPIONSHIP	
1. Jack Nicklaus	69 – 73 – 69 – 68 – 279
2. Dave Ragan	75 – 70 – 67 – 69 – 281
3. Bruce Crampton	70 – 73 – 65 – 74 – 282
Dow Finsterwald	72 – 72 – 66 – 72 – 282
5. Al Geiberger	72 – 73 – 69 – 70 – 284
Billy Maxwell	73 – 71 – 69 – 71 – 284

Jack remains a cool customer in the sweltering Dallas heat. After his victory, he and Barbara need towels to handle the sunbaked Wanamaker trophy.

1965 Masters Tournament

Augusta National Golf Club
Augusta, Georgia
April 8 - 11, 1965

6,925 Yards   Par-72   103 Invitees
64 Players made the cut at nine over par

The 1965 Masters was the 30th anniversary of greatest shot in golf history — Gene Sarazen's double-eagle two on the 15th hole during the fourth round in 1935.

So as to add an exclamation point to the celebration, Jack Nicklaus's victory at Augusta featured a third-round, eight-under 64, equalling the mark set by Lloyd Mangrum in 1940, and established a new tournament scoring record of 271, which bettered Ben Hogan's tournament record set in 1953 by three strokes. Jack's nine-stroke margin of victory eclipsed the previous record set by Cary Middlecoff in 1955 by two strokes, as Jack three-putted only one green over 72 holes.

Jack's record-setting performance was such a significant accomplishment that tournament host Bob Jones famously remarked at the presentation ceremony, "Jack Nicklaus is playing an entirely different game — a game I'm not even familiar with."

Jack was consistently long and straight off the tees, reducing the 6,925-yard course to virtually a pitch and putt course. In the third round, on the par 4s, the longest club he needed for a second shot was a 6-iron. And on the par-5 15th, then some 35 yards longer than when Sarazen holed a 4-wood for his second shot, Jack hit an easy 5-iron for his second to the green. (It was reported that he could have used a full 7-iron instead!)

A record-tying 64 in the third round propels Jack to his second Masters victory.

HOLE	Prev	1	2	3	4	5	6	7	8	9		10	11	12
PAR	Score	4	5	4	3	4	3	4	5	4		4	4	3
PALMER	6	6	6	6	5	5	4	5	6	6		6		
AARON	3	3	2	2	2	2	2	2	2			0		
SANDERS	3	3	4	3	1	1	2	2	2	2				
CASPER												1	2	2
LEMA	4	4	4		2	2	2	1	0	0		0	1	0
PLAYER	8	9			7	7	7	7	8	8		7	7	6
RUDOLPH		0		0	1	0	0	0	1	2		3	4	4
SIKES, D.		4	4	4	4	4	4	5	5			6	6	6
NICKLAUS			7	7	8	9	10	11	11			11	11	11
LITTLER		0	1	1	1	1	1	2	2			3	4	4

NICKLAUS 13

S S DAN 7

HRU·NO·15

16	17	18
3	4	4

5	5

NOTES
J MARTIN
RIVERS

3	3

"...Jack Nicklaus played what may well have been the finest round of golf ever recorded in the celebrated Masters tournament."

— Al Laney

The New York Herald Tribune, April 10, 1965

On the first day, the conditions were ideal for scoring with no wind, soft greens and accessible pins. Jack went out in 32 and came back in 35 for 67, as Gary Player led with a seven-under 65. On Friday, conditions toughened with gusting winds and faster greens, as only four people broke par. Jack's 71 tied him for the second-round lead with Arnold Palmer and Player, as he played Amen Corner in three over par. He recovered well, however, as he birdied 15 and 16 to finish strongly.

Jack's third round started inauspiciously as he hit a sand wedge from the middle of the fairway 50 feet past the hole. On the second he hit a dreadful drive into the right woods, a 3-iron out and a wedge to the green, where he made a 25-foot putt for birdie. He only missed one fairway the rest of the way, en route to his record-tying 64. His best shot of the day was a low half-wedge to the seventh green that landed just over the front bunker and stopped 20 inches short of the hole.

Jack, at the second (above) and 16th (left), reinforces his dominance at Augusta with a nine-stroke winning margin over runners-up Palmer and Player.

to win every major title since 1962 — Jack carded a four-under-par 68 in the first round to lead by three strokes over Billy Casper, Don January, Mike Souchak and amateur Charley Coe.

In the second round Jack shot a 76, the highest round he had at Augusta to date, and fell one back of Peter Butler of England and Paul Harney. Using 38 putts to get around the course, Jack had a poor day on the greens as he missed putts from distances he usually made them and had five three-putt greens. Ben Hogan, the winner in 1951 and 1953, shot a one-under 71 on the strength of 17 pars and one birdie, and was two back of the leaders at 145.

With the third-round lead in his grasp on the front, Jack let it get away on the back, ending with a 38, even par for the round and a tie for first with Tommy Jacobs. Hogan and Palmer, playing together to enthusiastic applause at each green, ended the day two back at 218 with Gay Brewer. January was in solo third at 217.

Playing with Hogan in the final round, Jack had numerous opportunities, but missed a 3½-foot putt on the 17th for the outright lead to end up in an 18-hole playoff with Brewer and Jacobs, set for Monday. Brewer had a chance for the victory on 18, but three-putted for his only bogey of the round. His 70 was the best round of the day.

After his round on Sunday, Jack happened to watch a videotape replay of his missed 3½-foot putt on the 17th hole and noticed what was wrong with his erratic putting — at address his head was bent too far forward so that he was actually looking back at the ball and was, in fact, aiming too far left. He immediately went to the practice green to test his hypothesis — moving his eyes back over the ball and practiced with this corrected position.

With Don January looking on, Jack finishes the third round tied with Jacobs for the lead.

At the 1961 PGA Championship in Chicago, the year before Jack became a professional, Don January reacted to all of the talk about this hot-shot amateur named Nicklaus, saying, "He's a great amateur, but if he really thinks he can play, let him come out here."

In the third round of the 1966 Masters, January had a chance to see Jack play up close, as he played with him in the third round. Jack shot a 73, as January shot 72.

By Monday afternoon, after prevailing in a playoff with Jacobs and Brewer, Jack had won his third Masters to add to his 1963 PGA and 1962 U.S. Open.

Later that summer he would go on to win the British Open for his sixth major championship in five years as a professional.

At the Masters, January finished tied for sixth, four strokes back.

In the Monday playoff he did not hit a single bad putt, as he shot a two-under-par 70 to edge Jacobs by two and Brewer by eight. Jack Nicklaus became the first golfer to successfully defend his Masters title.

1966 MASTERS

1. Jack Nicklaus*	68 – 76 – 72 – 72 – 288
2. Tommy Jacobs*	75 – 71 – 70 – 72 – 288
Gay Brewer*	74 – 72 – 72 – 70 – 288
4. Arnold Palmer	74 – 70 – 74 – 72 – 290
Dan Sikes	74 – 70 – 75 – 71 – 290

*Playoff; Nicklaus, 70; Jacobs, 72; Brewer, 78.

ABOVE: The new champion helps himself on with the winner's jacket.

RIGHT: In Monday's playoff with Brewer (inset) and Jacobs, Jack and his caddie, Willie Peterson, react with delight at his birdie on the 15th.

The 1966 British Open

The Honourable Company of Edinburgh Golfers
Muirfield, Gullane, Scotland
July 6 - 9, 1966

6,887 Yards   Par-71   129 Starters   63 made the 36-hole cut at eight over par

*T*he 1966 British Open championship was played at what is formally the Honourable Company of Edinburgh Golfers — what we call Muirfield, perhaps the finest course in the British Isles.

Clearly, Jack was comfortable playing at Muirfield. He was part of the eight-man U.S. Walker Cup team that soundly defeated the Great Britain and Ireland team, 9-3, in 1959, as Jack, then age 19, won both of the matches he played.

Even for the day and age, the Muirfield course was on the short side for a major championship, only 6,887 yards to a par of 71, with two par 5s on the front and one on the back; each one reachable by many players if one were to use a driver off the tee. There was what one British writer called "kilt-high" rough on either side of the fairways that resembled a Midwestern wheat field waving in the breeze, but this one purple-colored. (Given the height and color of the rough, from the tees, the fairways appeared even narrower than they actually were.)

On the eve of the Championship, easygoing Julius Boros — the two-time U.S. Open champ with the laconic swing — said of the rough, "I don't think this is the way golf is meant to be played." It was a sentiment many of the players shared. Further complicating the calculus of the tournament were 170 deep pot bunkers spread around the course, many coming into play off the tees. With the wind howling off the Firth of Forth, blowing Muirfield's purple-hued hay, brute force just wouldn't do it. Given the conditions, it was to be "The Thinking Man's Open."

Early in the week Jack said, "The way to win here is to use good common sense in the choice of irons." And use irons he did, hitting driver only 17 times on the 56 non-par-3 holes during the tournament.

On the first day, one shot off the lead and playing the 18th hole, Jack hit his drive into the rough just off the fairway. His second shot was off to the left and struck a grandstand and buried in the walked-on grass. With a thoughtful drop away from the grandstand, he calmly hit his third shot over a four-foot fence close to the pin and made the putt for a sterling thinking-man's par. He never hit one shot from the fairway in tying for the lead.

On the second day, with the wind drying out the greens — making them hard to hold approach shots from the narrow fairways — Jack was way ahead of the field after nine holes. Playing with Phil Rodgers, Jack was seven strokes up on Rodgers, who had just shot a 40 on the outward nine.

Then Muirfield bared its teeth. On the inward half, Jack made four bogeys and Rodgers, he of the mystical short game, shot an unbelievable 30. Thus, in the

On the first day, Jack checks his backswing near the grandstand at the 18th green.

space of nine holes, Jack lost nine strokes and the lead.

At dinner that evening, Jack confided, "It's someone else's turn to blow."

And so it was. In the third round Jack took the lead back from Rodgers and stretched it to two strokes. Out on the course, Doug Sanders, who would challenge Jack for his second win in this oldest of golf championships four years later at St. Andrews, was making his move along with long-hitting Welsh professional Dave Thomas.

With Jack, Sanders and Thomas all tied at one under par, Sanders and Thomas finished early at 283. After pars on 15 and 16, Jack played the 17th cautiously, hitting a 3-iron off the tee short of the trouble, and then hit an absolutely immense 5-iron 238 yards, to within 15 feet of the pin. Narrowly missing his eagle putt, Jack made birdie, going to the final tee with a one-stroke lead. He carefully hit a 1-iron off the 18th tee, another iron to the green and two-putted for a routine par on the 72nd hole, becoming the "Champion Golfer of the Year", as the Brits call their Open Champion.

Jack used the power of his mind, not the power of length off the tee, to win his first Open Championship. At the age of 26, it was the last of golf's four major championships that had eluded him. Now he had won each major at least one time.

1966 BRITISH OPEN

1. Jack Nicklaus	70 – 67 – 75 – 70 – 282
2. Doug Sanders	71 – 70 – 72 – 70 – 283
Dave Thomas	72 – 73 – 69 – 69 – 283
4. Phil Rodgers	74 – 66 – 70 – 76 – 286
Kel Nagle	72 – 68 – 76 – 70 – 286
Bruce Devlin	73 – 69 – 74 – 70 – 286
Gary Player	72 – 74 – 71 – 69 – 286

HOW JACK PLAYED MUIRFIELD

Hole	Yardage	Par	Times Driver Used	Other Clubs Used
1	429	4	0	1-iron; 3-iron
2	363	4	0	1-iron
3	385	4	0	1-iron
4	187	3	(par-3)	
5	516	5	4	
6	473	4	3	3-wood 1X
7	187	3	(par-3)	
8	451	4	3	3-iron 1X
9	495	5	0	1-iron
10	475	4	0	3 wood
11	363	4	1	3-wood 2X; 1-iron 1X
12	385	4	1	3-wood 2X; 1-iron 1X
13	154	3	(par-3)	
14	462	4	3	3-wood 1X
15	407	4	2	3-wood 2X
16	198	3	(par-3)	
17	528	5	0	3-wood 1X; 1-iron 2X
18	429	4	0	1-iron
Total	6,887	71	17	

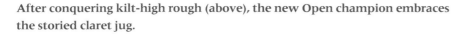

After conquering kilt-high rough (above), the new Open champion embraces the storied claret jug.

"... a victory that has to rank as the most gratifying of my career."

— Jack Nicklaus

1967 U.S. Open

Baltusrol Golf Club (Lower Course)
Springfield, New Jersey
June 15–18, 1967

7,015 Yards   Par-70   2,651 Entries   150 Qualifiers
64 Players made the cut at eight over par

*B*altusrol Golf Club, situated in leafy Springfield, New Jersey just 20 miles from New York City, is a classic parkland A.W. Tillinghast design that was brought up-to-date for the 1967 Open by golf course architect Robert Trent Jones. Featuring Tillinghast's signature bunkers with the flashed-up faces, the course — including the re-designed 194-yard, par-3 fourth hole over a small pond — would play to 7,015 yards and a par of 70. On the eve of the Open, Jack called the course,"… marvelously fair and yet exceptionally challenging … a pure test of golf."

Baltusrol's roots run deep in the history of the Open, having hosted the National Championship four times previously, although on three different courses, the last time in 1954 when Ed Furgol won playing the 72nd hole of the tournament from the adjoining fairway of Baltusrol's Upper Course. And the long-time Baltusrol head pro, Johnny Farrell, while the co-head professional at another Tillinghast course, Quaker Ridge, in nearby Scarsdale, New York, won the Open in a playoff against Bobby Jones in 1928 at Olympia Fields.

Jack came to this Open in the midst of the first serious slump of his career. Having won at the Crosby Clambake in January, he went into a swoon that lasted right up to the eve of the Open, including missing the cut at the Masters for the first time since his maiden trip to Augusta in 1959 as an amateur.

Jack summed up his play in the months leading up to the Open, "There is no question

LEFT: **With a four-stroke lead, Jack hits a 1-iron off the 18th tee in the last round.**

that I had been playing bad golf. I was hooking my drives, hitting my iron shots — especially the short ones — quite indifferently and putting worse than I can ever remember."

So what did he do to turn it around?

First Jack realized that he had to go back to his old swing, hitting the ball with a pronounced left-to-right ball flight, a gentle fade, instead of the hooking draw swing he had developed. Next, his short game was erratic, so he learned to keep his left arm rigid on his approach shots — instead of letting his left arm move all around in the swing, as it had been doing, thus letting the club head come into the ball on a different trajectory each time he hit it. And finally, his putting was the antithesis of what it had been in winning six major championships in the first five years of his professional career, so he borrowed a putter from one of Deane Beman's friends on the eve of the Open, a center-shafted Bulls Eye putter painted white to eliminate glare (which his wife, Barbara, nicknamed "White Fang"). He then took an ad hoc putting lesson on the practice putting green from fellow touring pro Gordon Jones on the Tuesday of Open week, "Go back to the way you used to putt…take it back shorter and hit it harder."

Incorporating all of these changes into his game, Jack's practice round on the day before the tournament began sent a clarion's warning to the field, as he shot an astounding eight-under-par 62, including six birdies in a row. Part of it had to do with the hard work he put in to make the necessary changes in his full swing and approach shots in the run-up to the Open, part had to do with the putting tip, and part had to do with his high level of comfort at Baltusrol, as it was a classically designed course similar to the one he played as a youngster, Scioto.

RIGHT: **Nicklaus played the opening round at Baltusrol with Mason Rudolph and Bob Goalby.**

In the first round, amateur Marty Fleckman surprisingly had a 67 to take a two-stroke lead over seven others including Billy Casper, Gary Player, Arnold Palmer and Deane Beman, who had turned pro two months earlier. (Interestingly, when Beman left the amateur ranks, he forfeited his spot on the Walker Cup team to the first alternate, Marty Fleckman.) Jack was in at one-over 71 and 54-year old Ben Hogan, the sentimental favorite, shot 72 after making a bogey on the home hole.

In the second round, Fleckman slipped with a 73, as Jack came in with a three-under 67, Palmer had a 68 and Casper scored a 70.

Fleckman, a former NCAA champion, added a 69 in the third round to take a one-stroke lead over Casper, Palmer and Jack. Fleckman had good training, working extensively with two legendary teachers, Open champion and golf mentor Byron Nelson and

TOP: Fleckman faltered in the fourth round, bogeying the first three holes on his way to an 80.

LEFT: Jack took only 29 putts in the fourth round while Arnold (above), his playing partner, winced as he watched his chances fade. That's USGA official and future Masters Chairman Hord Hardin at far left.

also his college coach at the University of Houston, Dave Williams. Through three rounds Fleckman had fewer putts, 92, than anyone in the field.

Playing in the last group of the final round with Casper, Fleckman, understandably, appeared tighter than a drum as he teed off — after all, he was leading the National Open with the biggest names in the game hot on his

heels. Driving erratically, he bogeyed the first three holes and had five three-putt greens in the round. He finished the Open tied for 18th place with a final-round 80.

Going to the 18th tee with a four-stroke lead, Jack's thought was not of besting Ben Hogan's Open scoring record of 276, set in 1948 at Riviera, but of winning the Open.

Playing safely with a 1-iron off the tee of the 542-yard, par-5 hole, his shot ended in an area off to the right rough that permitted him a free drop. He played his second with an 8-iron, just short of a wide creek and then hit another 1-iron to 22 feet of the flagstick on the elevated green. With his 29th putt of the round finding the bottom of the cup, Jack Nicklaus won his second U.S. Open with a stellar 65 in the last round and set a new Open scoring record of 275.

After a birdie at 18, Jack kicks up his heels to celebrate as runner-up Palmer looks on in disappointment. Note Arnie's Army, out in force.

So what were the results of his swing changes in winning the Open? Throughout the entire tournament he did not hit one hook or even have one shot move right to left; his approach shots were accurate and, mostly, right on the flag time and time again; and his putting was perhaps the key to his victory — only three three-putt greens and 17 one-putt ones. In all, he hit 61 of 72 greens in regulation and had the most birdies, 16, of all the contestants.

Quite a metamorphosis!

1967 U.S. OPEN

1. Jack Nicklaus	71 – 67 – 72 – 65 – 275
2. Arnold Palmer	69 – 68 – 73 – 69 – 279
3. Don January	69 – 72 – 70 – 70 – 281
4. Billy Casper	69 – 70 – 71 – 72 – 282
5. Lee Trevino	72 – 70 – 71 – 70 – 283

The champion and his scorecards (right). Barbara and Jack at the trophy ceremony (above).

18TH RYDER CUP MATCHES

UNITED STATES		GREAT BRITAIN		UNITED STATES		GREAT BRITAIN	
Morning Foursomes (Day One)				**Morning Singles (Day Three)**			
Miller Barber and Ray Floyd	0	Neil Coles and Brian Huggett (3 and 2)	1	Lee Trevino (2 and 1)	1	Peter Alliss	0
Lee Trevino and Ken Still	0	Bernard Gallacher and M. Bembridge (2 and 1)	1	Dave Hill (5 and 4)	1	Peter Townsend	0
Dave Hill and Tommy Aaron	0	Tony Jacklin and Peter Townsend (3 and 1)	1	Tommy Aaron	0	Neil Coles (1 up)	1
Billy Casper and Frank Beard (halved)	½	Christy O'Connor Sr. and Peter Alliss (halved)	½	Billy Casper (1 up)	1	Brian Barnes	0
Afternoon Foursomes (Day One)				Frank Beard	0	Christy O'Connor Sr. (5 and 4)	1
Dave Hill and Tommy Aaron (1 up)	1	Neil Coles and Brian Huggett	0	Ken Still	0	Maurice Bembridge (1 up)	1
Lee Trevino and Gene Littler (1 up)	1	Bernard Gallacher and Maurice Bembridge	0	Ray Floyd	0	Peter Butler (1 up)	1
Billy Casper and Frank Beard	0	Tony Jacklin and Peter Townsend (1 up)	1	Jack Nicklaus	0	Tony Jacklin (4 and 3)	1
Jack Nicklaus and Dan Sikes (1 up)	1	Peter Butler and Bernard Hunt	0	**Afternoon Singles (Day Three)**			
DAY ONE TOTAL	**3½**	**DAY ONE TOTAL**	**4½**	Dave Hill (4 and 2)	1	Brian Barnes	0
Morning Four-Balls (Day Two)				Lee Trevino	0	Bernard Gallacher (4 and 3)	1
Dave Hill and Dale Douglass	0	Christy O'Connor Sr. and Peter Townsend (1 up)	1	Miller Barber (7 and 6)	1	Maurice Bembridge	1
Ray Floyd and Miller Barber (halved)	½	Brian Huggett and Alex Caygill (halved)	½	Dale Douglass	0	Peter Butler (3 and 2)	1
Lee Trevino and Gene Littler (1 up)	1	Brian Barnes and Peter Alliss	0	Dan Sikes (4 and 3)	1	Neil Coles	0
Jack Nicklaus and Dan Sikes	0	Tony Jacklin and Neil Coles (1 up)	1	Gene Littler (2 and 1)	1	Christy O'Connor Sr.	1
Afternoon Four-Balls (Day Two)				Billy Casper (halved)	½	Brian Huggett (halved)	½
Billy Casper and Frank Beard (2 up)	1	Peter Butler and Peter Townsend	0	Jack Nicklaus (halved)	½	Tony Jacklin (halved)	½
Dave Hill and Ken Still (2 and 1)	1	Brian Huggett and Bernard Gallacher	0	**DAY THREE TOTAL**	**8**	**DAY THREE TOTAL**	**8**
Tommy Aaron and Ray Floyd (halved)	½	Maurice Bembridge and Bernard Hunt (halved)	½				
Lee Trevino and Miller Barber (halved)	½	Tony Jacklin and Neil Coles (halved)	½	**UNITED STATES**	**16**	**GREAT BRITAIN**	**16**
DAY TWO TOTAL	**4½**	**DAY TWO TOTAL**	**3½**				
TWO DAY TOTAL	**8**	**TWO DAY TOTAL**	**8**				

Non-Playing Captains:

Sam Snead   Eric Brown

The 1969 Ryder Cup

Royal Birkdale Golf Club
Southport, England
September 18 - 20, 1969

7,140 Yards   Par-74

*D*espite having won 27 tournaments on the PGA Tour since turning pro in 1962 — including seven major championships — Jack was never named to the Ryder Cup team prior to 1969 for a fascinating reason.

At the time the eligibility rules required that a player be a Class A member of the PGA of America for five years. In an effort to correct the slight, Leo Fraser, a vice president of the PGA of America, helped Jack cut through the red tape in 1966 which made him eligible for the 1967 Ryder Cup. However, that only gave him nine months to earn enough points to be selected for the 1967 team, as opposed to the usual two years. As a result, the 1967 Masters would be an important one. However, a few weeks before the Masters, while visiting his neighbor Gardner Dickinson, Jack contracted mumps from Gardner's children. The medication the doctor prescribed led to a stiff neck and back in the week before the Masters, with an additional side effect of poor coordination. After opening with a 72 at Augusta, Jack skied to a 79 in the second round, just missing the cut by one, his only missed cut at the Masters between 1963 and 1993. Needless to say, Jack didn't make the 1967 Ryder Cup team, but that U.S. squad went on to post its largest margin of victory in history, winning 23½ to 8½ over the British team.

By contrast, the 1969 Ryder Cup Matches, played at Royal Birkdale in Southport, England, were the closest matches ever contested. Jack was held out of the morning foursomes on Day One, as the British side went on to a 3½ to ½ lead at the lunch break. He played with Dan Sikes in the afternoon foursomes, and they defeated Peter Butler and Bernard Hunt.

The pattern was reversed on the second day as Jack played in the morning four-ball match, again with Dan Sikes, but this time lost to Tony Jacklin and Neil Coles. Captain Sam Snead again sat Jack out in the afternoon matches, explaining that he wanted Jack to be rested so he could play him twice in the singles matches on the last day.

Playing Jacklin in both rounds, Jack lost in the morning 4 and 3, but halved the final match in the afternoon as he conceded Jacklin's two-foot putt, after making his four-footer for par on the last green, resulting in the first tie in Ryder Cup history. It was one of the great shows of sportsmanship in the history of the game, as the U.S. side retained the Cup as it had won the previous match.

Jack made his inaugural play in the Ryder Cup a most memorable one.

INSET: **(left to right) Tony Jacklin, Neil Coles, Dan Sikes and Jack Nicklaus.**

LEFT: **The famous handshake. Jack's act of conceding Jacklin's putt for the tie has been called the greatest show of sportsmanship in the history of the game.**

1970 British Open

St. Andrews Golf Links, The Old Course
St. Andrews, Fife, Scotland
July 8-11, 1970

6,951 Yards   Par-72   134 Starters
78 Players made the 36-hole cut at five over par
57 Players made the 54-hole cut at seven over par

*W*hen the British Open is played at St. Andrews, the revered home of golf, it is a very special occasion for both the fans and competitors. But to win the Open Championship, and be crowned the Champion Golfer of the Year, as the Brits put it, is something to be prized and cherished.

On the eve of the 99th Open, Peter Thomson, the five-time winner of the claret jug, perhaps summed it up best, "In its best condition — reasonably firm and fast — the Old Course is the ultimate test of iron play. You cannot fire at the stick. You have to run the ball close to the hole. And if the greens are hard and fast, there are only a handful of players of the standard to win."

The first round produced what appeared to be the finest round ever shot in the history of the Open Championship. Low scores were the rule and it appeared that the Old Course would be defenseless. When torrential rains halted play, defending Open champion Tony Jacklin was eight under par at the 13th, but contemplating an unplayable lie as play was suspended. When play was resumed the next morning in a cold rain with gusty wind, Jacklin made bogeys on three of the last five holes and posted a first-round score of 67, his hopes of a record round washed away with the rain.

In the second round, a wind out of the west provided the course with a defense. The best scores came from Christy O'Connor, widely considered the world's best bad weather player, and Lee Trevino, who learned to play in the winds of a flat Texas countryside. At the end of the second day, Trevino led on the strength of a pair of 68s, one stroke ahead of Jacklin and Jack. Doug Sanders was three behind the leader with a 71, for a 139 two-round total.

The wind would continue throughout the remainder of the championship, as Trevino held the lead through the third round as he added an even-par 72 to lead

In front of the R&A clubhouse, officials with Jack and his caddie, Jimmy Dickinson (seventh and sixth from left), watch as Sanders tees off in the Sunday playoff.

Sanders, Jacklin and Jack by two strokes at eight under par for the tournament. Peter Oosterhuis, the home side hope, had a pair of 69s after an opening round of 73, to end up three behind. (In those days, there was a third round cut and Gary Player was victimized.)

In the fourth round, strong wind, gusting to gale force strength, continued to plague the players both on approach shots and on the greens. Jack did yeoman's work in shooting a one-over 73, as did Sanders, who'd had to qualify simply to enter the tournament. Sanders putted like a whirling dervish, making some and missing others that were seemingly right in his wheelhouse. On 14, he missed from three feet for birdie; on 17, the Road hole, Jack missed birdie from 12 feet, as Sanders blasted out superbly from the riveted bunker fronting the green to 1½ feet to save his par. On the 18th tee, Jack hit a monstrous drive of some 340 yards with the small British ball, to the front edge of the green, but rapped his uphill eagle putt 20 feet past and lipped out coming back.

Sanders, playing behind Jack, cautiously hit his drive out to the left leaving a clear shot to a wide open green. His pitch left a 35-foot putt for birdie, but all he needed was a simple par for the victory. His first putt was tentative and he left it three feet short. Not bad, but certainly makeable. As he started to stroke the ball, he thought he noticed a pebble in his line and stopped. He putted and the putt went wide. Stunned silence. Bogey. 18-hole playoff.

Afterwards Sanders was forthright, "I guess I never really got set, but there is not room on the scorecard for explanations." And Jack commented, "I'm just darned lucky to be sitting here with five three-putt greens and 39 putts in all."

And the playoff, especially the last five holes, was a thing to behold.

With five holes to go in the playoff round,

Jack and Sanders are all about focus during the playoff.

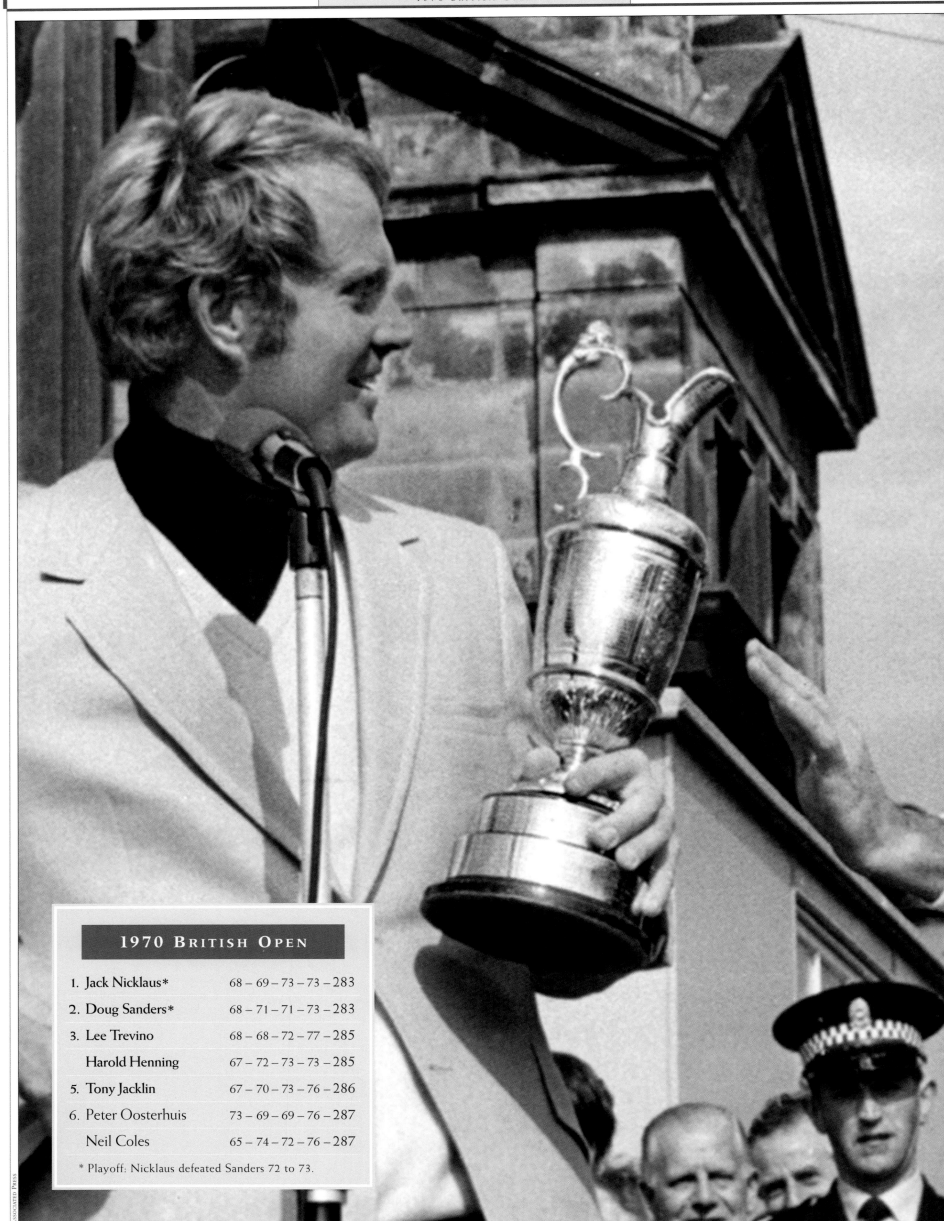

1970 BRITISH OPEN

1.	Jack Nicklaus*	68 – 69 – 73 – 73 – 283
2.	Doug Sanders*	68 – 71 – 71 – 73 – 283
3.	Lee Trevino	68 – 68 – 72 – 77 – 285
	Harold Henning	67 – 72 – 73 – 73 – 285
5.	Tony Jacklin	67 – 70 – 73 – 76 – 286
6.	Peter Oosterhuis	73 – 69 – 69 – 76 – 287
	Neil Coles	65 – 74 – 72 – 76 – 287

* Playoff: Nicklaus defeated Sanders 72 to 73.

Jack was four strokes up when Sanders began a charge worthy of Arnie in his prime. From 14 to 16, Sanders picked up three shots. On the 14th Sanders hit a sand wedge to within four feet for his four. On the 15th he carved an iron to 13 feet and made it. On the 16th Jack's putt somehow stayed on the lip of the cup for his only bogey of the day, as Sanders made his par.

Next came the Road hole, considered by some the most famous hole in golf. Knowledge-able golfers will tell you it requires a run-up shot to the green; a pitch just won't do it. Sanders hit a running 5-iron up the slope — the essence of a links-style shot, but it ended up 18 feet beyond the cup. Jack chose a 7-iron and got it to 10 feet. Both made their pars. Jack was still one up.

On the 18th tee, Sanders had the honor and laced a 275-yard drive on the 359-yard hole. Now Jack had center stage. He removed his yellow sweater, deciding to try and drive the green. With a mighty swing, he drove the ball up to, then on, and then over the back of the green into the rough — a wallop of some 370 yards. Seemingly he had hit his drive too far.

Sanders hit a fine run-up 4-iron from about 85 yards through the Valley of Sin, the depression on the front of the 18th green, to five feet. Jack's eagle chip out of the rough ended up eight feet away.

Away, Jack putted first, and, when he holed it for a birdie three, he flung his putter high into the air, almost hitting Sanders when it came down.

It was Jack's first win in a major in three years, but at 30 years of age, Jack won in truly memorable fashion at the home of golf.

Jack nearly beans Sanders when he flings his putter in the air at 18. Later the runner-up waves to the claret jug in the new champion's grip.

1971 PGA Championship

PGA National Golf Club
Palm Beach Gardens, Florida
February 25-28, 1971

7,096 Yards   Par-72   Field: 144
81 Players made the cut at five over par

*A*lthough the PGA Championship has traditionally been played as the fourth major of the year, usually a mid-summer date, the 1971 championship was moved to the end of February to accommodate the PGA of America's desire to have the tournament near its home in Palm Beach Gardens, Florida. The decision was made so as to play the championship in the balmy late winter climate of Florida, rather than the sometime oppressive heat of August.

Staying at his home in nearby North Palm Beach and commuting to his "office" for the week, along with houseguest Gary Player, Jack led the tournament wire-to-wire.

With a strong field that included Lee Trevino, Johnny Miller, Bruce Devlin, Al Geiberger, Bob Rosburg, Tom Weiskopf, Bob Goalby, Bobby Nichols, Jackie Cupit, Labron Harris, Jr., Gene Littler and Dave Hill, Jack was the only competitor to break 70 in the first two rounds as he shot 69-69.

In the first round Jack was paired with 69-year-old Gene Sarazen, resplendent in knickers and a straw Panama hat, who won his first of three PGA Championships in 1922. Sarazen commented after the round, "I saw a real champion today. I never saw such power and Nicklaus putted magnificently." In his first-round 69 Jack one-putted eight of the last 10 holes as he made brilliant recoveries time-and-time again. With a bogey five on the last hole in the first round, 58-year-old Sam Snead and his sidesaddle putting style just missed falling

With concentration that never wavers, Jack is the wire-to-wire leader.

"He may be the best the game ever had."

— **Dan Jenkins**
Sports Illustrated, March 8, 1971

1971 PGA CHAMPIONSHIP

1. Jack Nicklaus	69 – 69 – 72 – 73 – 281	
2. Billy Casper	71 – 73 – 71 – 68 – 283	
3. Tommy Bolt	72 – 74 – 69 – 69 – 284	
4. Miller Barber	72 – 68 – 75 – 70 – 285	
Gary Player	71 – 73 – 68 – 73 – 285	

into a tie for second place. With a 75 in the first round — including a missed six-inch putt on the ninth green for a 40 on the outgoing nine — Arnold Palmer essentially played himself out of the only professional major he would never win.

In the second round, Jack added another 69, as Miller Barber, the ever-popular Mr. X, was two strokes in back of Jack with a strong 68. Floridian Bob Murphy — suffering from a case of the flu — also shot 68, to finish the second round four shots behind Jack.

In the windblown third round, Jack increased his lead to four strokes with a two-under 70. In second place was Player, with the day's low round of 68. Player, the first foreign golfer to win the PGA in 1962, jocularly claimed, "Oh, I get a lot to eat at the Nicklaus home, but I don't like the way Jack is outscoring me."

With a cautious one-over-par 73 in the final round, Jack won the 53rd PGA Championship on the strength of marvelous putting — 30 one-putt greens, with six on the final day. Smooth-putting Billy Casper birdied the last two holes to finish second, while 58-year-old Tommy Bolt, who won the PGA Seniors on this same course in 1969, shot a wonderful 69 to finish alone in third place. Player made a double bogey on the 15th hole, as he hit his tee shot out of bounds, to finish tied for fourth with Barber.

With his victory, Jack Nicklaus became the first person to ever win all four Grand Slam events two times.

Jack offers a relaxed smile as he awaits the trophy presentation.

1971 U.S. Open

Merion Golf Club (East Course)
Ardmore, Pennsylvania
June 17 - 20, 1971

6,544/6,528 Yards Par-70 4,279 Entries 64 Players made the cut at eight over par

*C*oming into the U.S. Open at storied Merion Golf Club, Jack was the heavy favorite. Although many had felt that Merion might not stand up to the play of the current crop of players, their fears proved to be unfounded for Merion required a deft touch and shrewd course management, not a power game off the tee. Accuracy was the key to playing the hallowed ground of Bobby Jones's 1930 Grand Slam finale and Hogan's stirring victory in the 1950 Open. And besides, Jack had good memories from the World Amateur Team of 1960 where he blitzed the course setting an improbable scoring record of 11 under par.

Similar to his strategy emphasizing cautious play at Muirfield in 1966, Jack only used driver three times on the 12 par 4s in the first round, en route to a 69. In the second round he had an indifferent 72, with a double-bogey six on the famed 11th hole — the very hole where Jones closed out Gene Homans to capture the Grand Slam. Jack added a 68 in the third round, as amateur Jim Simons shot a spectacular 65 to take the 54-hole lead at 207, two ahead of Jack.

Simons continued to hold the lead through nine holes of the final round, but he bogeyed the 10th hole to fall into a three-way tie with Lee Trevino and Jack. Trevino birdied the 12th and 15th for a one-stroke lead, which he held until he pushed a six-footer for par on 18, making bogey five and moving into a tie with Jack, who was still out on the course. Jack kept close with par-saving putts of six feet on 15 and seven feet on 16, and had still another on 17. Needing a three on the 458-yard 18th hole for an outright win, Jack hit perhaps his best drive of the Open — a 280-yard beauty right down the middle of the fairway. Off a hanging downhill lie, Jack hit a high-flying, soft-landing 4-iron to 15 feet, then he slightly pulled the putt for the win, but tapped in the next one for a par four and the tie.

In the Monday playoff, both Jack and Lee got off to a scratchy start. After that, they both settled down, but it seemed each time Jack would make a move, Lee was there to counter it. In the end, Lee edged Jack by three, firing a 68 to Jack's 71.

Over the next five weeks, Trevino went on to win two more national championships — the Canadian Open and the British Open.

RIGHT: **The big story in the third and fourth rounds was the superlative play of amateur Jim Simons.**

INSET: **Jack (top) on the 11th green, where Bobby Jones completed the Grand Slam in 1930. Trevino (bottom) exhults, with Jack looking on, after winning the Monday playoff.**

1971 U.S. OPEN

1.	Lee Trevino*	70 – 72 – 69 – 69 – 280
2.	Jack Nicklaus*	69 – 72 – 68 – 71 – 280
3.	Bob Rosburg	71 – 72 – 70 – 69 – 282
	Jim Colbert	69 – 69 – 73 – 71 – 282
5.	Jim Simons**	71 – 71 – 65 – 76 – 283
	Johnny Miller	70 – 73 – 70 – 70 – 283
	George Archer	71 – 70 – 70 – 72 – 283

* Playoff: Trevino defeated Nicklaus 68 to 71.
** Amateur

19TH RYDER CUP MATCHES

UNITED STATES		GREAT BRITAIN	
Morning Foursomes (Day One)			
Billy Casper and Miller Barber	0	Neil Coles and Christy O'Connor Sr. (2 and 1)	1
Arnold Palmer and Gardner Dickinson (2 up)	1	Peter Townsend and Peter Oosterhuis	0
Jack Nicklaus and Dave Stockton	0	Brian Huggett and Tony Jacklin (3 and 2)	1
Charles Coody and Frank Beard	0	Maurice Bembridge and Peter Butler (1 up)	1
Afternoon Foursomes (Day One)			
Billy Casper and Miller Barber	0	Harry Bannerman and Bernard Gallacher (2 and 1)	1
Arnold Palmer and Gardner Dickinson (1 up)	1	Peter Townsend and Peter Oosterhuis	0
Lee Trevino and Mason Rudolph (halved)	½	Brian Huggett and Tony Jacklin (halved)	½
Jack Nicklaus and J.C. Snead (5 and 3)	1	Maurice Bembridge and Peter Butler	0
DAY ONE TOTAL	**3½**	**DAY ONE TOTAL**	**4½**
Morning Four-Balls (Day Two)			
Lee Trevino and Mason Rudolph (2 and 1)	1	Christy O'Connor Sr. and Brian Barnes	0
Frank Beard and J.C. Snead (2 and 1)	1	Neil Coles and John Garner	0
Arnold Palmer and Gardner Dickinson (5 and 4)	1	Peter Oosterhuis and Bernard Gallacher	0
Jack Nicklaus and Gene Littler (2 and 1)	1	Peter Townsend and Harry Bannerman	0
Afternoon Four-Balls (Day Two)			
Lee Trevino and Billy Casper	0	Bernard Gallacher and Peter Oosterhuis (1 up)	1
Gene Littler and J.C. Snead (2 and 1)	1	Tony Jacklin and Brian Huggett	0
Arnold Palmer and Jack Nicklaus (1 up)	1	Peter Townsend and Harry Bannerman	0
Charles Coody and Frank Beard (halved)	½	Neil Coles and Christy O'Connor Sr. (halved)	½
DAY TWO TOTAL	**6½**	**DAY TWO TOTAL**	**1½**
TWO DAY TOTAL	**10**	**TWO DAY TOTAL**	**6**

UNITED STATES		GREAT BRITAIN	
Morning Singles (Day Three)			
Lee Trevino (1 up)	1	Tony Jacklin	0
Dave Stockton (halved)	½	Bernard Gallacher (halved)	½
Mason Rudolph	0	Brian Barnes (1 up)	1
Gene Littler	0	Peter Oosterhuis (4 and 3)	1
Jack Nicklaus (3 and 2)	1	Peter Townsend	0
Gardner Dickinson (5 and 4)	1	Christy O'Connor Sr.	0
Arnold Palmer (halved)	½	Harry Bannerman (halved)	½
Frank Beard (halved)	½	Neil Coles (halved)	½
Afternoon Singles (Day Three)			
Lee Trevino (7 and 6)	1	Brian Huggett	0
J.C. Snead (1 up)	1	Tony Jacklin	0
Miller Barber	0	Brian Barnes (2 and 1)	1
Dave Stockton (1 up)	1	Peter Townsend	0
Charles Coody	0	Bernard Gallacher (2 and 1)	1
Jack Nicklaus (5 and 3)	1	Neil Coles	0
Arnold Palmer	0	Peter Oosterhuis (3 and 2)	1
Gardner Dickinson	0	Harry Bannerman (2 and 1)	1
DAY THREE TOTAL	**8½**	**DAY THREE TOTAL**	**7½**
UNITED STATES	**18½**	**GREAT BRITAIN**	**13½**

Non-Playing Captains:

Jay Hebert   Eric Brown

The 1971 Ryder Cup

Old Warson Country Club
St. Louis, Missouri
September 16 - 18, 1971

7,272 Yards   Par-71

A strong American team was beset by health problems as Lee Trevino, winner of the U.S., British and Canadian Opens within just six weeks early in the summer, had undergone an appendectomy in August and, as U.S. captain Jay Hebert said, "He's under par physically." Billy Casper was among the walking wounded, too, as he had broken a toe.

The British side carried the morning foursomes, 3-1, while the U.S. side eked out a victory in the afternoon, 2½-1½, to conclude Day One with the British side up 4½-3½. Brian Huggett and Tony Jacklin defeated Dave Stockton and Jack in the morning by a score of 3 and 2, while J.C. Snead and Jack soundly beat Maurice Bembridge and Peter Butler, 5 and 3, in the afternoon.

On Day Two, the U.S. side exerted its dominance, earning all four available points in the morning, while gaining a one point advantage in the afternoon four-balls, garnering 2½ points to 1½ points.

In the morning singles on Day Three the U.S. side won 4½ points, to 3½ points for the British, while each side won four points in the afternoon singles to conclude the 19th Ryder Cup Matches with the U.S. winning, 18½-13½.

Despite his medical condition, Trevino played extremely well, winning 3½ points while losing one match. Jack won five points, while only losing one.

Seated, from left: Gene Littler, Jack Nicklaus, Billy Casper, Arnold Palmer, Lee Trevino, Gardner Dickinson. Standing: Mason Rudolph, Dave Stockton, J.C. Snead, Jay Hebert, Charles Coody, Miller Barber, Frank Beard.

1972 Masters Tournament

Augusta National Golf Club
Augusta, Georgia
April 6-9, 1972

6,925 Yards   Par-72   103 Invitees
64 Players made the cut at nine over par

*I*t is widely acknowledged it was Arnold Palmer, dominating the game in 1960, who resurrected the concept of the Grand Slam to fit the modern professional game. The Slam of Bobby Jones — the U.S. and British Amateurs along with the U.S. and British Opens — was somewhat outdated in the modern game as the best players now were professionals and therefore not eligible to play the amateur events. It was against this backdrop that Arnold formalized what many had discussed, the idea of achieving the modern version of the Grand Slam — the Masters, the U.S. Open, the British Open and the PGA Championship. In fact, it was to become the Holy Grail of golf.

By 1972, Jack's desire to capture this grand prize in one year was out in the open. Playing in the New Orleans tour event two weeks before the Masters, Jack acknowledged "it is not an impossible dream," although he thought the chances were one in a 100,000. Linc Werden, writing in *The New York Times*, commented, "Nevertheless he is planning his 1972 campaign with that in mind."

Though not a serious challenger at Augusta, Trevino, who played with Jack, would loom large in the bid for the Grand Slam.

After all, at 32 Jack was at the height of his abilities and had already won 11 major championships, including each one of the majors at least twice, the only person to have ever accomplished the career slam twice. And 1972 apparently provided a "perfect storm" of venues as the majors were to be played at his very favorite courses — the Masters, of course, at Augusta National Golf Club, where he had already won three times; the U.S. Open at Pebble Beach, where he had won the 1961 U.S. Amateur and played exceptionally well in the Crosby each year; the British Open at Muirfield, where he was on the winning 1959 Walker Cup team, winning both his foursomes and singles matches, and winning his first British Open in 1966; and the PGA Championship at Oakland Hills. "When they were scheduled, I thought I had a good chance to win all four," Jack said at the time, "but to put them together in the same year is something else." If Jack were to ever achieve the Slam, chances were, it was going to be in 1972.

It was the one goal that he wanted to achieve, perhaps most, but would elude him after coming so tantalizingly close.

Jack led the first round with a 68, but was followed in second place by 59-year-old Sam Snead. Palmer was two strokes back at two-under-par 70, along with Paul Harney and amateur Jim Simons.

In the second round, three-time Masters winner Snead started fast, by one-putting the first four holes to begin the round three under, taking only 31 putts for the entire round. Jack continued his steady play, adding a one-under-par 71 to hold his lead by one stroke.

In the third round, Jack stayed one shot in front of the field with a 73. With two holes to go, Jack was six under par for the tournament, but bogeyed the last two holes to finish one

Jack tees off from the 10th tee.

over for the day and two under for the tournament. As the greens became harder and faster, only seven players shot sub-par rounds.

Paired with fellow Ohio Stater Tom Weiskopf in the final round, Jack held off all challengers as he shot a two-over 74 on the slippery greens with exceedingly difficult pin positions. Bruce Crampton, Bobby Mitchell and Weiskopf finished tied for second, three back. Jack was the only contestant to break par in aggregate for the tournament with his two-under-par total of 286.

In winning his fourth Masters, and leading the tournament after each round as Craig Wood did in 1941 and Arnold Palmer in 1960, Jack was just one victory away from tying Bobby Jones's record of 13 major championship victories.

As for the Grand Slam, it was alive and still possible.

1972 MASTERS	
1. Jack Nicklaus	68 – 71 – 73 – 74 – 286
2. Bruce Crampton	72 – 75 – 69 – 73 – 289
Bobby Mitchell	73 – 72 – 71 – 73 – 289
Tom Weiskopf	74 – 71 – 70 – 74 – 289
5. Homero Blancas Jr.	76 – 71 – 69 – 74 – 290
Bruce Devlin	74 – 75 – 70 – 71 – 290
Jerry Heard	73 – 71 – 72 – 74 – 290
Jim Jamieson	72 – 70 – 71 – 77 – 290
Jerry McGee	73 – 74 – 71 – 72 – 290

Jack accepts his fourth green jacket from last year's winner, Charles Coody, as Augusta member Frank Broyles, then Arkansas football coach, watches.

1972 U.S. Open

Pebble Beach Golf Links
Pebble Beach, California
June 15 - 18, 1972

6,812 Yards   Par -72   4,196 Entries; 150 Starters
70 Players made the cut at 10 over par

*I*f Riviera and Colonial vie for the title of "Hogan's Alley"— because of Ben's consistent winning performances at both courses — Pebble Beach could rightfully be considered in the same vein for Jack Nicklaus, whose record at Pebble Beach is stellar.

In 1961 Jack won his second U.S. Amateur crown in match play at Pebble Beach; in his sophomore year on Tour, he finished one stroke behind Billy Casper in the Bing Crosby tournament in 1963; then in 1967 he bested Casper by five strokes to win at Pebble Beach for the second time; in 1970 he again finished second in the Crosby, this time by one stroke to Bert Yancey; and, uniquely, won the Crosby in the early winter of 1972, on the same course that was to host the U.S. Open that June, for his third win at Pebble.

With the backdrop of his strong historical showings at Pebble Beach and his win in the Masters in April, Jack was clearly the pre-tournament favorite.

Based on the condition of the course — fast, hard-slick greens cut down to 3/32 inch in height, rather than the usual 3/16 inch for the Crosby, and five-inch tall rough off the 30-yard wide fairways — combined with typically blustery conditions on the Monterey Peninsula in June, the president of the USGA, Lynnford Lardner, predicted, "If the wind blows, the winning score could go to 290." This would prove to be quite prescient.

One of the problems virtually all of the competitors found was new sand in the bunkers (from a nearby beach) that made playing out

All eyes are on Jack as he escapes from a bunker at the 8th hole in the third round.

problematical, as balls hit into them tended to bury in the soft, loose sand.

In the first round Jack shot a one-under 71, to join six others tied for the lead. It was the highest first-round lead in the history of the modern Open. In the second round Jack added a one-over 73 to share the 36-hole lead with five others, including Lanny Wadkins, who shot a sizzling 68. Arnold Palmer also had a 68 for a 145 two-round total, one stroke behind the leaders. The defending champion, Lee Trevino, who had been ill with bronchitis, was one more back at 146. The cut came at 154, as second year Tour member Tom Watson made the cut with scores of 74-79 – 153 along with Tony Jacklin.

Jack added an even-par 72 in the third round to take the solo lead for the first time, with Trevino, Bruce Crampton and Kermit Zarley one stroke back in second place. Through three rounds Jack had seven birdies but said, "I'd have said you were cracked if you told me I'd be leading with even par after three rounds here."

In the final round, the greens were particularly difficult as many of them had died with the tight mower heights used combined with the wind. The feeling was that the greens each played to a different speed, bringing three putts into the equation on each green.

Playing with Trevino, the only real trouble Jack encountered was on the 10th hole as a gust of wind caught his tee shot and pushed it over the right hand rough and down the hill to the beach below. With the ball buried in the sand, Jack declared an unplayable lie and scrambled to make a double-bogey six. He added a bogey on the 12th.

Standing on the 17th tee, Jack had a three-stroke lead over Crampton. With the wind blowing and the pin positioned just over the left-

Jack hits a long iron off the fourth tee, a 325-yard, par-4.

hand bunker in the back portion of the green, Jack hit one of the very finest shots in the history of championship golf. With a 1-iron to the 218-yard, par-3 hole, Jack's tee shot clanged against the flagstick and ended up just four to five inches away for a kick-in birdie and a four-shot cushion playing the beautiful, par-5 18th hole bordering Carmel Bay.

Although he three-putted the 18th, Jack shot a two-over 74 for an aggregate score of 290 — precisely the number that USGA president Lardner had predicted.

1972 U.S. OPEN

1. Jack Nicklaus	71 – 73 – 72 – 74 – 290	
2. Bruce Crampton	74 – 70 – 73 – 76 – 293	
3. Arnold Palmer	77 – 68 – 73 – 76 – 294	
4. Lee Trevino	74 – 72 – 71 – 78 – 295	
Homero Blancas	74 – 70 – 76 – 75 – 295	

Trevino congratulates Jack after his victory as they walk off the 18th green.

1972 British Open

The Honourable Company of Edinburgh Golfers
Muirfield, Gullane, Scotland
July 12 - 15, 1972

6,892 Yards   Par-71   150 Starters
88 Players made the 36-hole cut at 10 over par
64 Players made the 54-hole cut at 12 over par

*M*uirfield was always one of Jack's favorite courses — he was a member of the victorious 1959 U.S. Walker Cup team, winning both his matches; he also won his first Open Championship in strong winds there in 1966 by one stroke.

And now, after wins in the first two majors, the Grand Slam was very definitely in play, as Jack came to Muirfield with high hopes, great expectations and the small British ball against a backdrop of previous substantial success.

Through the first three rounds of the 1972 British Open the weather was more benign than when Jack last won here in 1966. Even so, Jack reprised his previous strategy of cautious play with long irons off most of the tees to stay away from the numerous fairway bunkers and the penal rough.

In hindsight, it was clear that Jack had stuck with this guarded strategy for too long as the course played much easier than it had in 1966, as he aggressively attacked the course in the last round.

And it almost worked.

Starting the final round six strokes back in fifth place behind third-round leader Lee Trevino, Jack began to finally go after the course hard, hitting driver and 3-wood on the driving holes. Even though he birdied six of the first 11 holes — and at one point even led the tournament by one stroke — unbelievably, there were six makeable putts that refused to drop on the way back to the clubhouse. In a heroic but somewhat belated effort, Jack shot 66 to tie the course record.

As for Trevino, he had what could be considered a lucky round, as he holed out four times from off the green, but no more so than his half-skulled sand wedge out of the greenside bunker on 16 that clanged against the flagstick and dropped in for a birdie. It was a shot that had bogey or worse written all over it when he struck it.

With a few slightly different turns of the ball, or a change in strategy just a little bit earlier, Jack might have had the first honest-to-goodness shot at the professional Grand Slam going into the PGA Championship at Oakland Hills.

1972 BRITISH OPEN	
1. Lee Trevino	71 – 70 – 66 – 71 – 278
2. Jack Nicklaus	70 – 72 – 71 – 66 – 279
3. Tony Jacklin	69 – 72 – 67 – 72 – 280
4. Doug Sanders	71 – 71 – 69 – 70 – 281
5. Brian Barnes	71 – 72 – 69 – 71 – 283

RIGHT: At Muirfield, Jack was shy a birdie — not to be confused with shooing a bird on this tee—to keep Trevino from snatching the title and spoiling his Grand Slam bid.

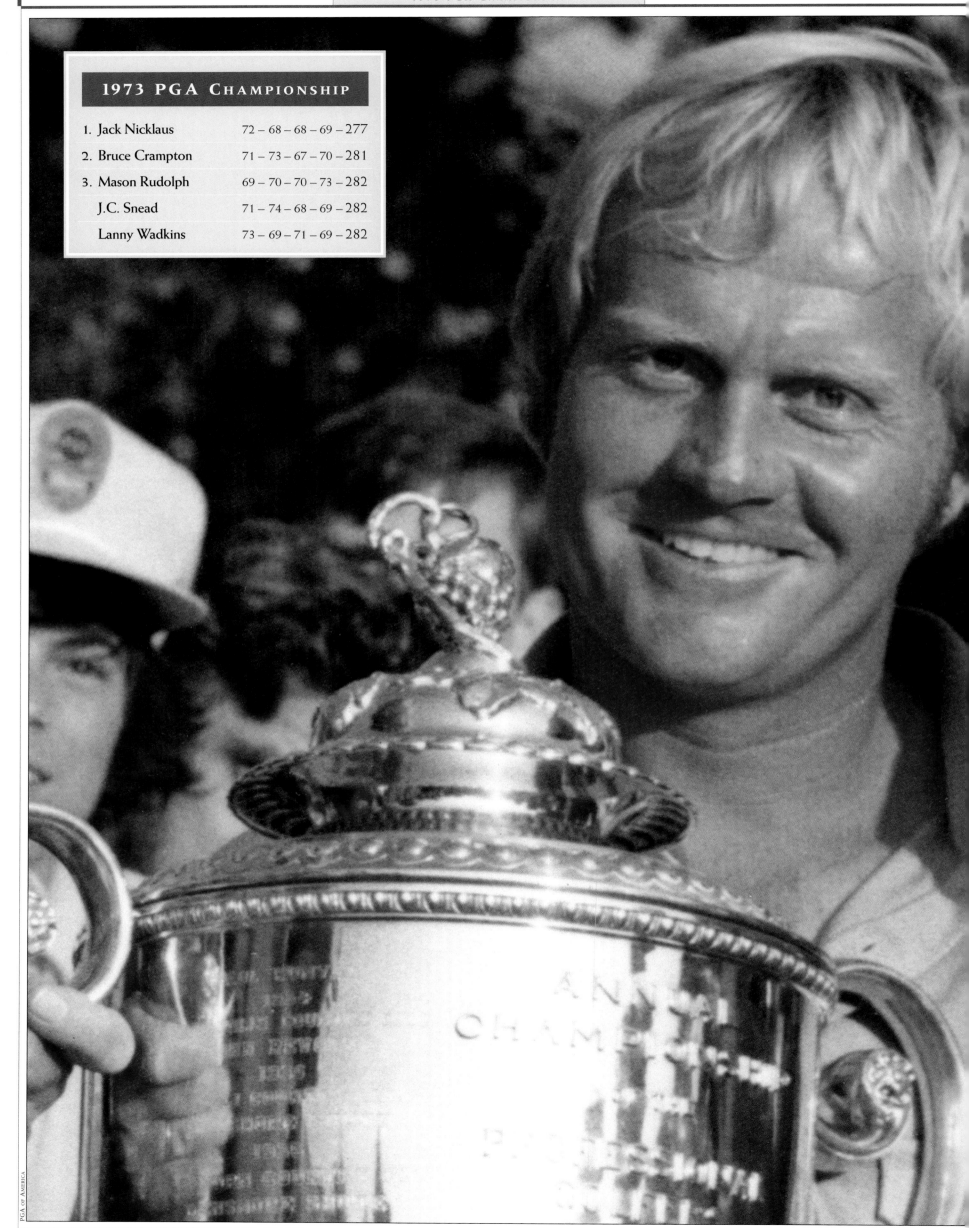

1973 PGA CHAMPIONSHIP

1.	Jack Nicklaus	72 – 68 – 68 – 69 – 277
2.	Bruce Crampton	71 – 73 – 67 – 70 – 281
3.	Mason Rudolph	69 – 70 – 70 – 73 – 282
	J.C. Snead	71 – 74 – 68 – 69 – 282
	Lanny Wadkins	73 – 69 – 71 – 69 – 282

1973 PGA Championship

Canterbury Golf Club
Cleveland, Ohio
August 9 - 12, 1973

6,825 Yards   Par-71   Field: 148   75 Players made the cut at seven over par

*W*ith 13 major championships to his credit — two U.S. Amateurs, three U.S. Opens, four Masters, two British Opens, and two PGA Championships — Jack needed one more victory to move ahead of Bobby Jones's record. Clearly this was one of his lifelong goals.

Jack was in the hunt in the previous three majors, but didn't quite make it as 1973 was a year that saw Tommy Aaron, Johnny Miller and Tom Weiskopf win their first major championships.

The 55th PGA Championship was to be played at Canterbury, an old tree-lined course in Shaker Heights, featuring blind shots among the numerous hills. It was a course that required good short irons with a premium on putting the ball in play off the tees. The final three holes, however, were extremely long and required long drives. It was said that Canterbury, with its emphasis on short iron play, was really not the ideal course for Jack's 14th major championship win.

Having hosted the 1940 U.S. Open, won in a playoff by Lawson Little, and the 1946 Open as well, fittingly won — also in a playoff — by returning war hero Lloyd Mangrum, Canterbury had a history of championship play.

Starting with a so-so first round of one-over 72, Jack added a pair of 68s in the second and third rounds to take a one-stroke lead going into the third round. Playing with Mason Rudolph, who was one stroke back, and Bruce Crampton, three strokes back, Jack never once gave a hint that he would falter as he breezed to a four-stroke win.

At the end, Jack quieted the critics who claimed this wasn't his type of course, as he continued to hit his short irons right at the flagstick through virtually the entire round — leaving himself with numerous birdie tries. Even with a bogey at the last hole for a three-under 69, Jack bettered his hero Bobby Jones's 43-year-old record of 13 major championships.

Doing double duty, Jack carried son Gary from the 18th green at Canterbury before hoisting the PGA Wanamaker trophy.

The 1973 Ryder Cup

The Honourable Company of Edinburgh Golfers
Muirfield, Gullane, Scotland
September 20 - 22, 1973

6,917 Yards   Par-71

The Ryder Cup had never been played in Scotland before the 20th matches, scheduled in 1973 at Muirfield, or rather — the proper name — at The Honourable Company of Edinburgh Golfers. By whatever name you might wish to use, Muirfield certainly enjoys a special spot in Jack's heart as it was the site of his first British Open victory in 1966 and also the venue for the winning U.S. Walker Cup team in 1959.

In the morning foursomes on the first day, Jack and Arnold defeated Maurice Bembridge and Eddie Polland 6 and 5, then lost to Bembridge and Brian Huggett, 3 and 1, in the afternoon. At the end of the first day, the Great Britain/ Ireland side was leading, 5½ to 2½.

In the morning foursomes on the second day, Jack teamed with Tom Weiskopf to defeat Brian Barnes and Peter Butler, 1 up. However, the host team's effort to break the U.S. side's winning streak over the previous seven Ryder Cups took a downward turn as Britain's Bernard Gallacher, who had helped win two points on the first day, developed a case of food poisoning and had to be replaced by Peter Butler. In the afternoon, the Ohio State pairing of Weiskopf and Nicklaus scored another victory, this time a 3-and-2 defeat of Clive Clark and Eddie Polland. At the end of the day, the matches were tied 8-8.

In the morning singles on Day Three Jack halved his match with Maurice Bembridge, but in the afternoon he scored a 2-up victory over Bembridge. In all, Jack won 4½ points and lost 1½ points as he played in six matches over three days.

Although Gallacher recovered from his illness in time to play two single matches on the last day, he lost both as the U.S. team went on to win the 20th Ryder Cup Matches, 19-13, for its eighth victory in a row.

ABOVE: **Jack comes out of the deep rough at Muirfield.**

RIGHT: **Leading a strong U.S. team, Casper and Palmer (third and fourth from left), along with non-playing Captain Burke and Trevino (fourth and third from right) practice with Jack, teeing off, at Muirfield.**

20TH RYDER CUP MATCHES

UNITED STATES		GREAT BRITAIN/IRELAND	
Morning Foursomes (Day One)			
Lee Trevino and Billy Casper	0	Brian Barnes and Bernard Gallacher (1 up)	1
Tom Weiskopf and J.C. Snead	0	Christy O'Connor Sr. and Neil Coles (3 and 2)	1
Chi Chi Rodriguez and Lou Graham (halved)	½	Tony Jacklin and Peter Oosterhuis (halved)	½
Jack Nicklaus and Arnold Palmer (6 and 5)	1	Maurice Bembridge and Eddie Polland	0
Afternoon Four-Balls (Day One)			
Tommy Aaron and Gay Brewer	0	Brian Barnes and Bernard Gallacher (5 and 4)	1
Jack Nicklaus and Arnold Palmer	0	Maurice Bembridge and Brian Huggett (3 and 1)	1
Tom Weiskopf and Billy Casper	0	Tony Jacklin and Peter Oosterhuis (3 and 1)	1
Lee Trevino and Homero Blancas (2 and 1)	1	Neil Coles and Christy O'Connor Sr.	0
DAY ONE TOTAL	**2½**	**DAY ONE TOTAL**	**5½**
Morning Foursomes (Day Two)			
Jack Nicklaus and Tom Weiskopf (1 up)	1	Brian Barnes and Peter Butler	0
Arnold Palmer and Dave Hill	0	Peter Oosterhuis and Tony Jacklin (2 up)	1
Chi Chi Rodriguez and Lou Graham	0	Maurice Bembridge and Brian Huggett (5 and 4)	1
Lee Trevino and Billy Casper (2 and 1)	1	Neil Coles and Christy O'Connor Sr.	0
Afternoon Four-Balls (Day Two)			
J.C. Snead and Arnold Palmer (2 up)	1	Brian Barnes and Peter Butler	0
Gay Brewer and Billy Casper (3 and 2)	1	Tony Jacklin and Peter Oosterhuis	0
Jack Nicklaus and Tom Weiskopf (3 and 2)	1	Clive Clark and Eddie Polland	0
Lee Trevino and Homero Blancas (halved)	½	Maurice Bembridge and Brian Huggett	½
DAY TWO TOTAL	**5½**	**DAY TWO TOTAL**	**2½**
TWO DAY TOTAL	**8**	**TWO DAY TOTAL**	**8**

UNITED STATES		GREAT BRITAIN/IRELAND	
Morning Singles (Day Three)			
Billy Casper (2 and 1)	1	Brian Barnes	0
Tom Weiskopf (3 and 1)	1	Bernard Gallacher	0
Homero Blancas (5 and 4)	1	Peter Butler	0
Tommy Aaron	0	Tony Jacklin (3 and 1)	1
Gay Brewer (halved)	½	Neil Coles (halved)	½
J.C. Snead (1 up)	1	Christy O'Connor Sr.	0
Jack Nicklaus (halved)	½	Maurice Bembridge (halved)	½
Lee Trevino (halved)	½	Peter Oosterhuis (halved)	½
Afternoon Singles (Day Three)			
Homero Blancas	0	Brian Huggett (4 and 2)	1
J.C. Snead (3 and 1)	1	Brian Barnes	0
Gay Brewer (6 and 5)	1	Bernard Gallacher	0
Billy Casper (2 and 1)	1	Tony Jacklin	0
Lee Trevino (6 and 5)	1	Neil Coles	0
Tom Weiskopf (halved)	½	Christy O'Connor Sr. (halved)	½
Jack Nicklaus (2 up)	1	Maurice Bembridge	0
Arnold Palmer	0	Peter Oosterhuis (4 and 2)	1
DAY THREE TOTAL	**11**	**DAY THREE TOTAL**	**5**
UNITED STATES	**19**	**GREAT BRITAIN/IRELAND**	**13**

Non-Playing Captains:

Jack Burke   Bernard Hunt

1975 Masters Tournament

Augusta National Golf Club
Augusta, Georgia
April 10 - 13, 1975

6,925 Yards   Par-72   76 Invitees
46 Players made the cut at four over par

*G*iven the pyrotechnics that transpired in Augusta, it may have been the most thrilling and suspenseful Masters to date.

The focus of attention in the 1975 Masters was Lee Elder, the first African-American to qualify and play in the tournament since its inception in 1934.

And, as before, the overwhelming favorite was Jack Nicklaus — already a winner twice in 1975, looking for a record fifth green jacket, a feat no one had ever achieved. Other contenders were expected to be Johnny Miller, the 27-year-old winner of eight PGA Tour events in 1974; Tom Weiskopf, the runner-up at Augusta three times; Lee Trevino, the winner of five major championships; and stalwart Gary Player, who won both the Masters and the British Open in 1974.

The name on top of the star-studded leaderboard in the first round was Bobby Nichols, after shooting a five-under-par 67. Jack was in

Paired with Palmer the third round, Jack shoots a one-over 73.

"From the confidence standpoint, I'm on top of my game. I'm better prepared for this Masters than I've ever been before."

— Jack Nicklaus
Sports Illustrated, April 9, 1975

second with a solid four-birdie, no-bogey 68, while 45-year-old Arnold Palmer, clearly the fans' favorite and sporting eyeglasses for the first time in competition, was just behind with a 69, along with long-hitting Weiskopf, who putted erratically on the slowish greens, consistently leaving his putts short throughout the first round. Close on their heels were Billy Casper and Tom Watson at two-under 70.

With a five-under 67 in the second round, Jack leapt to a five-stroke lead over Casper, Watson and the surprising Palmer, trying to turn back the clock. Arnie was five under par after nine holes before losing some ground. One stroke behind these three future Hall of Famers was Trevino.

The featured pairing in the third round was pure adrenaline — Jack and Arnie, the only four-time winners of the Masters. However, Jack gave up his five-stroke second-round lead as he and Arnie went at each other, rather than playing for a score. Both admitted after the round that neither played particularly well when they play with each other when they are in contention in a big tournament. Jack went on to say, "We want to beat each other so bad, we don't play the golf course, we play each other. I think this is the only time that Arnie's gallery is to his detriment. I don't like to be beat by Arnie — I never have and I never will." Arnie agreed, acknowledging that they try harder to play well against each other when they are paired together, simply because they are on stage together.

The talk of the third round was Miller's red-hot front-side score of 30, a Masters record as he shot a 65.

Jack was paired with Tom Watson in the final round and there probably has never been a more exciting day at the Masters.

In a traditional first-round pairing of a former winner and a top amateur, Jack played with Wake Forest standout, and future U.S. Open champion, Curtis Strange.

"I don't think there's ever been a more exciting day."
— **Jack Nicklaus**
Sports Illustrated, April 14, 1975

©BETTMANN/CORBIS

Playing the 16th green and faced with a 40-foot double breaking putt for birdie, Jack incredibly thought he could make it. "Sometimes you get a feeling that I think I can make this one. It's silly on a 40-foot putt, but I thought I could make the putt. I knew the line. The line was very clear to me," Jack said after the round. Standing over that putt for what seemed like an eternity, he finally stroked it. Up the hill it went, breaking one way, then the other. When the putt improbably dropped into the cup for a birdie two, Jack leaped into the air with his putter held high in salute and excitedly ran across the green while his long-time Augusta caddie excitedly pumped his arm in the air. It was the one stroke that won the Masters.

Later Miller was asked if he saw Jack's putt on 16 as he stood on the 16th tee. "See it?," he said, "I had to walk through the bear tracks."

ASSOCIATED PRESS

TOP: **After missing the tying putt at 18, Miller is visibly annoyed with himself.**

LEFT: **His improbable 40-foot birdie putt on 16 drops in the cup and Jack leaps in the air.**

HISTORIC GOLF PHOTOS/THE RON WATTS COLLECTION

Miller ended up shooting a 66 to go with the previous day's 65 and set a Masters record for the final 36 holes. But he had a chance to tie at the 18th green, just missing a 20-footer for birdie. Miller said, "I've dreamed of a finish like this since I was a kid. You can't imagine how exciting that last putt was on 18 unless you were in my shoes trying it."

Then it was left to the star-crossed Tom Weiskopf, who held the lead three times in the final round, as he narrowly missed an eight-foot putt on the final hole also to tie. To this day, Tom can't believe it didn't drop for a birdie. It was the fourth time Weiskopf had finished second in the Masters.

Now Jack had a record five green jackets.

1975 MASTERS	
1. Jack Nicklaus	68 – 67 – 73 – 68 – 276
2. Johnny Miller	75 – 71 – 65 – 66 – 277
Tom Weiskopf	69 – 72 – 76 – 70 – 277
4. Hale Irwin	73 – 74 – 71 – 64 – 282
Bobby Nichols	67 – 74 – 72 – 69 – 282

"At the awards ceremony Jack leaned over to me and said, 'I just want you to know how much fun you made it for me.'"

— Johnny Miller

LEFT: Player with runners-up Weiskopf and Miller listen as Jack is introduced as the 1975 Masters champion.

ABOVE: Player, the 1974 winner, presents the green jacket.

Muirfield Village Golf Club

Dublin, Ohio

7,337 Yards   Par-72

*M*uirfield Village Golf Club, ranked 18th on *Golf Digest's* list of "America's Greatest Courses," was designed by Jack and Desmond Muirhead and opened in 1974.

The initial layout, influenced by Donald Ross's Scioto Country Club in nearby Columbus where Jack learned to play golf, measured 7,101 yards from the championship tees, 6,455 yards from the members' tees, and played to a par of 72. Distinctive features of the course include downhill tee shots on all but three of the par 5s and par 4s, greens that are among the fastest and firmest in the country, and wonderful spectator viewing areas on each hole, as Jack knew this was to be the site of an annual tournament. Just as Augusta National has evolved over time, so too has Muirfield Village, which now plays to 7,337 yards.

And just like Bobby Jones's collaboration with Dr. Alistair Mackenzie yielded a course that would be enjoyable for the members and would also provide a stern test for the best professionals, so, too, did Jack's efforts at Muirfield Village result in a similar course.

In designing the course, Jack took inspiration from several of his favorite holes in golf — his 12th at Muirfield Village, a 184-yard par 3 over a pond, is reminiscent of the 12th at Augusta National; the eighth, a 182-yard one-shotter almost completely surrounded by sand, reminds one of the third at Pine Valley; and the 15th, a shortish par 5 of 508 yards, plays to a decidedly Donald Ross-style crowned green which is equally difficult to hold with either a long second shot from the fairway or with a little pitch third shot.

However, many of the best holes are Nicklaus originals. Of particular note is the 567-yard, par-5 11th, which features a meandering brook which starts from the left-hand rough and continues down the middle of the fairway in the drive area.

Also highly regarded is the 14th hole, a 363-yard par 4 that plays to a narrow sliver of a long, thin green with a pond that guards the entire right-hand side of the putting surface and a left side protected by bunkers.

Although the course was not molded after Jack's game — after all, it requires more right-to-left shots than controlled fades and precise placement off the tees rather than prodigious length — it is a thinking man's golf course, i.e., shots need to be well thought out from the green back to the tee. In this regard, Muirfield Village is very much in keeping with Jack's greatest strength as a player — his ability to devise a strategy and then execute it. Clearly, Muirfield Village requires the mental aspects of the game in spades.

Over time, it is perhaps Jack's crowning glory as a golf course architect and a course worthy of an event considered almost as prestigious as the four major professional championships.

The 11th hole at Muirfield Village.

1975 PGA Championship

Firestone Country Club (South Course)
Akron, Ohio
August 7 - 10, 1975

7,180 Yards   Par-70   Field: 136   71 Players made the cut at eight over par

*T*he 1975 PGA Championship was again played in Jack's home state of Ohio, but this time at the 7,180-yard Firestone Country Club.

With rounds of 70, 68, 67 and 71, Jack won his sixth major over Bruce Crampton by two, and by three over fellow Buckeye Tom Weiskopf. Billy Casper, Hale Irwin, Gene Littler and Tom Watson all made runs at the title, but came up short, finishing in the top 10.

It was Jack's sixth win at Firestone — four wins in the World Series of Golf and one in the American Golf Classic. The key hole turned out to be a routine par in Saturday's third round on the 16th hole — a long par 5 with loads of room on the right, but lots of trouble on the left. What Jack did was to pull his drive to the left and into a ravine. Taking a drop about 50 yards behind the hazard, he then hit his third shot way right, behind a big tree. Taking a 9-iron, he hit it a long way — a long way up in the air to clear the tree and a long way, for a 9-iron, to the green about 30 feet from the pin. And all he did was knock it in for your standard garden-variety par.

With a 67 in the third round, Jack took a four-stroke lead into the last round. After an up-and-down beginning with two bogeys and a birdie in the first three holes, Jack settled down, making pars on the way in, and adding birdies at 11 and 15 for the win.

It was a year similar to 1972, when he won the first two majors and came tantalizingly close to winning the Grand Slam, but this time he won the Masters and PGA, and lost the British and U.S. Opens by a total of three strokes.

1975 PGA CHAMPIONSHIP	
1. Jack Nicklaus	70 – 68 – 67 – 71 – 276
2. Bruce Crampton	71 – 63 – 75 – 69 – 278
3. Tom Weiskopf	70 – 71 – 70 – 68 – 279
4. Andy North	72 – 74 – 70 – 65 – 281
5. Billy Casper	69 – 72 – 72 – 70 – 283
Hale Irwin	72 – 65 – 73 – 73 – 283

A family affair with, from left, Barbara, Steve and Jackie joining Jack at the trophy presentation.

21ST RYDER CUP MATCHES

UNITED STATES		GREAT BRITAIN/IRELAND	
Morning Foursomes (Day One)			
Jack Nicklaus and Tom Weiskopf (5 and 4)	1	Brian Barnes and Bernard Gallacher	0
Gene Littler and Hale Irwin (4 and 3)	1	Norman Wood and Maurice Bembridge	0
Al Geiberger and Johnny Miller (3 and 1)	1	Tony Jacklin and Peter Oosterhuis	0
Lee Trevino and J.C. Snead (2 and 1)	1	Tommy Horton and John O'Leary	0
Afternoon Four-Balls (Day One)			
Billy Casper and Raymond Floyd	0	Peter Oosterhuis and Tony Jacklin (2 and 1)	1
Tom Weiskopf and Lou Graham (3 and 2)	1	Eamonn Darcy and C. O'Connor Jr.	0
Jack Nicklaus and Bob Murphy (halved)	½	Brian Barnes and Bernard Gallacher (halved)	½
Lee Trevino and Hale Irwin (2 and 1)	1	Tommy Horton and John O'Leary	0
DAY ONE TOTAL	6½	DAY ONE TOTAL	1½
Morning Four-Balls (Day Two)			
Billy Casper and Johnny Miller (halved)	½	Peter Oosterhuis and Tony Jacklin (halved)	½
Jack Nicklaus and J.C. Snead (4 and 2)	1	Tommy Horton and Norman Wood	0
Gene Littler and Lou Graham (5 and 3)	1	Brian Barnes and Bernard Gallacher	0
Al Geiberger and Raymond Floyd (halved)	½	Eamonn Darcy and Guy Hunt (halved)	½
Afternoon Foursomes (Day Two)			
Lee Trevino and Bob Murphy	0	Tony Jacklin and Brian Huggett (3 and 2)	1
Tom Weiskopf and Johnny Miller (5 and 3)	1	C. O'Connor Jr. and John O'Leary	0
Hale Irwin and Billy Casper (3 and 2)	1	Peter Oosterhuis and Maurice Bembridge	0
Al Geiberger and Lou Graham (3 and 2)	1	Eamonn Darcy and Guy Hunt	0
DAY TWO TOTAL	6	DAY TWO TOTAL	2
TWO DAY TOTAL	12½	TWO DAY TOTAL	3½

UNITED STATES		GREAT BRITAIN/IRELAND	
Morning Singles (Day Three)			
Bob Murphy (2 and 1)	1	Tony Jacklin	0
Johnny Miller	0	Peter Oosterhuis (2 up)	1
Lee Trevino (halved)	½	Bernard Gallacher (halved)	½
Hale Irwin (halved)	½	Tommy Horton (halved)	½
Gene Littler (4 and 2)	1	Brian Huggett	0
Billy Casper (3 and 2)	1	Eamonn Darcy	0
Tom Weiskopf (5 and 3)	1	Guy Hunt	0
Jack Nicklaus	0	Brian Barnes (4 and 2)	1
Afternoon Singles (Day Three)			
Raymond Floyd (1 up)	1	Tony Jacklin	0
J.C. Snead	0	Peter Oosterhuis (3 and 2)	1
Al Geiberger (halved)	½	Bernard Gallacher (halved)	½
Lou Graham	0	Tommy Horton (2 and 1)	1
Hale Irwin (2 and 1)	1	John O'Leary	0
Bob Murphy (2 and 1)	1	Maurice Bembridge	0
Lee Trevino	0	Norman Wood (2 and 1)	1
Jack Nicklaus	0	Brian Barnes (2 and 1)	1
DAY THREE TOTAL	8½	DAY THREE TOTAL	7½
UNITED STATES	**21**	**GREAT BRITAIN/IRELAND**	**11**

Non-Playing Captains:

Arnold Palmer   Bernard Hunt

The 1975 Ryder Cup

Laurel Valley Golf Club
Ligonier, Pennsylvania
September 19-21, 1975

7,045 Yards   Par-71

*T*he 1975 Ryder Cup was played at Laurel Valley Golf Club, a handsome 7,045-yard layout in Ligonier, Pennsylvania.

Jack came to Ligonier "playing the best golf of his life." After all, he had won the Masters in April's stirring finish, in August he won his fourth PGA Championship, and, just before the Ryder Cup, Jack won the World Open at Pinehurst in front of the Great Britain/Ireland Ryder Cup team.

Given the relative inexperience of the British and Irish Team, and the strength of the American side, many conjectured that the 22nd Ryder Cup Matches would be a cakewalk.

As it turned out the U.S. team did win, but what transpired in Jack's two matches in the singles on the third day was perhaps the biggest upset in the history of the Ryder Cup.

At the end of the first day, the U.S. team led 6½-1½. At the end of the second day, the U.S. side extended its dominance, 12½-3½. With a total of 16 points available on the last day in two sets of singles matches, all the American team needed was 3½ points to retain the cup.

Playing in the final twosome in the morning singles against Brian Barnes, Jack was defeated by the improbable score of 4 and 2. In the afternoon match and still playing in the final twosome, Jack said to Barnes on the first tee, "You've beaten me once, but there ain't no way you're going to beat me again." Although Jack began with birdies on the first two holes, Barnes sprinted and went on to beat the best player in the game by a score of 2 and 1.

Seated from left: Billy Casper, Al Geiberger, Tom Weiskopf, Johnny Miller, J.C. Snead and Raymond Floyd. Standing from left: Jack Nicklaus, Hale Irwin, Lee Trevino, Arnold Palmer, Bob Murphy, Lou Graham and Gene Littler.

1977 British Open

Turnberry Golf Links (Ailsa Course)
Turnberry, Scotland
July 6-9, 1977

6,875 Yards   Par-70   156 Starters
87 Players made the 36-hole cut at 10 over par
64 Players made the 54-hole cut at 11 over par

*Q*uite simply, this one may have been the best — the very best golf tournament of all time.

In the first British Open played on the Ailsa course at Turnberry, hard by the Irish Sea on the West Coast of Scotland, Jack and Tom Watson shot identical scores of 68-70 over the first two rounds.

Playing together in the third round, they matched each other birdie-for-birdie, as each shot a five-under-par 65. In the round Tom kept fighting back — when he was two back, he scrapped his way to tie the match.

Tied going into the last round and three strokes up on the field, Tom came back again, not just one time, but twice — once from three down to tie and then again from two down to tie once again.

On the par-3, 15th hole Tom found his tee shot on hardpan, 10 feet off the green with 60 feet to the pin. Just your basic tough two-putt. With a bold stroke, his putt rapped against the flagstick and dropped into the cup to bring him even with Jack once again. Both then parred the 16th.

On the short par-5 17th Tom hit a 3-iron to 20 feet of the pin, maybe an eagle, but surely a birdie. The iron seemed to unnnerve Jack — just a wee bit — as he hit a 4-iron that was a little off, leaving him a tough chip shot from off the green. Tom two-putted for his birdie. Jack chipped to four feet, but missed. After two days of punch and counter-punch — essentially a dead-even match. Now Tom had taken a one-shot lead to the last tee.

Tom hit a 1-iron off the tee into the fairway, 180 yards from the pin. For his part, Jack hit a driver that got away from him, ending up in the right rough inches from a bush and buried in deep grass. Tom played his second, as he lofted a monstrous 7-iron 30 inches from the pin. Surely it was over now.

But Jack wasn't quite finished. With a mighty swing of an 8-iron, Jack dislodged his ball from the gunk. Somehow it ended up on the right side of the green, some 32 feet from the flag.

Tom later said that he knew, just knew, that Jack would make his birdie. Jack hit it — left to

Jack and Tom matched each other's scores after three rounds 68-70-65–213, setting up Sunday's epic battle.

"...what took place was the most colossal head-to-head shotmaking and low scoring in the history of golf."

— Dan Jenkins
Sports Ilustrated, July 18, 1977

right, down a slope, then up — all 32 feet of it — and then — improbably, incredibly — Jack's putt found the bottom of the cup. Birdie three from the hay.

Now for Tom — only 30 inches to glory — he made his putt. It was almost anticlimactic, but hugely heroic nonetheless. Tom finished with a 65, Jack one stroke back at 66.

In all, Tom made four birdies over the final six holes to win with a score of 268, eight strokes below the previous British Open record. It was Tom's second Open Championship.

But what made this tournament unique was that Tom and Jack played together at an incredibly high level over the last two rounds, essentally playing each other head-to-head in what turned out to be perhaps the best tournament ever played.

1977 BRITISH OPEN

1. Tom Watson	68 – 70 – 65 – 65 – 268
2. Jack Nicklaus	68 – 70 – 65 – 66 – 269
3. Hubert Green	72 – 66 – 74 – 67 – 279
4. Lee Trevino	68 – 70 – 72 – 70 – 280
5. Ben Crenshaw	71 – 69 – 66 – 75 – 281
George Burns	70 – 70 – 72 – 69 – 281

ABOVE: Jack and Tom during a respite in the third round.

RIGHT: Only one stroke separated the champion and runner-up after the final round.

22ND RYDER CUP MATCHES

UNITED STATES		GREAT BRITAIN/IRELAND	
Foursomes (Day One)			
Lanny Wadkins and Hale Irwin (3 and 1)	1	Bernard Gallacher and Brian Barnes	0
Dave Stockton and Jerry McGee (1 up)	1	Neil Coles and Peter Dawson	0
Raymond Floyd and Lou Graham	0	Nick Faldo and Peter Oosterhuis (2 and 1)	1
Ed Sneed and Don January (halved)	½	Eamonn Darcy and Tony Jacklin (halved)	½
Jack Nicklaus and Tom Watson (5 and 4)	1	Tommy Horton and Mark James	0
DAY ONE TOTAL	**3½**	**DAY ONE TOTAL**	**1½**
(Four-Balls (Day Two)			
Tom Watson and Hubert Green (5 and 4)	1	Brian Barnes and Tommy Horton	0
Ed Sneed and Lanny Wadkins (5 and 3)	1	Neil Coles and Peter Dawson	0
Jack Nicklaus and Raymond Floyd	0	Nick Faldo and Peter Oosterhuis (3 and 1)	1
Dave Hill and Dave Stockton (5 and 3)	1	Tony Jacklin and Eamonn Darcy	0
Hale Irwin and Lou Graham (1 up)	1	Mark James and Ken Brown	0
DAY TWO TOTAL	**4**	**DAY TWO TOTAL**	**1**
TWO DAY TOTAL	**7½**	**TWO DAY TOTAL**	**2½**

UNITED STATES		GREAT BRITAIN/IRELAND	
Singles (Day Three)			
Lanny Wadkins (4 and 3)	1	Howard Clark	0
Lou Graham (5 and 3)	1	Neil Coles	0
Don January	0	Peter Dawson (5 and 4)	1
Hale Irwin	0	Brian Barnes (1 up)	1
Dave Hill (5 and 4)	1	Tommy Horton	0
Jack Nicklaus	0	Bernard Gallacher (1 up)	1
Hubert Green (1 up)	1	Eamonn Darcy	0
Ray Floyd (2 and 1)	1	Mark James	0
Tom Watson	0	Nick Faldo (1 up)	1
Jerry McGee	0	Peter Oosterhuis (2 up)	1
DAY THREE TOTAL	**5**	**DAY THREE TOTAL**	**5**
UNITED STATES	**12½**	**GREAT BRITAIN/IRELAND**	**7½**

Non-Playing Captains:
Dow Finsterwald   Brian Huggett

The 1977 Ryder Cup

Royal Lytham and St. Annes
St. Annes, England
September 15 - 17, 1977

6,822 Yards   Par-71

*T*he format for the 22nd Ryder Cup Matches was changed once again so that five foursomes matches would be played the first day, five four-balls matches would be played on the second day and 10 singles matches would be played on the last day, totaling 20 points to be decided.

The U.S. team moved to a 3½-1½ point lead on the first day, as Jack played with Tom Watson to win by a margin of 5 and 4 over Tommy Horton and Mark James. On the second day, Jack was teamed with Raymond Floyd — one of the game's toughest match play competitors — but this time lost to Peter Oosterhuis and Nick Faldo, the strongest pairing on the Great Britain and Ireland side, 3 and 1. At the end of Day Two the U.S. team led by a score of 7½-2½.

On the last day, each team won five singles matches, with the U.S team winning the cup 12½-7½. However, Jack lost to Bernhard Gallacher 1 up.

Significantly, this was the last Ryder Cup with the Americans playing a team composed of players from Britain and Ireland only, as the newly agreed upon format expanded eligibility to include players from all of the European countries. Jack was instrumental in making the change, meeting with Lord Derby during the Ryder Cup Matches to discuss the expansion of the European team.

The 1977 U.S. Ryder Cup Team, (left-to-right)
Raymond Floyd, Lou Graham, Hubert Green, Dave Hill,
Hale Irwin, Don January, Captain Dow Finsterwald,
Jerry McGee, Jack Nicklaus, Ed Sneed, Dave Stockton,
Lanny Wadkins and Tom Watson.

WALTER IOOSS JR./SPORTS ILLUSTRATED

The 1978 British Open

St. Andrews Golf Links (The Old Course)
St. Andrews, Fife, Scotland
July 12 - 15, 1978

6,933 Yards   Par-72   156 Starters
80 Players made the 36-hole cut at four over par
64 Players made the 54-hole cut at 10 over par

At 38 years of age and three years since Jack's last victory in a major, the 1975 Masters Tournament, some pros and several in the media were quietly speculating that Jack would never win another major. Only the year before, in fact, Jack was tied for the lead through 70 holes in three majors — the Masters, the British and the PGA — and yet failed to win any of them. After 16 victories in the major championships over a span of 19 years, the string had played out — so these "experts" seemed to be saying.

Had he lost just enough of his game — a wee bit, as the Scots would say — to bring him down to the level of, say, your regular PGA Tour superstar?

In an effort to recapture some of the old magic and provide him with some additional knowledge of the Old Course, Jack brought back his old caddie, Yorkshire-born Jimmy Dickinson, who had been on the bag when Jack last won at St. Andrews in 1970 in an 18-hole playoff against Doug Sanders.

Through two rounds, the answer appeared to be yes, he had lost just enough to find himself in the middle of a scrum of Seve Ballesteros, Ben Crenshaw, Peter Oosterhuis, Isao Aoki, Tom Watson and little-known New Zealander Simon Owen. Although Jack had hit the ball well from tee to green, all he could muster was a 71 in the first round and a 72 in the second. It seemed to be his putting, always a singular hallmark of Jack's game, that wasn't quite there. In fact, in the second round he two-putted every hole. It wasn't the Jack of old — seemingly willing in putts from all over the place.

Four shots off the lead starting the third round, Jack birdied the 14th and 15th holes, to finish with a 69. Watson and Oosterhuis began the fourth round as the leaders, and Jack was one stroke back.

With Watson, Oosterhuis and Crenshaw falling behind in the fourth round, it was Jack and, improbably, Owen, playing together in the next-to-last-group, in the lead with four holes to play. On the 15th Owen chipped in for a birdie from 25 yards away. He was now one shot ahead of Jack.

On the 16th tee Jack gathered himself. He knew what he had to do. He'd been there before. Owen hit his second shot over the back of the green. Bogey. Now Jack went back to character, as he hit a 9-iron to within six feet and a birdie. Tied.

Two holes to go: first the 461-yard Road hole, considered by many to be the toughest hole in the world (and by some the very best), and then the shortish 18th.

Always a fan favorite in Scotland, Jack tees off at the fifth hole in the opening round and on the 18th hole (inset) in the final round.

Uncharacteristically, Jack had bogeyed 17 all three previous days. Now he hit a 3-wood off the tee, away from the out-of-bounds where the old coal sheds used to be on the right-hand side, to the middle of the fairway and then a 6-iron safely to the front part of the green, some 50 feet away. With all of his powers, Jack struck a putt just like Jack had always putted — up over the various humps and bumps on the old green to within one foot.

With the weight of the golf world seemingly on his shoulders, Owen bogeyed. Jack now had a one-stroke lead playing 18.

With a par at the last, Jack had won his 17th major championship and quieted the critics who said that he had somehow slipped — just a wee bit.

1978 BRITISH OPEN	
1. Jack Nicklaus	71 – 72 – 69 – 69 – 281
2. Ben Crenshaw	70 – 69 – 73 – 71 – 283
Simon Owen	70 – 75 – 67 – 71 – 283
Tom Kite	72 – 69 – 72 – 70 – 283
Raymond Floyd	69 – 75 – 71 – 68 – 283

Sharing the emotional victory with caddie Jimmy Dickinson, after the final moments with runner-up Owen (inset).

THE PLAYERS Championship

The first ever PLAYERS Championship was held in 1974 at the Atlanta Country Club in intermittent heavy rains. Contending for the lead in the first two rounds were J.C. Snead and Lou Graham. J.C. played well as he shot a third-round 67 to go to the final round 14 under par as he made eagle by holing out from a bunker at the back of the 18th green.

Beginning three strokes ahead of Jack, Snead increased his lead to five after two holes, but by the sixth, Jack caught him. By the 13th hole Jack made birdie to lead by two as a rainstorm forced play to be suspended for the day. When play

resumed on Monday, Jack continued his strong play, winning by two at 16 under par. PGA Tour Commissioner Joe Dey presented the trophy to the fitting inaugural winner.

When Jack next contended in THE PLAYERS Championship, in 1976, poor weather again followed the tournament, this time to Inverrary Golf and Country Club, in Fort Lauderdale, Florida. The second-round surprise leader was 46-year-old Don January, who had just returned to the Tour after 2½ years designing and building golf courses. Two shots behind were Jack and his opponent from the inaugural PLAYERS, J.C. Snead. This time Jack defeated J.C. by three shots.

In 1978 THE PLAYERS was at Sawgrass Country Club in Ponte Vedra, Florida, in stiff winds and chilly 35 degree temperatures. Leading after three rounds, Jack shot a 75 to win by one over Lou Graham. It was the only round that Jack could remember where he had won a tournament without making a birdie on the final day. There was only one sub-par round, a 69 by Mike McCollough, in the entire tournament. Given the conditions, Jack remarked, "I didn't win this tournament. I was just the only one to survive." It was Jack's 65th Tour victory.

Not a bad beginning for the championship of the players on the PGA Tour — having the best player in the world win three of the first five events. Quite a start.

ABOVE: **In 1974 Jack, with Barbara, receives the Joseph C. Dey Jr. Trophy from the man for whom it is named, the first PGA Tour commissioner, Joe Dey.**

ABOVE RIGHT: **Winning again in 1976, Jack and Barbara receive the winner's trophy from the PGA Tour commissioner Deane Beman, Dey's successor.**

RIGHT: **Jack tees off at Sawgrass, the site of his third PLAYERS win in 1978.**

1980 U.S. Open

Baltusrol Golf Club (Lower Course)
Springfield, New Jersey
June 12 - 15, 1980

7,076 Yards   Par-70   4,812 Entries   154 Starters
63 Players made the cut at six over par

*A*t 40 years of age, and not playing up to his standards, Jack was not considered a serious contender for the U.S. Open at the course where he won his second Open as a 27-year-old in 1967. In the past year he had not even won a tournament, the first time since he burst on the professional golf scene when he won the 1962 Open in a playoff against Arnold Palmer at Oakmont. In fact, the previous week he even missed the cut in the Atlanta Golf Classic — his putting was off, his drives found the rough and his approach shots to the greens weren't sharp — a very un-Nicklaus style of golf, despite the fact that he started training at the beginning of the year like a rookie venturing out on the circuit.

As the 1980 U.S. Open unfolded, the concept of an "over-the-hill" Jack could not be further from the truth, as he regained his old form to become the only player ever to win a major championship in three decades.

When Jack arrived at Baltusrol, he didn't have high hopes of winning and couldn't imagine how he won in 1967, claiming, "I must have been some kind of gorilla."

The scoring in the first round of the Open was incredible — both Jack and fellow Ohio State product Tom Weiskopf fired 63's, tying the single-round scoring record set by Johnny Miller at Oakmont in 1973, while 17 other players also broke par. Jack's round seemed to be one out of the old-time Nicklaus archive of play — his driving was long and true, his iron play was sharp, his putting deft, even his new-found short game, recently taught to him by

Up periscopes in Jack's Pack: Nicklaus opened his attack on Baltusrol with a record-tying 63.

his friend, short-game wizard Phil Rodgers, was right on — as his confidence was buoyed with one good shot after another. It was so good, in fact, that he missed a three-foot putt on 18 that would have given him a 62!

Playing with Japan's Isao Aoki and his unique heel-down-and-toe-in-the-air putting style, Jack had a workmanlike one-over-par 71 to finish the second day two strokes ahead of Aoki.

Jack was moving along smoothly in the third round, as he was two under for the front nine and eight under for the tournament, but he bogeyed the 14th and 15th, and parred in for a 204 aggregate total and a tie with Aoki.

Playing again with Aoki for the fourth consecutive day, Jack nursed a two-stroke lead through the final round, as Aoki stayed even with Jack — with both going birdie-birdie on the last two holes.

At the end, Jack seemingly agreed with the sign put up by the teenager working the giant leaderboard at the 18th hole — JACK IS BACK. "The putt on 17 was the kind I had been making for 15 years when I needed it. But it was the kind I hadn't made for nearly two years."

INSETS: The *Sports Illustrated* cover after the Open; second-place finisher Isao Aoki was paired with Jack all four days.

RIGHT: With the leaderboard looming, Jack lines up (above), then strokes his birdie putt at the 17th in the final round.

DON EMMERT/AFP/GETTY IMAGES

In winning the 1980 U.S. Open Jack smashed the Open scoring record of 275, which he shared with Lee Trevino, by three strokes, and joined the threesome of Willie Anderson, Bobby Jones and Ben Hogan as four-time National Open champions.

1980 U.S. OPEN

1. Jack Nicklaus	63 – 71 – 70 – 68 – 272
2. Isao Aoki	68 – 68 – 68 – 70 – 274
3. Keith Fergus	66 – 70 – 70 – 70 – 276
Tom Watson	71 – 68 – 67 – 70 – 276
Lon Hinkle	66 – 70 – 69 – 71 – 276

ABOVE: At the 2005 PGA Championship, members of Baltusrol unveil a plaque at the 18th tee, commemorating Jack's two U.S. Open victories there, in 1967 and 1980.

LEFT: USGA officials Jim Hand (far left) and P.J. Boatwright (leaning in with white hat) lead the applause for Jack, who is joined by son Michael and Barbara. Joe Dey leans in to talk to Barbara as Will Nicholson (at far right) looks on.

"It is hard to imagine a more dramatic climax to an Open than the one we had at Baltusrol. There was Nicklaus, one of the greatest golfers of all time — there has never been a better one — reasserting his genius just when the pundits had decided that he was definitely over the hill, wrapping up his victory with birdies on the last two holes... for a round of 68 and a total of 272, a new Open record."

— **Herbert Warren Wind**
The New Yorker, August 11, 1980

1980 PGA CHAMPIONSHIP

1. Jack Nicklaus	70 – 69 – 66 – 69 – 274	
2. Andy Bean	72 – 71 – 68 – 70 – 281	
3. Lon Hinkle	70 – 69 – 69 – 75 – 283	
Gil Morgan	68 – 70 – 73 – 72 – 283	
5. Curtis Strange	68 – 72 – 72 – 72 – 284	
Howard Twitty	68 – 74 – 71 – 71 – 284	

1980 PGA Championship

Oak Hill Country Club
Rochester, New York
August 7 - 10, 1980

6,964 Yards   Par-70   Field: 148   77 Players made the cut at nine over par

O n the eve of the 62nd PGA Championship at beautiful Oak Hill Golf Club, Jack's son, Jack Jr., gave his dad a putting lesson, as he was struggling on the practice green. Jack Jr. told his father that his putting stance looked peculiar, that he was quitting on the stroke after impact and pulling his putter to the left.

Jack made some corrections and started putting like, well, Jack Nicklaus, and in so doing he made golf history by winning the PGA Championship for a fifth time, tying Walter Hagen's record. What is more, Jack set a PGA record for the largest winning margin, as he finished at six-under-par 274, seven shots ahead of Andy Bean.

With a 66 in the third round, Jack took a three-stroke lead over Lon Hinkle, who had a spectacular par four on the 18th hole to stay close. Jack played the first 14 holes in six under par, but stumbled a bit coming in, as he made two bogeys, which easily could have been doubles, and two saved pars, that could also have been bogeys.

Just as he salvaged a 69 in Friday's play with terrific scrambling, he did so again in the final four holes on Saturday. The par-4 17th was a good example. Jack hit his tee shot into the rough and then his second into a greenside bunker. He then hit his sand shot 40 feet past the flag and his first putt six feet by. With a double bogey definitely a possibility, Jack, concentrating intently, stared down the putt and made the six-footer for bogey. But it still added up to 66, the low round of the tournament.

In the final round, Jack played steadily, shooting a one-under-par 69, while Bean edged Hinkle for second place, as both played in the last group with Jack.

It was Jack's 19th major championship and his second of the year, after winning the U.S. Open at Baltusrol in June.

With his win in the 1980 PGA Jack became only the third man in history to win both the U.S. Open and PGA Championship in the same year, joining Gene Sarazen who accomplished the feat in 1922 and Ben Hogan who did it in 1948.

Jack, with Oak Hill president Allen Brewer and tournament general chairman Jack Hoff, after winning his fifth PGA Championship.

The 1981 Ryder Cup

Walton Health Golf Club
Surrey, England
September 18-20, 1981

7,067 Yards   Par-73

his was the last Ryder Cup team that Jack was to play on as a competitor. And he went out in grand fashion.

U.S. Ryder Cup Captain Dave Marr teamed Nicklaus and Tom Watson with spectacular success — in the morning foursomes on Day One they defeated Peter Oosterhuis and Nick Faldo, 4 and 3; in the morning four-balls on Day Two they defeated Jose Maria Canizares and Des Smyth, 3 and 2; and in the afternoon foursomes on Day Two they defeated Ryder Cup rookies Bernhard Langer and Manual Pinero, 3 and 2. Three matches, three wins.

Finally, playing in the anchor position on Day Three in the singles, Jack defeated Eamonn Darcy, 5 and 3.

That's four out of four total points available to be won — truly a dominating performance.

The most success that the European team could muster was the afternoon four-balls on Day One, when they edged the U.S. 4½-3½, as Captain Marr rested Tom and Jack.

In a strange quirk, Seve Ballesteros, who had won the 1980 Masters and had spent most of the season playing outside of Europe, was kept off the European team for not playing a sufficient number of events on the European PGA Tour.

For his part, Jack played seven different members of the 12-man European team and defeated each of them.

It was the American side's 22nd consecutive win in the Ryder Cup Matches, as the U.S. defeated the Europeans, 18½-9½.

24TH RYDER CUP MATCHES

UNITED STATES		EUROPE	
Morning Foursomes (Day One)			
Lee Trevino and Larry Nelson (1 up)	1	Bernhard Langer and Manuel Pinero	0
Bill Rogers and Bruce Lietzke	0	Sandy Lyle and Mark James (2 and 1)	1
Hale Irwin and Raymond Floyd	0	Bernard Gallacher and Des Smyth (3 and 2)	1
Tom Watson and Jack Nicklaus (4 and 3)	1	Peter Oosterhuis and Nick Faldo	0
Afternoon Four-Balls (Day One)			
Tom Kite and Johnny Miller (halved)	½	Sam Torrance and Howard Clark (halved)	½
Ben Crenshaw and Jerry Pate	0	Sandy Lyle and Mark James (3 and 2)	1
Bill Rogers and Bruce Lietzke	0	Des Smyth and Jose Maria Canizares (6 and 5)	1
Hale Irwin and Raymond Floyd (2 and 1)	1	Bernard Gallacher and Eamonn Darcy	0
DAY ONE TOTAL	3½	DAY ONE TOTAL	4½
Morning Four-Balls (Day Two)			
Lee Trevino and Jerry Pate (7 and 5)	1	Nick Faldo and Sam Torrance	0
Larry Nelson and Tom Kite (1 up)	1	Sandy Lyle and Mark James	0
Raymond Floyd and Hale Irwin	0	Bernhard Langer and Manuel Pinero (2 and 1)	1
Jack Nicklaus and Tom Watson (3 and 2)	1	Jose Maria Canizares and Des Smyth	0
Afternoon Foursomes (Day Two)			
Lee Trevino and Jerry Pate (2 and 1)	1	Peter Oosterhuis and Sam Torrance	0
Jack Nicklaus and Tom Watson (3 and 2)	1	Bernhard Langer and Manuel Pinero	0
Bill Rogers and Raymond Floyd (3 and 2)	1	Sandy Lyle and Mark James	0
Tom Kite and Larry Nelson (3 and 2)	1	Des Smyth and Bernard Gallacher	0
DAY TWO TOTAL	7	DAY TWO TOTAL	1
TWO DAY TOTAL	10½	TWO DAY TOTAL	5½
Singles (Day Three)			
Lee Trevino (5 and 3)	1	Sam Torrance	0
Tom Kite (3 and 2)	1	Sandy Lyle	0
Bill Rogers (halved)	½	Bernard Gallacher (halved)	½
Larry Nelson (2 up)	1	Mark James	0
Ben Crenshaw (6 and 4)	1	Des Smyth	0
Bruce Lietzke (halved)	½	Bernhard Langer (halved)	½
Jerry Pate	0	Manuel Pinero (4 and 2)	1
Hale Irwin (1 up)	1	Jose Maria Canizares	0
Johnny Miller	0	Nick Faldo (2 and 1)	1
Tom Watson	0	Howard Clark (4 and 3)	1
Raymond Floyd (1 up)	1	Peter Oosterhuis	0
Jack Nicklaus (5 and 3)	1	Eamonn Darcy	0
DAY THREE TOTAL	8	DAY THREE TOTAL	4
UNITED STATES	**18½**	**EUROPE**	**9½**
Non-Playing Captain:	Dave Marr	*Non-Playing Captain:*	John Jacobs

Standing (from left): Tom Kite, Bill Rogers, Jerry Pate, Johnny Miller (obscured) Bruce Lietzke, Dave Marr, Raymond Floyd, Hale Irwin, Jack Nicklaus and Tom Watson. Crouching, from left: Lee Trevino, Ben Crenshaw and Larry Nelson.

1982 U.S. Open

Pebble Beach Golf Links
Pebble Beach, California
June 17 - 20, 1982

6,825/6,791 Yards Par-72 Entries: 5,255 Starters: 153
68 Players made the cut at seven over par

*J*ack's record at Pebble Beach was beyond reproach. Over time, no one has played Pebble better than Jack — he won his second U.S. Amateur title in 1961, blitzing his final two opponents by a score of 9 and 8 in the semi-final and 8 and 6 in the final; here he won the 1972 U.S. Open with Arnold Palmer and Lee Trevino in close pursuit; and at Pebble he won the Crosby three times, while finishing second several times as well.

The other dominant player in the game, Tom Watson, who by this time had already won five majors, was equally fond of Pebble, as he would come down to play while he was a student at Stanford.

Through the three rounds, Watson — with scores of 72-72-68 — was tied for the lead with Bill Rogers at 212. Two strokes back were 44-year-old Bruce Devlin, defending champion David Graham, Scott Simpson and George Burns, with Jack one stroke further back at 215 after rounds of 74-70-71.

Jack started the fourth round indifferently, as he bogeyed the first hole and parred the relatively easy par-5 second. He then went on a tear with birdies on the third, fourth, fifth, sixth (with a good drive and a stupendous 1-iron to the uphill par-5 hole and two putts from 35 feet) and the seventh — that's four under par playing the eighth which he bogeyed. Making the turn at four under par for the tournament, Jack was just one stroke in back of the leader, Rogers, and tied with Watson.

Although the key to Tom's eventual win was the incredible chip-in at 17, the one hole that made it possible was his play on the 10th. Jack, playing just ahead, three-putted the 11th green from 20 feet, to slip back to three under par. From the tee on the 424-yard, par-4 10th, Tom hit the 27-yard wide fairway, but pushed his 7-iron to the right and, luckily, caught the deep bunker on the cliff side of the green. His bunker shot was long — some 25 feet from the cup — but he acquitted himself well as he ran in the putt to improbably save his par. It could have been worse — a six or seven was certainly a possibility, with an eight not out of the question if the approach shot missed the bunker and tumbled down to the beach. With a big tee shot on the par-4 11th, Tom birdied, to go five under and two ahead of Jack. But his play on the 204-yard, par-3 12th turned into a bogey and he was now only one up on Jack, four under par. With Watson carefully playing the par-5 14th, Jack posted a birdie on 15 to tie for the lead. Watson parried with a bold 35-foot birdie putt from the back edge of the 14th green and a one-stroke

Watson's miraculous chip-in at the 17th ended Nicklaus's hopes for a fifth Open crown.

"The 1982 Open turned out to be one of the great Opens of all time."

— **Herbert Warren Wind**
The New Yorker, July 26, 1982

1982 U.S. OPEN

1. Tom Watson	72 – 72 – 68 – 70 – 282
2. Jack Nicklaus	74 – 70 – 71 – 69 – 284
3. Bill Rogers	70 – 73 – 69 – 74 – 286
Dan Pohl	72 – 74 – 70 – 70 – 286
Bobby Clampett	71 – 73 – 72 – 70 – 286

lead again. Watson parred 15 and then made a very good bogey on 16 as he hit his tee shot into a recently redone bunker on the right side of the dogleg, leaving himself with no shot at the green.

Tied now with Jack with two holes to play, Tom came to the fateful par-3, 209-yard 17th, which again turned out to be the pivotal hole in the Open, as it had been for Jack in 1972 when he sealed his victory as he hit the flag-stick with his 1-iron tee shot and left himself with a kick-in birdie. Watson hit a 2-iron to the hourglass-shaped green, with the pin in the back, a bit too good as his tee shot hooked just a little, ending up 20 feet from the pin and about eight feet off the fringe, in the tangled rough but somehow sitting up.

Opening up his sand wedge, Tom slipped the club underneath the ball, and watched as it hit the green, took the break and found the bottom of the cup for a birdie two.

Standing behind the 18th green, Jack — watching on a small TV monitor in an official's tent — was stunned when he saw Tom's little pitch jump into the hole on 17. He knew, just knew, that this was the shot that had won Tom his first Open and the one that had denied Jack his record fifth Open.

In a show of great sportsmanship, Nicklaus waited behind the 18th green for Watson to finish so he could congratulate him as he came off the final green.

Famously gracious in defeat, Jack is there to congratulate Watson coming off the 18th green, as caddie Bruce Edwards (left) and USGA President Jim Hand (behind cameraman) look on.

VICTORIES IN TEAM CHAMPIONSHIPS

Team Championship	Year	Partner	Location
Canada Cup	1963*	Arnold Palmer	Paris, France
Canada Cup	1964*	Arnold Palmer	Maui, Hawaii
PGA National	1966	Arnold Palmer	Palm Beach Gardens, Florida
World Cup**	1967	Arnold Palmer	Mexico City, Mexico
National Four Ball	1970	Arnold Palmer	Ligonier, Pennsylvania
World Cup	1971*	Lee Trevino	Palm Beach, Florida
World Cup	1973	Johnny Miller	Marbella, Spain
Chrysler Team	1983	Johnny Miller	Boca Raton, Florida

* Individual champion   ** Formerly the Canada Cup

Team Championships

Canada Cup/World Cup
PGA National Team Championship
National Four Ball
Chrysler Team Championship

*J*ack played in and won a number of significant two-man team championship events with a variety of partners.

Most prominent was the pairing of Jack and Arnold Palmer, an American dream team if there ever was one, in the Canada Cup, an event founded by Canadian industrialist John Jay Hopkins in 1953 in an effort to promote good will among nations. The name was changed to the World Cup in 1967. The format consists of a combined score for the two-man team competition over 72 holes and an individual competition for the International Trophy for the player with the best 72-hole score.

Jack and Arnie won the Canada Cup/World Cup three times, in 1963, 1964 and 1967. Jack won the event two more times, in 1971 with Lee Trevino and again in 1973 with Johnny Miller. Jack was the individual low scorer three times — in 1963, 1964 and 1971.

In addition Jack won the PGA Team Championship in 1966 and the National Four Ball in 1971, both times partnering with Arnie, and also the Chrysler Team Championship in 1983 with Miller.

ABOVE: **Jack and Lee Trevino share a laugh after winning the 1971 World Cup in Palm Beach.**

LEFT: **Although Jack and Arnold were totally in sync during this round in Tokyo, for one of the few times they failed to win.**

The New York Times

THE ROUND JACK NICKLAUS FORGOT
(The 1963 Canada Cup)

By RED SMITH

JACK NICKLAUS' golf is better than his memory. When he came charging home in the Inverrary Classic last weekend, picking up four strokes on Grier Jones, three on Jerry Pate and Andy Bean, and two on Hale Irwin with five birdies on the last five holes, he was asked whether he had ever put on such a finish before. "I can't imagine any other time," he said. "It was the most remarkable thing I've ever seen in my life," said Lee Trevino, comparing it with Reggie Jackson's three home runs in the last World Series game and Leon Spinks' victory over Muhammad Ali. Well, it was remarkable but it wasn't unprecedented.

Fifteen years ago, Nicklaus and Arnold Palmer represented the United States in the World Cup competition at Saint-Nom-la-Breteche near Versailles in France. If Jack has forgotten his performance there, perhaps he wanted to forget it. Maybe he deliberately put it out of his mind as too outrageously theatrical to bear remembering.

The things he did on the very first hole were downright scandalous. The hole was a legitimate par 5 for club members but a trifle short for a pro with Jack's power, measuring somewhere between 450 and 500 yards. In his four rounds, Jack played it eagle, eagle, eagle, birdie, and that was just for openers.

Breteche may have been a trifle shorter than Inverrary's 7,127 yards, but this was no exhibition on a pitch-and-putt course, and the opposition was at least as distinguished as the field Nicklaus encountered last week. The World Cup, now twenty-five years old, is a moveable feast that leaps from continent to continent, usually playing national capitals, matching two-man teams from virtually every land where the game is known. Though it hasn't the prestige of the United States or British Open, it is probably the closest thing there is to a world championship.

In 1963, Saint-Nom-la-Breteche was a comparatively new course built on land that had been the royal farm when Louis XIV was top banana. The clubhouse, once the royal cow barn, was a splendid building of ivy-covered stone set in a terraced stableyard ablaze with roses, snapdragon, chrysanthemum, and pansies.

The galleries had a touch of quality seldom associated with, say, Maple Moor in Westchester County. Among those who followed the play were two former kings and one former Vice President — Leopold of Belgium, the Duke of Windsor, and Richard M. Nixon.

Before play started, Prince Michel de Bourbon-Parme, the club president, dispatched ten dozen fresh eggs to a nearby convent. This, he explained, was an ancient custom in the Ile de France. Anyone planning an outdoor binge like a wedding or garden party sent eggs to the poor and this assured him of good weather. The standard fee was one dozen eggs, but the Prince had laid it on to guarantee a week of sunshine.

Morning of the opening round found the Prince glowering through a clammy fog. "So, " he said, "I am sending to the sisters to get back my eggs."

Soggy turf made the course play long for little guys, but not for Nicklaus. His second shot on the opening hole was twenty feet from the pin, and he ran down the putt for his first eagle 3. After that he had five birdies and three bogeys for a 67. Palmer's 69 gave the pair a tie for first place with Al Balding and Stan Leonard of Canada.

Prince Michel changed his mind about reclaiming the eggs, but the weather didn't relent. Day by day the fog thickened, until the green hills and yellow bunkers were all but blotted out. Realizing that if a hitter like Nicklaus tried to fire a tee shot into that soup the ball would never be seen again, officials postponed the final round for twenty-four hours.

It didn't help much. Next day a gray soufflé garnished the fairways. The climate dripped sullenly from the trees. Windsor and Leopold showed up as they had for each earlier round, but the weather reduced the gallery to a minimum. Reluctantly, the committee decided to cut the final round to nine holes. At this point Nicklaus and Palmer were tied with Spain's Ramon Sota and Sebastian Miguel for the team trophy, with Nicklaus and Gary Player all square in individual competition.

Automobiles were driven out past the first green, where they made a U-turn and parked with headlights on. From the tee, lights were blurred but visible, giving the players a target. For the first time in four rounds, Nicklaus needed four shots to get down. Then he got serious.

With that birdie for a start, he played the next five holes as follows: 3-3-3-3. When he walked toward the seventh tee, a spectator asked, "What are you going to do for an encore?"

"Try to finish," Jack said.

On the first six holes he had taken 19 shots. On the last three he took 13 for a 32. It won.

— March, 1978

INSET: Johnny Miller and Jack successfully pair for two team titles — the 1973 World Cup and the 1983 Chrysler Team Championship, pictured here.

LEFT: Arnold and Jack team up to win the 1963 Canada Cup at St-Nom-La-Breteche, France. Giving the prizes are (center) Prince Michael Bourbon de Parme and Howard Clark, President of the International Golf Association.

The 1983 Ryder Cup Captain

PGA National Golf Club
Palm Beach Gardens, Florida
October 14 - 16, 1983

7,137 Yards   Par-72

*I*n retrospect, the 1983 Ryder Cup, played at PGA National Golf Club in Palm Beach Gardens, Florida, was a portent of things to come as the U.S. side almost lost for the first time on U.S. soil to a surprisingly strong European team. The European team's performance set the stage for the watershed years of 1985 and 1987.

Jack had one of the strongest Ryder Cup records of all time, playing on six teams with a record of 17-8-3. He missed playing in the matches in the first several years of his career, despite being the most dominant player in the game, because of the eligibility rules in effect at that time. He also missed the team in 1979 due to the first real slump of his career. But it was altogether fitting that he was named U.S. Ryder Cup Captain in 1983.

With the matches tied at 8-8 after two days of play, European captain Tony Jacklin went for offense as he set his team with his strongest players — Seve Ballesteros, Nick Faldo and Bernhard Langer — leading off the singles matches on the third day. Captain Nicklaus opted for defense placing his strongest players — Lanny Wadkins, Raymond Floyd and Tom Watson — at the tail end of the draw. Jack's strategy proved to be correct, but just barely.

With the score tied 12½ - 12½, three matches were left on the course. Sam Torrance and Tom Kite halved, as Watson was 1 up on Bernard Gallacher on the 16th and Wadkins was one down to Jose Maria Canizares playing 18. With the Watson-Gallacher match apparently well in hand, all of the pressure was on Wadkins. After a good drive and a fairway wood on the par-5 18th hole, Wadkins was lying cleanly in the fairway about 80 yards from a pin tucked just behind a large bunker. He almost holed his shot, as it ended up just 18 inches from the cup. With Wadkins's birdie to win the hole, the match was halved and he earned the crucial ½ point. Almost simultaneously, Watson closed out Gallacher on 17. The U.S. had eked out the win over the Europeans, 14½ - 13½.

A self-assured Wadkins later told a relieved captain Nicklaus, "It was only the most important shot of my life, Jack. There's nobody I'd rather have hit it for."

The victorious 1983 U.S. Ryder Cup team: (back row, left to right) Craig Stadler, Jay Haas, Gil Morgan, Bob Gilder, Captain Jack Nicklaus, Tom Watson, Raymond Floyd, Curtis Strange and Fuzzy Zoeller; (kneeling) Tom Kite, Ben Chrenshaw, Calvin Peete, and Lanny Wadkins.

25TH RYDER CUP MATCHES

UNITED STATES		EUROPE	
Morning Foursomes (Day One)			
Tom Watson and Ben Crenshaw (5 and 4)	1	Bernard Gallacher and Sandy Lyle	0
Lanny Wadkins and Craig Stadler	0	Nick Faldo and Bernhard Langer (4 and 2)	1
Tom Kite and Calvin Peete (2 and 1)	1	Seve Ballesteros and Paul Way	0
Raymond Floyd and Bob Gilder	0	Jose Maria Canizares and Sam Torrance (4 and 3)	1
Afternoon Four-Balls (Day One)			
Gil Morgan and Fuzzy Zoeller	0	Brian Waites and Ken Brown (2 and 1)	1
Tom Watson and Jay Haas (2 and 1)	1	Nick Faldo and Bernhard Langer	0
Raymond Floyd and Curtis Strange	0	Seve Ballesteros and Paul Way (1 up)	1
Ben Crenshaw and Calvin Peete (halved)	½	Sam Torrance and Ian Woosnam (halved)	½
DAY ONE TOTAL	**3½**	**DAY ONE TOTAL**	**4½**
Morning Four-Balls (Day Two)			
Lanny Wadkins and Craig Stadler (1 up)	1	Brian Waites and Ken Brown	0
Ben Crenshaw and Calvin Peete	0	Nick Faldo and Bernhard Langer (4 and 2)	1
Gil Morgan and Jay Haas (halved)	½	Seve Ballesteros and Paul Way (halved)	½
Tom Watson and Bob Gilder (5 and 4)	1	Sam Torrance and Ian Woosnam	0
Afternoon Foursomes (Day Two)			
Tom Kite and Raymond Floyd	0	Nick Faldo and Bernhard Langer (3 and 2)	1
Jay Haas and Curtis Strange (3 and 2)	1	Brian Waites and Ken Brown	0
Gil Morgan and Lanny Wadkins (7 and 5)	1	Sam Torrance and Jose Maria Canizares	0
Tom Watson and Bob Gilder	0	Seve Ballesteros and Paul Way (2 and 1)	1
DAY TWO TOTAL	**4½**	**DAY TWO TOTAL**	**3½**
TWO DAY TOTAL	**8**	**TWO DAY TOTAL**	**8**
Singles (Day Three)			
Fuzzy Zoeller (halved)	½	Seve Ballesteros (halved)	½
Jay Haas	0	Nick Faldo (2 and 1)	1
Gil Morgan	0	Bernhard Langer (2 up)	1
Bob Gilder (2 up)	1	Gordon Brand Sr.	0
Ben Crenshaw (3 and 1)	1	Sandy Lyle	0
Calvin Peete (1 up)	1	Brian Waites	0
Curtis Strange	0	Paul Way (2 and 1)	1
Tom Kite (halved)	½	Sam Torrance (halved)	½
Craig Stadler (3 and 2)	1	Ian Woosnam	0
Lanny Wadkins (halved)	½	Jose Maria Canizares (halved)	½
Raymond Floyd	0	Ken Brown (4 and 3)	1
Tom Watson (2 and 1)	1	Bernard Gallacher	0
DAY THREE TOTAL	**6½**	**DAY THREE TOTAL**	**5½**
UNITED STATES	**14½**	**EUROPE**	**13½**
Non-Playing Captain:	Jack Nicklaus	*Non-Playing Captain*	Tony Jacklin

Jack Nicklaus's quite unbelievable drive to victory on the final ten holes at the Augusta National Golf Club this year must be regarded as nothing less than the most important accomplishment in golf since Bobby Jones's Grand Slam in 1930.

— Herbert Warren Wind

The New Yorker, June 2, 1986

1986 Masters Tournament

Augusta National Golf Club
Augusta, Georgia
April 8 - 11, 1965

6,925 Yards   Par-72   88 Invitees   48 Players made the cut at at five over par

*T*here was nothing that would lead anyone but the ultimate romantic to believe that Jack Nicklaus would be a serious contender for the Masters at the age of 46. Over the early part of the 1986 season his best finish was a tie for 39th in the Hawaiian Open — not exactly the performance to inspire confidence. He hadn't won a tournament since his own Memorial Tournament in 1984, not a major since the PGA in 1980. It had been a long time.

But somehow Jack started playing like the Nicklaus of old.

As is so often the case in major championships — most typically in the U.S. and British Opens — the leaders in the first round are solid, but many times, little-known players. In this case form held true as Ken Green and Bill Kratzert led with a pair of 68s. Green's round was fashioned with his putter, as he made seven birdie putts, including one from 50 feet and one from 75 feet. In all there were 16 sub-par rounds and two at par. The scoring was surprising as the first round was played in strong, gusty winds that started to dry out, and then speed up, the already fast greens. Jack came in with a 74. Given the sub-par scoring in the first round, it seemed that he would have to press just to make the cut.

In the second round, the winds continued, further drying out the greens, as the scores went higher. Making the cut at 149 were 48 players out of the starting field of 88, with as a strong contingent of foreign players, including Spain's Seve Ballesteros, the leader after two rounds at 139. Jack added a 71 to the previous day's 74 to sit six strokes back.

Conditions changed on Saturday, as the winds stopped and a front moved in, carrying with it much more humidity. With softer greens and more accessible pin positions, the competitors were able to attack the course.

As a result, scores were much lower. In fact, Nick Price, who opened with a 79 and followed with a 69 to make the cut by one, had a phenomenal round, setting the all-time, single-round scoring record, a gaudy nine-under 33-30 – 63. On the

LEFT: **At 46, Jack was not among the pre-tournament favorites. Nick Price's dazzling 63 in the third round (above) set a course record.**

front side Price made bogey on the first hole and then four birdies through the ninth. Then the fireworks began — four birdies on the next four holes, a par on the 14th, birdies on 15 and 16 and pars on the last two for 30. And he scored all of his 10 birdies without reaching even one of the par-5 holes in two. In all there were 18 rounds of three under par or better.

One of those rounds was recorded by one Jack Nicklaus, though no one seemed to give him much of a chance, as there were so many other more *au courant* players in the hunt. Greg Norman, with a 68, led by one at 210, Price at 211 along with Ballesteros, Bernhard Langer, Tom Watson, Tom Kite and Donnie Hammond. Jack was at 214, four back, tied for ninth. Seeing his name on the leaderboard on Saturday evening seemed more like an exercise in nostalgia than a plausible run at yet another green jacket.

It is axiomatic to say that the Masters Tournament begins on the back nine on Sunday. In this case it began on the ninth hole.

After eight holes on Sunday Jack was at even par with 12 players ahead of him.

In his salad days Jack was known for his exceptionally long, accurate drives and incredibly deft putting.

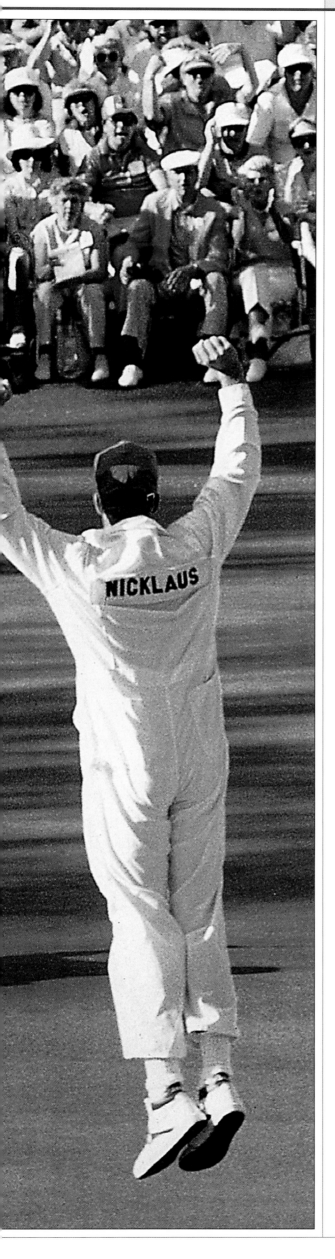

NICKLAUS

Then somehow, on the ninth hole, it was the Jack Nicklaus of old, not an old Jack Nicklaus, as he made a run as he had never done in a major championship.

As Jack was lining up his birdie putt from 11 feet on the ninth hole, big things were happening out on the course — first Kite holed a wedge from 100 yards for eagle on eight; Ballesteros,

playing with Kite, incredibly did the same, but from 60 yards.

Jack holed his putt on nine for birdie.

On 10, he hit a huge drive on the 485-yard, par-4 hole that left him with a 4-iron, and made the 25-footer for birdie. On 11, he hit another big drive and then an 8-iron to 20 feet for his third birdie. It seemed that the entire course was abuzz with Nicklaus's run of three birdies in a row.

LEFT: **The putt that sunk Seve. Son Jackie, caddieing, leaped up when Jack made this birdie on 16. After hearing the cheers, Ballesteros (above) dunked his approach on 15 in the water.**

DAVID CANNON/GETTY IMAGES

Could he do it? Most thought not, he was still too far back, but this was certainly getting interesting.

On the dangerous par-3 12th, with the pin in the usual back right position, Jack hit what he thought was a safe, low-flying 7-iron to the "smarter" left-hand side of the green. But he pulled it a little as his tee shot ended up on the fringe of the green, some few feet below the level of the putting surface. A chip and a missed par putt from six feet. Bogey.

But as Jack would later admit, the bogey on 12 was the turning point in the round, as he realized he had to be aggressive, not defensive, to have a chance.

He then reached the par-5 13th in two. Two putts later, a birdie — back to five under. Still a chance. Through 13 Jack was two behind Ballesteros, one behind Kite and tied with Jay Haas, Payne Stewart and Greg Norman, with all but Stewart playing behind him.

After a garden variety par on 12, Ballesteros hit a 6-iron as his second shot to the par-5 13th and made his second eagle of the day, from eight feet, seemingly taking charge of the tournament. Now Jack was four back.

But he answered Ballesteros's eagle with a big drive on 15, over the crest of the hill in the drive area, about 200 yards from the pin. Then he hit a Nicklaus signature high-flying soft-landing 4-iron — right out of his playbook from the olden days — to 12 feet.

Now the institutional memory kicked in — after all, he had missed this very same putt in the 1975 Masters — he knew, just knew, that his putt would break about 16 inches from left to right. All he had to do was to hit it on the right line with the proper pace. As his putt caught the right edge of the cup, it tumbled in for an eagle three to a truly deafening roar.

LEFT: **Jack immediately followed his birdie at 16 with another at 17 (inset).**

While in the Press Room…

Like the everything else that afternoon, it defied explanation.

There is no cheering in a press room. You take notes. You interview. You write your story.

But for one magic Sunday afternoon in 1986, things changed. Really changed.

The curmudgeons, the cynical ink-stained wretches who worked in the old Quonset hut that served as the press facility were fans. As Jack Nicklaus was coming down the stretch, they gathered around the television sets and cheered. When that putt fell at the 17th a few writers whistled *God Bless America*.

And when the final putt dropped? The room erupted in cheers and applause.

At the end of the night when everyone was filing out, some of the top veterans left shaking their heads. This one, they said, was too big to write.

So, they let it write itself.

— MELANIE HAUSER, *VETERAN GOLF WRITER*

Seven under par. Jack holding his putter high in the air. Suddenly it's 1975 again — but this time it's his caddie, son Jackie, jumping in excitement.

With a 5-iron on the par-3, 170-yard 16th hole, Jack's tee shot landed some 20 feet over the flag, but came back down the hill to within three feet of the hole, just missing a hole-in-one by inches. One more birdie. Eight under.

Standing in the 15th fairway after a drive of over 300 yards, Ballesteros heard the roars for Jack's birdie on 16. He first chose a 5-iron but switched to a 4-iron, figuring he'd rather be long than short in the water. Take the water out of play he thought. Hitting his 4-iron from a downhill lie, Ballesteros hit it fat — right in the water. Bogey. End of the Spanish challenge.

On the par-4, 400-yard 17th Jack dramatically made his move, but it started out badly, as he pushed his drive right. Hitting a punched wedge from 125 yards, circumventing a tree limb to a raised green, it ended up close, just 12 feet away. Birdie.

With a 3-wood off the 18th tee, Jack had 175 yards to the pin on the upper level of the green. He hit it well, but a little breeze picked up just as he hit, leaving his putt 40 feet away on the lower level of the green. Jackie later said that the first putt on 18 was the best shot of the day, as it ended up just a few inches short of the cup. Par.

A record-tying 30 on the back nine; 33 strokes over the last 10 holes.

Now all that remained to challenge Nicklaus was Norman. With four birdies in a row — at 14, 15, 16, 17 — he needed a par on 18

ABOVE: Once again, Norman came up short at the finish.

LEFT: Father and son close out the round at 18, then bask in the applause of the Augusta gallery.

A CHARGE FOR THE AGES

Hole	Par	Result	+/-
9	4	3	-1
10	4	3	-1
11	4	3	-1
12	3	4	+1
13	5	4	-1
14	4	4	-
15	5	3	-2
16	3	2	-1
17	4	3	-1
18	4	4	-
Total	40	33	-7

for a tie with Jack and a playoff, or better yet, a birdie for the outright win. Hitting a 3-wood from the 18th tee, Norman had 186 yards left. Wanting to get back to the upper level of the green — and give himself a chance at the three and the victory — he chose a 4-iron, deciding to take a little off and cut it. But Norman came off the shot a little too much as his approach went wide of the green to the right. Now Norman had to get up and down from about 15 feet off the green, just to tie. Chipping rather than putting, he left his pitch about 10 feet above the pin.

When Norman missed the putt to the left, it was as the romantic had dreamed: Jack Nicklaus had won his sixth Masters.

1986 MASTERS

1.	Jack Nicklaus	74 – 71 – 69 – 65 – 279
2.	Tom Kite	70 – 74 – 68 – 68 – 280
	Greg Norman	70 – 72 – 68 – 70 – 280
4.	Seve Ballesteros	71 – 68 – 72 – 70 – 281
5.	Nick Price	79 – 69 – 63 – 71 – 282

LEFT: In the now familiar winner's ritual, Jack is all smiles as 1985 champion Bernhard Langer presents the green jacket.

1987 Ryder Cup Captain

Muirfield Village Golf Club
Dublin, Ohio
September 25-27, 1987

7,104 Yards   Par-72

*T*he tide had started to turn as the European team came close to winning the Ryder Cup in 1983. In 1985, in fact, the Europeans did win for only the fifth time — all in Europe. But 1987 would prove to be different.

Jack was named captain of the American team for the second time and, once again, Tony Jacklin captained the European team. These leaders of their respective teams constitute an organic linkage to the first playing for the Ryder Cup in 1927, not only because of their historic singles match in 1969 — when Jack conceded a two-foot putt to Jacklin, thereby ending those matches in a tie — but also to the roots of the cup in 1927 as the matches came to represent the very essence of competition and sportsmanship at the highest levels.

After two days, the strong European team led by a score of 10½-5½, virtually requiring a complete U.S. domination of the 12 singles matches on the last day if the Americans were to have any reasonable chance of winning back the cup.

But it was not to be, despite a valiant rally by the Americans on the last day as they scored 7½ points — taking many of the matches to the last few holes — as the European team won, 15-13.

It was altogether fitting that the Ryder Cup was clinched for the European side by Seve Ballesteros, the most dominant player on the European team and, in some experts' opinion, the most talented player in the world.

It was the first time in the 60-year history of the Ryder Cup Matches that the U.S. lost on its home soil. Given the globalization of golf that had been taking place in the past decade and a half, the result was a virtual equalization of talent among the major golfing countries around the world. Thus, the result of the 1987 Ryder Cup was by no means surprising.

ABOVE: The European team celebrating its first win on U.S. soil.

RIGHT: Captains Jacklin and Nicklaus before the start of the matches.

27TH RYDER CUP MATCHES

UNITED STATES		EUROPE	
Morning Foursomes (Day One)			
Curtis Strange and Tom Kite (4 and 2)	1	Sam Torrance and Howard Clark	0
Hal Sutton and Dan Pohl (2 and 1)	1	Ken Brown and Bernhard Langer	0
Lanny Wadkins and Larry Mize	0	Nick Faldo and Ian Woosnam (2 up)	1
Larry Nelson and Payne Stewart	0	Seve Ballesteros and J.M. Olazabal (1 up)	1
Afternoon Four-Balls (Day One)			
Ben Crenshaw and Scott Simpson	0	Gordon Brand Jr. and Jose Rivero (3 and 2)	1
Andy Bean and Mark Calcavecchia	0	Sandy Lyle and Bernhard Langer (1 up)	1
Hal Sutton and Dan Pohl	0	Nick Faldo and Ian Woosnam (2 and 1)	1
Curtis Strange and Tom Kite	0	Seve Ballesteros and J.M. Olazabal (2 and 1)	1
DAY ONE TOTAL	**2**	**DAY ONE TOTAL**	**6**
Morning Foursomes (Day Two)			
Curtis Strange and Tom Kite (3 and 1)	1	Jose Rivero and Gordon Brand Jr.	0
Hal Sutton and Larry Mize (halved)	½	Nick Faldo and Ian Woosnam (halved)	½
Lanny Wadkins and Larry Nelson	0	Sandy Lyle and Bernhard Langer (2 and 1)	1
Ben Crenshaw and Payne Stewart	0	Seve Ballesteros and J.M. Olazabal (1 up)	1
Afternoon Four-Balls (Day Two)			
Curtis Strange and Tom Kite	0	Nick Faldo and Ian Woosnam (5 and 4)	1
Andy Bean and Payne Stewart (3 and 2)	1	Eamonn Darcy and Gordon Brand Jr.	0
Hal Sutton and Larry Mize (2 and 1)	1	Seve Ballesteros and J.M. Olazabal	0
Lanny Wadkins and Larry Nelson	0	Sandy Lyle and Bernhard Langer (1 up)	1
DAY TWO TOTAL	**3½**	**DAY TWO TOTAL**	**4½**
TWO DAY TOTAL	**5½**	**TWO DAY TOTAL**	**10½**
Singles (Day Three)			
Andy Bean (1 up)	1	Ian Woosnam	0
Dan Pohl	0	Howard Clark (1 up)	1
Larry Mize (halved)	½	Sam Torrance (halved)	½
Mark Calcavecchia (1 up)	1	Nick Faldo	0
Payne Stewart (2 up)	1	Jose Maria Olazabal	0
Scott Simpson (2 and 1)	1	Jose Rivero	0
Tom Kite (3 and 2)	1	Sandy Lyle	0
Ben Crenshaw	0	Eamonn Darcy (1 up)	1
Larry Nelson (halved)	½	Bernhard Langer (halved)	½
Curtis Strange	0	Seve Ballesteros (2 and 1)	1
Lanny Wadkins (3 and 2)	1	Ken Brown	0
Hal Sutton (halved)	½	Gordon Brand Jr. (halved)	½
DAY THREE TOTAL	**7½**	**DAY THREE TOTAL**	**4½**
UNITED STATES	**13**	**EUROPE**	**15**
Non-Playing Captain:	Jack Nicklaus	*Non-Playing Captain*	Tony Jacklin

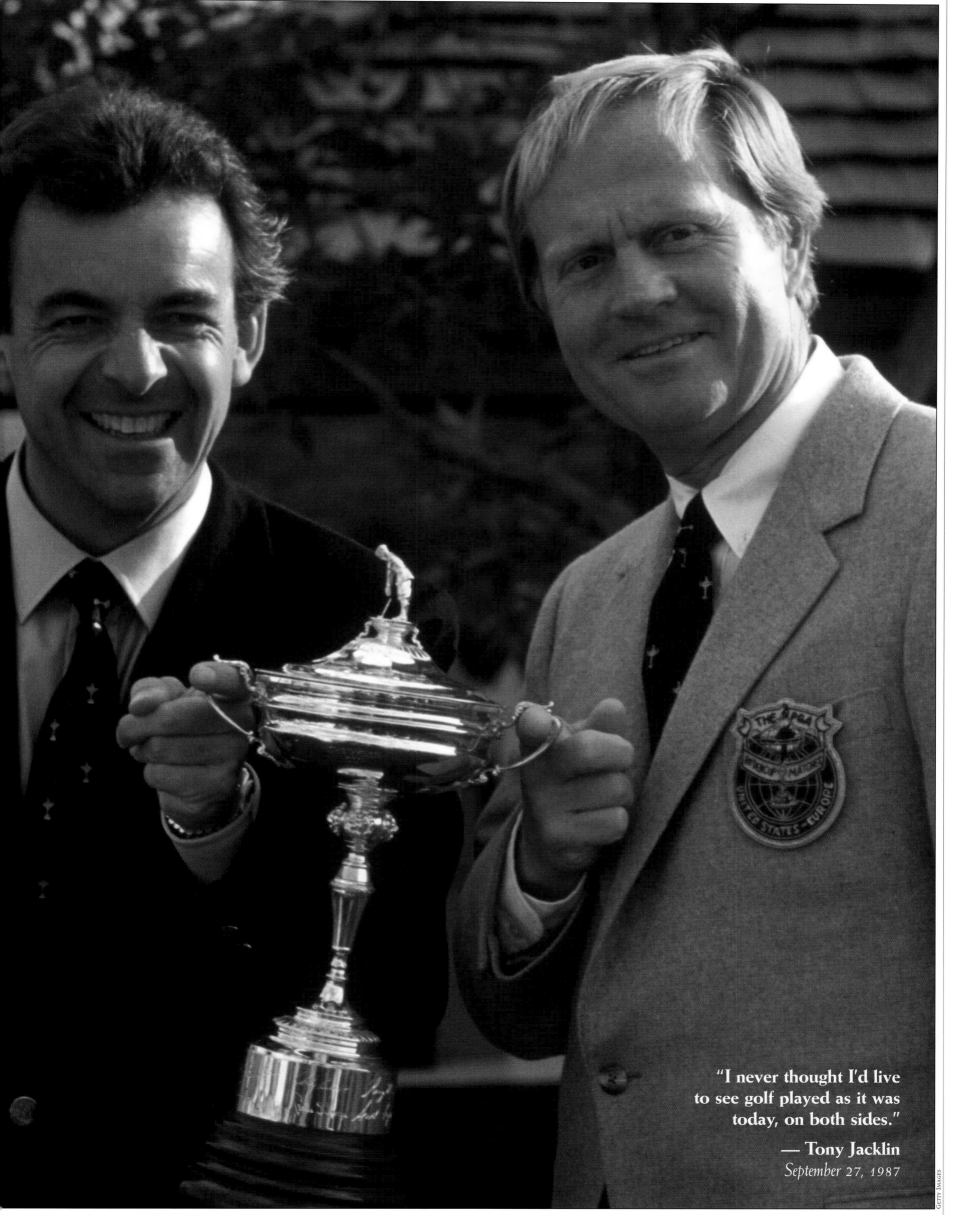

"I never thought I'd live
to see golf played as it was
today, on both sides."

— Tony Jacklin
September 27, 1987

THE MEMORIAL TOURNAMENT

Year	Winner	Score	Year	Winner	Score
1976	Roger Maltbie *	288	1992	David Edwards *	273
1977	Jack Nicklaus	281	1993	Paul Azinger	274
1978	Jim Simons	284	1994	Tom Lehman	268
1979	Tom Watson	285	1995	Greg Norman	269
1980	David Graham	280	1996	Tom Watson	274
1981	Keith Fergus	284	1997	Vijay Singh **	202
1982	Raymond Floyd	281	1998	Fred Couples	271
1983	Hale Irwin	281	1999	Tiger Woods	273
1984	Jack Nicklaus *	280	2000	Tiger Woods	269
1985	Hale Irwin	281	2001	Tiger Woods	271
1986	Hal Sutton	271	2002	Jim Furyk	274
1987	Don Pooley	272	2003	Kenny Perry	275
1988	Curtis Strange	274	2004	Ernie Els	270
1989	Bob Tway	277	2005	Bart Bryant	272
1990	Greg Norman **	216	2006	Carl Petterson	276
1991	Kenny Perry *	273			

* Won in playoff
** Weather shortened

The Memorial Tournament

Dublin, Ohio
Inaugural Tournament 1976

The Memorial Tournament, begun in 1976 and won by Roger Maltbie, has evolved into one of the finest and most respected tournaments on the PGA Tour. In fact, many rank it just behind the four majors in the quality of field, course conditioning and prestige.

Each year the tournament honors golf's greatest players, as befits the name Memorial. The inaugural honoree was the incomparable Bobby Jones. In subsequent years, the tournament has recognized the greats of the game — men and women, amateurs and professionals. The tournament also annually recognizes those who have made significant journalistic contributions to the game.

The Memorial Tournament has met Jack and Barbara's goal of giving back to the community, as the primary beneficiary of the tournament is the Columbus Children's Hospital, as well as several other Central Ohio area charities.

Jack had the grace not to win the first tour-

ABOVE: **Jack speaks at the inaugural Memorial Tournament which honored Bobby Jones in 1976. On the right are Hord Hardin, Gene Sarazen and Bob Hope.**

LEFT: **In 2001, Tiger Woods won his third consecutive Memorial.**

ASSOCIATED PRESS

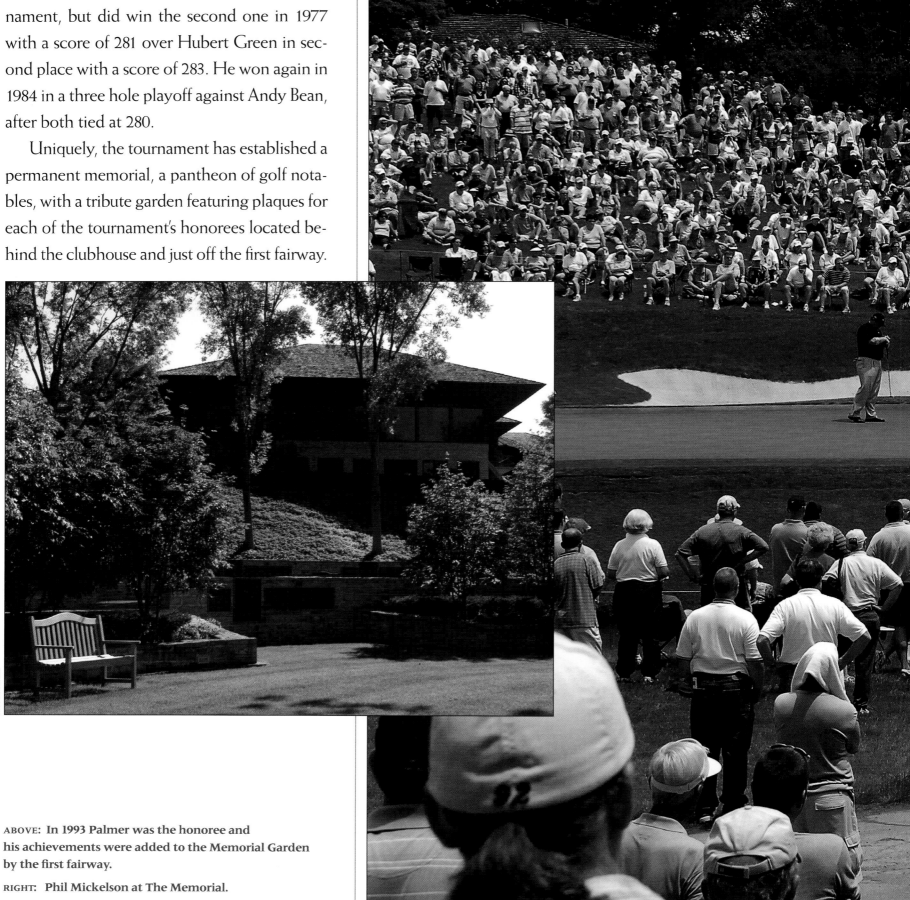

JIM MANDEVILLE

nament, but did win the second one in 1977 with a score of 281 over Hubert Green in second place with a score of 283. He won again in 1984 in a three hole playoff against Andy Bean, after both tied at 280.

Uniquely, the tournament has established a permanent memorial, a pantheon of golf notables, with a tribute garden featuring plaques for each of the tournament's honorees located behind the clubhouse and just off the first fairway.

ABOVE: **In 1993 Palmer was the honoree and his achievements were added to the Memorial Garden by the first fairway.**

RIGHT: **Phil Mickelson at The Memorial.**

THE JACK NICKLAUS MUSEUM

Ohio State University, Columbus, Ohio

Opened in 2002, this state-of-the-art, 24,000-square-foot facility offers visitors
a comprehensive view of Nicklaus's life and career, in and out of golf.
The galleries house an exhaustive collection of Jack's trophies and memorabilia,
as well as exhibits celebrating the history and legends of the game.

The par-3 second hole at The Bear's Club, in Jupiter, Florida, designed by Nicklaus in 2000, and (inset) the 18th hole and clubhouse.

Golf Course Design

Jack's first forays into the world of golf course design were in conjunction with Pete Dye, when the two collaborated in the late 1960s on Harbour Town Golf Links in Hilton Head, South Carolina. Jack then designed several courses with the input of Desmond Muirhead, including Muirfield Village Golf Club, regarded worldwide as one of Jack's finest efforts, just outside of his hometown of Columbus, Ohio.

By 1976, Jack unveiled his first solo design at Glen Abbey and that launched a 30-year career during which he has created some of the world's most acclaimed private, public and resort courses. Later, his four sons and son-in-law got involved in Nicklaus Design, and through the middle of 2007, the company had opened 315 courses in 30 countries.

On the following pages is a selection of Jack's most notable efforts.

Cabo del Sol - Ocean Course

Cabo San Lucas, Mexico • 1994 • 7,103/7,041 Yards, Par 72

JIM MANDEVILLE

Old Greenwood

Truckee, California •2004 • 7,518 Yards, Par 72

JIM MANDEVILLE

JIM MANDEVILLE

From his private jet Jack has a bird's eye view of the courses he's designed.

Jack uses the plane to effectively manage his time visiting the company's many projects all over the world.

PHOTOS ON GATEFOLD OPENER: JIM MANDEVILLE

Chapelco Golf and Resort
San Juan Martin de los Andes, Argentina • 2004 • 7,163 Yards, Par 72 • Co-designed with J.

Course

Jim Mandeville

Jim Mandeville

Sebonack Golf Club

Southampton, New York • 2006 • 7,220 Yards, Par 72 • Co-designed with Tom Doak

Steve Szurlej

Desert Mountain (Chiricahua)

Scottsdale, Arizona • 1999 • 7,300 Yards, Par 72

Jim Mandeville

Course

II

Cap Cana - Punta Espada Golf C

Punta Cana, Dominican Republic • 2006 • 7,368 Yards, Par 72

Mayacama Golf Club

Santa Rosa, California • 2001 • 6,761 Yards, Par 72

INSET LEFT: **Jack makes a point with Nicklaus Design colleagues, (from left) John Cop•**
Bill O'Leary, Troy Vincent and and Jack Nicklaus II.

The Presidents Cup

$\mathcal{T}$he original concept behind the Presidents Cup was to provide non-European golf professionals an opportunity to play in an international match-play competition against an American team, much like the biennial Ryder Cup Matches between the U.S. and Europe. It is played in non-Ryder Cup years, thus providing an international team competition each year.

The inaugural Presidents Cup was played in 1994 at the Robert Trent Jones Golf Club in Prince William County, Virginia. The U.S. side, captained by Hale Irwin, defeated the International Team, captained by David Graham, 20-12.

Former U.S. President Gerald Ford was the Honorary Chairman of the first event. Former President George Herbert Walker Bush chaired the 1996 Cup; Australian Prime Minister John Howard similarly chaired the 1998 Cup; sitting President Bill Clinton chaired the 2000 event; Thabo Mbeki, President of the Republic of South Africa, did the honors in 2003, while President George W. Bush was the Honorary Chair in 2005.

Members of the U.S. are selected from the money list beginning the year after the previous year's Presidents Cup through the PGA Championship the following year. Members of the International Team are selected from the Official World Ranking and do not include players eligible for the European Ryder Cup Team. The rankings are used to select the first 10 members of the 12-man teams, with each captain having two "free" selections to round out his respective team. The competition,

LEFT: **U.S. captain Jack Nicklaus with (from left) former Presidents George H.W. Bush and Bill Clinton and International captain Gary Player before the 2005 Presidents Cup, in Virginia.**

INSET: **PGA Tour Commissioner Tim Finchem presents the Presidents Cup to Jack Nicklaus on behalf of his winning U.S. team.**

played over three days, consists of 11 four-somes matches, 11 four-ball matches and 12 singles matches.

Jack has captained the U.S. Team on three separate occasions. In 1998, the International side, led by five-time British Open Champion Peter Thomson, defeated the American Team 20½-11½, over Royal Melbourne Golf Club.

The 2003 event, played at The Links at Fancourt in George, South Africa, provided a unique outcome. With the teams tied with 17 points each at the end of the three-day matches, Ernie Els, for the International Team, and Tiger Woods, for the American Team, began a sudden-death playoff. Still tied after three holes in the increasing darkness, American captain Nicklaus and International captain Gary Player huddled and decided that, in the spirit of the competition, the two teams would share the cup.

The 2005 President Cup, played for the fourth time at the Robert Trent Jones Golf Club, proved to be equally exciting, as Chris DiMarco birdied the 18th hole of his singles match to defeat Stuart Appleby, 1 up, for Jack's second win as team captain.

ABOVE: As darkness fell, captains Nicklaus and Player agreed to a tie in 2003.

LEFT: The 2005 U.S. Presidents Cup team. Seated from left: Justin Leonard, Fred Funk, Jim Furyk, Stewart Cink, Davis Love III. Standing from left: Scott Verplank, Phil Mickelson, assistant captain Jeff Sluman, Kenny Perry, Jack Nicklaus, David Toms, Tiger Woods, Fred Couples and Chris DiMarco.

INSET: DiMarco's winning putt at the last hole gave captain Nicklaus reason to cheer in 2005.

The Presidential Medal of Freedom

The White House
November 9, 2005

*E*stablished by an Executive Order signed by President John F. Kennedy in 1963, the Presidential Medal of Freedom is the nation's highest civilian award.

The medal may be awarded at the discretion of the President of the United States "to any person who has made an especially meritorious contribution to (1) the security or national interests of the United States, or (2) world peace, or (3) cultural or other significant public or private endeavors."

On November 9, 2005 in the East Room of the White House, President George W. Bush awarded Jack the Presidential Medal of Freedom. In his speech the President, in introducing Jack, said to much laughter, "Last year in Ohio, I ran into Jack Nicklaus and asked if he had any advice for my golf game. He said, 'Sure — quit.'"

In his comments, the President noted that Jack was receiving the award not only for his notable accomplishments on the golf course, but also for his significant charitable activities and contributions.

A signal honor, Jack is awarded the Presidential Medal of Freedom by President George W. Bush in a 2005 ceremony at the White House.

...o in the final round of the club junior championship.

...6, beats pros.

...State

1959
Wins first U.S. Amateur.
Member of winning Walker Cup Team.

1961
Jack II born.
Low amateur in U.S. Open for second year.
Wins second U.S. Amateur.
Member of winning Walker Cup Team; retires undefeated.
Appears on cover of Golf Digest for first of 50 times.

1963
Steve born.
Wins first Masters.
Wins first PGA.

1960
Finishes second in Open as amateur.
Wins NCAA individual and team crowns.
Leads U.S. team to victory in World Team Amateur at Merion.
Marries Barbara Bash.

1962
Turns pro, earns $33.33 in debut at L.A. Open.
Defeats Arnold Palmer in U.S. Open playoff at Oakmont.

...rade up Broadway.

...oadcast.

1958
Tommy Bolt wins U.S. Open; doesn't throw a club.

1960
Arnie wins his only U.S. Open.

1962
Julius Boros wins U.S. Open at The Country Club with easygoing swing.

Mickey Wright wins her fourth Women's Open; Ben Hogan opines "... best swing in golf."

1959
Billy Casper wins U.S. Open at Winged Foot.

1961
Shell's Wonderful World of Golf debuts on television with Gene Sarazen as host.

1963
"Champagne" Tony Lema finish... second in Masters, one stroke behind Jack.

1963
Barry Goldwater defeated for the Presidency; Conservatives emboldened.

1959
Castro takes Cuba.

1961
Berlin Wall erected.
Roger Maris breaks Babe Ruth's single season home run record, asterisk wrongly inserted in record book.

*

...hed into space.

1960
Nixon-Kennedy Presidential debates.
OPEC formed.

...958
...'hamO Corp. invents hula hoop.
...Chubby Checker twists.

1962
Cuban Missile Crisis, U.S. blockades Cuba.

TIMELINE
by Martin Davis

JACK'S YEAR

1950
Scioto CC Juvenile Championship. Wins with 61–60 – 121 for 18 holes

1954
Made first hole-in-one on the 145-yard 17th at Scio

1955
Shoots 63 five times over the summer.

1956
Wins Ohio Open at age
Wins Ohio High School
Championship with a 73

1951
Scioto CC Sub-Juvenile Championship. Wins with 90–84 – 174 for 36 holes.

1940
Jack William Nicklaus born.

1942
With dad.

1953
Wins Ohio State Jr. Amateur (13-15 year-old bracket) with 82-83 – 165.

1957
Qualifies for U.S. Open for first time; misses cut after shooting a pair of 80s.

1958
Medalist in U.S. Open regional qualifying, shoots 304 at Southern Hills to T-41.
Wins Trans-Mississippi Am at Prairie Dunes, with 9-and-8 victory in final.

THE YEAR IN GOLF

1946
Lloyd Magrum, war hero, wins first U.S. Open played after WWII.

1947
Herbert Warren Wind pens his opus, The Story of American Golf.

1948
Ike joins Augusta National Golf Club.

1953
Ben Hogan wins Masters, U.S. Open and British Open, has pa

1956
First Masters television b

1950
Jimmy Demaret wins his third Masters.
First issue of Golf Digest, 15¢.

1955
Byron Nelson, retired for nine years, wins French Open.

SIGNIFICANT WORLD EVENTS

...or at least my take on them.

1940
Radar invented in the UK.

1941
World War II begins.

1951
Joe D retires.

1953
Ike inaugurated.

1955
Bill Buckley launches
National Review,
liberals cringe.

1957
Sputnik lau.

1956
Suez crisis.
Mickey Mantle wins Triple Crown.
Don Larsen pitches perfect game in World Series as Yankees defeat the Brooklyn Dodgers.

Background Photo: Jack putts on first green at St. Andrews during final round at his last major championship, 2005 British Open.

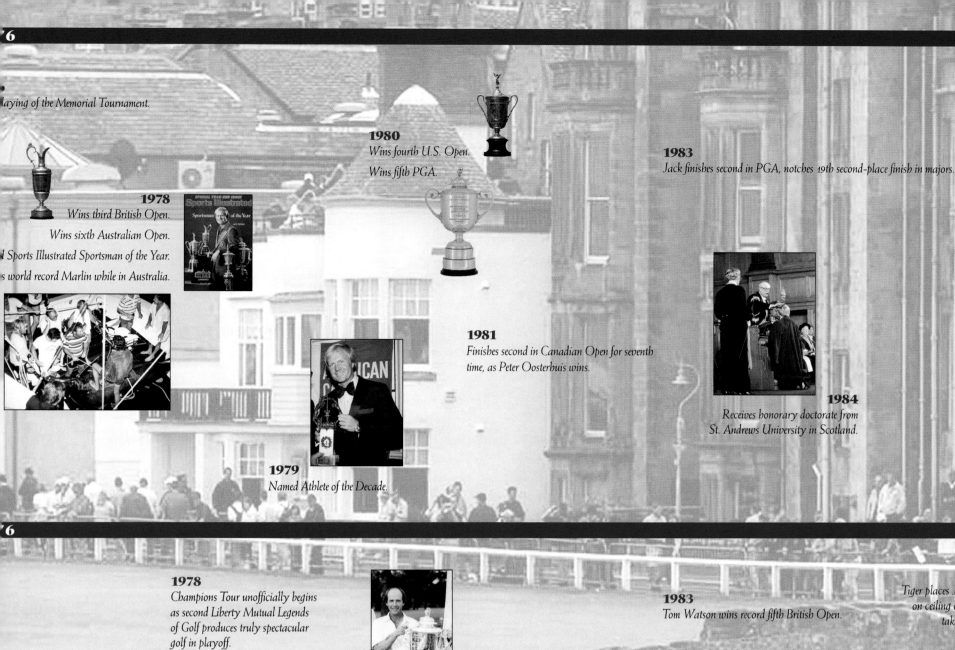

aying of the Memorial Tournament.

1978
Wins third British Open.

Wins sixth Australian Open.

d Sports Illustrated Sportsman of the Year.

s world record Marlin while in Australia.

1980
Wins fourth U.S. Open.

Wins fifth PGA.

1983
Jack finishes second in PGA, notches 19th second-place finish in majors.

1981
Finishes second in Canadian Open for seventh time, as Peter Oosterhuis wins.

1984
Receives honorary doctorate from St. Andrews University in Scotland.

1979
Named Athlete of the Decade.

1
W

1978
Champions Tour unofficially begins as second Liberty Mutual Legends of Golf produces truly spectacular golf in playoff.

1983
Tom Watson wins record fifth British Open.

Tiger places Jac
on ceiling ove
takes

1981
Future Hall of Famer Larry Nelson wins PGA Championship at The Atlanta Athletic Club.

1979
Seve Ballesteros wins British Open from car park.

1984
Ben Crenshaw wins Masters; Herb Wind appropriately calls it "…a great day for golf."

y in head-to-head
citing major ever.

1977

1982
Tom Watson's chip in thwarts Jack's bid for fifth U.S. Open.

1
R
at

Friedman wins Nobel Prize
nomics.

Bicentennial.

1978
Yankees win World Series for second year in a row, natural order restored.

1981
Dave Anderson wins Pulitzer Prize for Distinguished Commentary.

Sandra Day O'Connor first woman on Supreme Court.

1983
Reagan re-elected in landslide.

Apple introduces first user-friendly computer.

1
B
a
F

EIB broad
mo

1977
Elvis dies, leaves building.

1980
Al Michaels intones, "Do you believe in miracles?," as U.S. wins Olympic gold in hockey.

Reagan elected.

1982
Michael Jackson releases Thriller.

Al Gore claims to invent the Internet.

At Brandenberg Gate, President Reaga
"Mr. Gorbachev, tear down

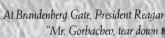

1966

First to go back-to-back at Augusta, wins third Masters.

Wins first British Open at Muirfield, Doug Sanders one back.
Completes career Grand Slam of all four professional majors, age 26 .

1970

Wins Byron's tournament after defeating Arnie
on first hole of sudden death

Wins second British
Open at Home of Golf
Doug Sanders second
again after playoff

1965
Nan born.
Wins second Masters.

1969
Gary born.
First golf course design —
Harbour Town Golf Links, with Pete Dye.

Wins second U.S. Open. Sets new Open scoring record of 275. Arnie
second, followed by Don January, Billy Casper and Lee Trevino.

1967

1965
Gary Player wins U.S. Open.
Peter Thomson wins 5th British Open.
Dave Marr wins PGA, West 52nd St. celebrates.
Carol Mann wins Women's Open.

1968
Bob Goalby defeats Roberto DiVicenzo by one stroke
in Masters as DiVicenzo signs incorrect scorecard.

Lee Trevino bursts onto scene with win in
U.S. Open at Oak Hill.

1969
Raymond Floyd wins PGA.
Walter Hagen,
golf's greatest showman, dies.

4
d wins fourth Masters.

1970
Billy Casper wins Masters, ignites fervor for buffalo meat

1966
Big Three, biggest thing in golf, dominates game.
Ping introduces Anser putter.

1965
First troops deployed to Vietnam.

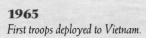

1968
Ohio State's Woody Hayes wins third National Championship.

Red Auerbach and the Boston Celtics win 10th NBA Championship
with Bill Russell and John Havlicek starring.

1967
First heart transplant.

1966
First Star Trek episode, Mr. Sulu three-putts.

1969
Neil Armstrong walks on moon.
Joe Willie Namath guarantees victory as

1972
Wins fourth Masters.
Wins third U.S. Open.

1973
Michael born.
Wins third PGA.

1975
Wins fifth Masters.
Wins fourth PGA.

1974
Muirfield Village Golf Club opens.
One of 13 original inductees into the World Golf Hall of Fame in Pinehurst. Hall later moves to St. Augustine.

1971
Wins second PGA.

1971
Bobby Jones dies, golf mourns.

1973
Johnny Miller, beginning six strokes behind the leaders, shoots spectacular 63 in final round of Open to win at Oakmont.

1975
Tiger Woods born.
U.S. Open won by Lou Graham at Medinah.

1974
Johnny Miller wins eight PGA Tour events.

1972
Lee Trevino defeats Jack by one in British Open at Muirfield; ends Jack's hope for Professional Grand Slam.

Gary Player wins PGA at tough Oakland Hills; hits 150-yard nine iron over a weeping willow tree on the 16th hole to seal victory.

Tom Watson wins British Open by one stroke at duel with Jack; considere

1973
Secretariat dominates Triple Crown.
Dan Jenkins's book Semi-Tough becomes best seller.
America still laughing.

970
e Beatles break up.
onday Night Football debuts, Howard Cosell
s new hairpiece.

1975
Saturday Night Live debuts.

1971
Starbucks opens first store.

1972
Bobby Fischer defeats Boris Spasky for World Chess Crown.

1974
Nixon resigns.

e Jets win Super Bowl III.

A singular honor, "dotting the i" with The Ohio State University marching band.

1991
Wins U.S. Senior Open at Oakland Hills in playoff over Chi Chi Rodriguez.

Does expert golf commentary for ABC Sports.

1998
Finishes T-6 at Masters, age 58.

2000
Plays in last U.S. Open and last PGA.

Named Sports Illustrated Best Individual Male Athlete of the 20th century.

1990
Wins Senior Tour debut at The Tradition.

86
ns record sixth Masters at age 46. Wow!

1999
Jack has hip replacement with a new ceramic and titanium joint.

2005
Plays in last Masters and last British Open.

1993
Wins second U.S. Senior Open by one over Tom Weiskopf at Cherry Hills.

1987
's record his bed; ad aim.

1989
Curtis Strange goes back-to-back with U.S. Open victories, The Country Club in 1988 and Oak Hill in 1989.

1996
Tiger wins third consecutive U.S. Amateur.

2003
Bob Hope, golf's great ambassador, dies at 100. Golf thankful for the memories.

Jim Furyk, with funky backswing, wins U.S. Open at Olympia Fields by three strokes.

1991
Ely Callaway introduces Big Bertha driver, persimmon trees thankful.

1993
Tiger wins third consecutive Boys Junior.

Greg Norman wins second British Open.

1992
Nick Faldo wins third British Open.

1994
George H.W. Bush sets new land speed record, plays 18 holes in under 1½ hours.

2004
Peter Jacobsen wins U.S. Senior Open at Bellerive.

86
ymond Floyd wins U.S. Open Shinnecock.

1998
Titliest introduces Pro V1 golf ball.

2006
Chasing Jack, Tiger wins 12th professional major.

1995
The Golf Channel airs first broadcast.

Byron Nelson, golf's Patron Saint, dies at 94.

86
Buckner muffs easy grounder, Red Sox find ther way not to win World Series.

OX network created.

1993
McDonald's sells 100 billionth burger.

2004
"Curse of the Bambino" apparently broken, Red Sox somehow win World Series. Sean McDonough still grinning.

1988
sts first radio show, cringing on the left.

1992
Johnny Carson retires from Tonight Show.

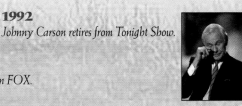

2000
W elected.

1990
The Simpsons debuts on FOX.

1989
Gorbachev complies, Berlin Wall falls; Evil Empire defeated.

1987
declares, is wall."

2001
Sean Hannity launches syndicated radio show, left now apoplectic.

The Complete Record of Jack Nicklaus

Jack Nicklaus, age 11, receiving the Scioto Country Club Juvenile Championship trophy.

AMATEUR RECORD

1950

| 1950 | Scioto CC Juvenile | 1 | 61 60 — — | 121 |

1951

| 1951 | Scioto CC Juvenile | 1 | 90 84 — — | 174 |
| 1951 | Columbus District Jr. Golf League | Qualified with 81, eliminated in first round | | |

1952

| 1952 | Columbus District Jr. Golf League Team Championship | | |
| | Youngest member of Scioto CC, 10-0 overall team record | | |

1953

1953	Ohio State Jr.	1	82 83 — —	165
1953	Columbus Jr. Match-Play	1	— — — —	—
1953	Columbus Jr. Stroke-Play	1	77 76 74 73 72	372
1953	U.S. Jr. Amateur	Eliminated in fourth round, 5 and 4		
1953	Columbus District Amateur	Eliminated in second round, 2 and 1		

1954

1954	Tri-State High School	Medalist, 68, member of winning team		
1954	Columbus Jr. Stroke-Play	1	70 69 — —	139
1954	Columbus Jr. Match-Play	1	Won final, 6 and 5	
1954	U.S. Jr. Amateur	Eliminated in second round, 4 and 3		
1954	Ohio State Jr.	1	74 85 — —	159
1954	Scioto CC Jr.	1	— — — —	—
1954	Columbus District Amateur	Eliminated in quarter final, 2 and 1		
1954	Ohio State Amateur	Eliminated in first round, 1 down		

1955

1955	Ohio Jaycees	1	67 68 — —	135
1955	Columbus Jr. Match-Play	1	Won final, 6 and 5	
1955	Columbus Jr. Stroke-Play	1	71 72 73 —	216
1955	Ohio State Jr. Class B(13-15 years)	1	72 73 — —	145
1955	Columbus Amateur Class A	Eliminated in semifinal, 3 and 2		
1955	National Jaycees	Medalist (tie), 144 for two rounds; thirteenth, 293 for four rounds		
1955	Ohio State Amateur	Medalist; eliminated in first round		
1955	U.S. Jr. Amateur	Eliminated in quarter finals, 4 and 2		
1955	**U.S. Amateur**	First time qualified for National Amateur; lost in first round		

1956

1956	Tri-State High School	Medalist, 67		
1956	Ohio High School State	1	73 — — —	73
1956	Columbus Amateur Match-play	1	Won final, 5 and 4	
1956	Columbus Jr. Match-Play	1	Won final, 2 up	
1956	Exhibition Match	Sam Snead, 68; Jack Nicklaus, 72		
1956	Ohio State Open	1	76 70 64 72	282
1956	Ohio Jaycees	1	72 70 — —	142
1956	Scioto CC Father/Son	1	— — — —	151
	Charlie Nicklaus, 77; Jack Nicklaus, 74		
1956	National Jaycees	2	Defeated in playoff, 69-71	
1956	U.S. Jr. Amateur	Eliminated in semifinal, 1 down		
1956	Ohio State Amateur	Medalist; eliminated in first round 2 and 1		
1956	Sunnehanna Amateur Invitational	5	— — — —	286
1956	**U.S. Open**	Second alternate; missed championship proper; did not play		
1956	**U.S. Amateur**	Eliminated in third round, 3 and 2		

Upon returning to Columbus after winning the 1959 U.S. Amateur, Jack received a royal welcome.

1957

1957	Tri-State High School	Medalist; led winning Upper Arlington team				
1957	Ohio High School State	1	72	76	—	—	148
1957	Ohio Jaycees	1	75	71	—	—	146
1957	Ohio HS Central District	1	69	—	—	—	
1957	National Jaycees	1	71	76	74	73	294
1957	U.S. Jr. Amateur	Eliminated in third round, 4 and 3				
1957	U.S. Open	CUT	80	80	—	—	160
	Qualified for first time with 68-71-139; missed cut, 80-80-160					
1957	U.S. Amateur	Eliminated in fourth round, 3 and 2				
1957	Columbus HS Golf League	Medalist, 74; member of winning team				

1958

1958	Trans-Mississippi Amateur	1	Won final, 9 and 8			
1958	Queen City Open	1	70	67	—	—	137
1958	Colonial Invitational		71	71	—	—	142
	Medalist					
1958	Rubber City Open	12	67	66	76	68	277
	(First PGA tour event)					
1958	U.S. Open	T41	79	75	73	77	304
1958	U.S. Amateur	Eliminated in second round, 1 down				

1959

1959	Masters	CUT	76	74	—	—	150
1959	North and South Amateur	1	Won final, 1 up			
1959	Trans-Mississippi Amateur	1	Won final, 3 and 2			—
1959	U.S. Open	CUT	77	77	—	—	154
1959	Gleneagles-Chicago Open	T26	67	69	76	73	285
1959	Motor City Open	T45	75	74	72	71	292
1959	Buick Open	T12	76	70	70	72	288
1959	U.S. Amateur	1				

In the first round (18 Holes) Jack defeated Robert T. Jones, III, 7 and 6

In the second round Jack defeated William Williamson, 2 and 1

In the third round, Nicklaus defeated Don Massengale, 6 and 5

In the fourth round Nicklaus defeated Orville Goens, 5 and 4

In the fifth round, Nicklaus defeated Richard Yost, 2 and 1

In the sixth and semi final round Nicklaus defeated Jean Andrews, 1up

In the final round (36 holes) Nicklaus defeated Charley Coe, 1 up

International

1959	Royal St. George's Challenge Cup	1	76	73	—	—	149
1959	British Amateur	Eliminated in quarter finals, 4 and 3				
1959	Walker Cup Match	1				

US wins at Honourable Company of Edindburgh Golfers, Muirfield, Scotland, (9 to 3)

Ward Wettlaufer and Jack teamed to defeat Michael Lunt and
　　Alec Shepperson in the foursomes (2 and 1).

In the singles, Jack defeated Dickson Smith (5 and 4)

1 9 6 0

1960	International Four-Ball	1	—	—	—	—	266
	(Partnered with Deane Beman)					
1960	Masters	T13	75	71	72	75	293
1960	Colonial Invitational	1	Won final, 4 and 2			—
1960	NCAA Big Ten Conference					
	Member of winning team (Ohio State); Runner up for individual title, 284-282					
1960	U.S. Open (Low amateur)	2	71	71	69	71	282
1960	NCAA	Eliminated in third round, 4 and 3				
1960	U.S. Amateur	Eliminated in fourth round, 5 and 3				

International

1960	World Amateur Team	Jack	—	66	67	68	68	269
		Team	1	208	205	203	218	834
	Led U.S. to team victory					
	Total best 3 of 4 scored daily					
	Jack Nicklaus 11 under par					
	US team won by 42 strokes					
1960	Americas Cup	1	Singles: won 2; Team: lost 2			

1 9 6 1

1961	Western Amateur	1	Won final, 4 and 3			—
1961	Masters	T7	70	75	70	72	287
1961	Colonial National Invitational	T38	75	74	76	72	297
1961	U.S. Open (Low amateur)	T4	75	69	70	70	284
1961	NCAA Big Ten Conference	1	68	70	73	72	283
1961	NCAA Individual	1	Won final, 5 and 3			—
1961	Buick Open	T24	74	72	72	74	292
1961	American Golf Classic	T55	76	73	74	76	299
1961	U.S. Amateur	1				

In the first round Jack drew a bye

In the second round (18 holes) Nicklaus defeated Don Krieger 4 and 3

In the third round, Nicklaus defeated William Edwards 5 and 4

In the fourth round Nicklaus defeated Dave Smith 2 and 1

In the fifth round, Nicklaus defeated Sam Carmichael 4 and 3

In the sixth and semi final round Nicklaus defeated Marion Mithvin 9 up and 8 to play

In the final round (36 holes) Nicklaus defeated Dudly Wysong 8 and 6

International

1961	Americas Cup	1	Singles: won 1, halved 1; Team: won 1, halved 1
1961	Walker Cup Match	1	

US wins at Seattle Golf Club, (11 to 1) for 17th time in 18 matches

In the foursomes Jack, teamed with Deane Beman; defeated the GBI team of
　　James Walker and H.G. Chapman, 6 and 5

In the singles, Jack defeated Irishman Joe Carr, 6 and 4

PROFESSIONAL RECORD

1962

1962	Los Angeles Open	T50	74	70	72	73	289	$33.33
1962	San Diego Open	T15	72	69	74	67	282	550.00
1962	Bing Crosby National Pro-Am	T23	71	77	72	76	296	450.00
1962	Lucky International Open	T47	71	73	73	73	290	62.86
1962	Palm Springs Golf Classic	T32	71 71 73 65 75				355	164.44
			P(5 round tournament)					
1962	Phoenix Open	T2	69	73	68	71	281	2,300.00
1962	Greater New Orleans Open	T17	71	80	70	71	292	650.00
1962	Baton Rouge Open	T9	72	68	69	71	280	753.33
1962	Pensacola Open	T16	71	71	74	64	280	450.00
1962	Doral Open	3	69	74	69	73	285	3,000.00
1962	**Masters**	T14	74	75	70	72	291	1,160.00
1962	Greater Greensboro Open	T7	70	72	74	70	286	1,300.00
1962	Houston Classic	T2	68	70	68	72	278	3,800.00
1962	Waco Turner Open	T3	71	73	70	71	285	1,233.33
1962	Colonial National Invitation	4	69	71	74	69	283	2,000.00
1962	500 Festival Open	T29	73	66	69	69	277	291.66
1962	Thunderbird Classic	2	69	73	65	70	277	10,000.00
1962	**U.S. Open**	1	72	70	72	69	283	15,000.00
			(Won in playoff, 71)					
1962	Western Open	T8	70	73	73	75	291	1,500.00
1962	**PGA**	T3	71	74	69	67	281	3,450.00
1962	American Golf Cassic	T3	72	70	71	71	284	1,450.00
1962	World Series of Golf	1	66	69	–	–	135	50,000.00
1962	Dallas Open	T5	72	71	68	72	283	1,420.00
1962	Seattle World's Fair Pro-Am	1	67	65	65	68	265	4,300.00
1962	Portland Open	1	64	69	67	69	269	3,500.00
1962	West Palm Beach Open Intl.	T13	73	71	69	71	284	550.00

International

1962	Piccadilly Tournament	43	79	71	70	78	298	0.00
1962	**British Open**	T34	80	72	74	79	305	90.20
1962	Canadian Open	T5	70	75	68	71	284	1,450.00
1962	Australian Open	5	74	70	71	71	286	–
1962	Wills Masters	5	–	–	–	–	–	2,200.00

JACK'S PROFESSIONAL RECORD

Major Championship Victories: 18
  U.S. Open: 1962, 1967, 1972, 1980
  Masters: 1963, 1965, 1966, 1972, 1975, 1986
  British Open: 1966, 1970, 1978
  PGA Championship: 1963, 1971, 1973, 1975, 1980

PGA TOUR Victories: 73

Champions Tour Victories: 10

Ryder Cup Teams: 8
  (17-8-3) 1969, 1971, 1973, 1975, 1977, 1981
  Captain: 1983, 1987

Presidents Cup Captain:
  1998, 2003, 2005, 2007

PGA Player of the Year:
  1967, 1972, 1973, 1975, 1976

Leading Money Winner:
  1964, 1965, 1967, 1971, 1972, 1973, 1975, 1976

Bob Jones Award: 1975

Jack won the Western Open in 1967.

1963

1963	Los Angeles Open	T24	71	74	68	67	280	$525.00
1963	Bing Crosby National Pro-Am	T2	71	69	76	70	286	2,140.00
1963	Lucky International Open	CUT	76	73	–	–	149	0.00
1963	Palm Springs Golf Classic	1	69 66 67 71 72				345	9,000.00
			(5 round tournament, won in playoff 65)					
1963	Phoenix Open	T3	67	70	67	71	275	2,200.00
1963	Greater New Orleans Open	T8	74	73	69	72	288	1,450.00
1963	Doral Open	T9	73	73	72	73	291	1,400.00
1963	**Masters**	1	74	66	74	72	286	20,000.00
1963	Houston Classic	4	65	69	68	71	273	3,000.00
1963	Tournament of Champions	1	64	68	72	69	273	13,000.00
1963	Colonial National Invitation	3	71	69	74	70	284	3,500.00
1963	Memphis Open	11	67	73	70	68	278	1,400.00
1963	Thunderbird Classic	T21	69	72	71	72	284	1,075.00
1963	**U.S. Open**	CUT	76	77	–	–	153	0.00
1963	Cleveland Open	7	68	68	69	70	275	3,450.00
1963	**PGA**	1	69	73	69	68	279	13,000.00
1963	Western Open	T2	69	74	71	66	280	4,450.00
1963	Insurance City Open	T5	73	67	67	71	278	1,675.00
1963	American Golf Classic	T5	70	70	71	72	283	2,200.00
1963	World Series of Golf	1	70	70	–	–	140	50,000.00
1963	Seattle Open	CUT	77	72	–	–	149	0.00
1963	Portland Open	T10	72	67	68	70	277	925.00
1963	Whitemarsh Open	T18	71	77	74	67	289	1,600.00
1963	Sahara Invitational	1	75	66	66	69	276	13,000.00
1963	Cajun Classic Open	T5	69	72	69	69	279	1,050.00

International

1963	**British Open**	3	71	67	70	70	278	2,240.00
1963	Canada Cup	1	67	72	66	32	237	2,000.00
			(Partnered with Arnold Palmer; won individual title)					
1963	Wills Masters	2	74	77	64	72	287	–

1964

Tournament	Place	R1	R2	R3	R4	R5	Total	Earnings
1964 Bing Crosby National Pro-Am	CUT	75	70	77	–		222	$0.00
1964 Lucky International Open	T12	74	72	66	68		280	1,200.00
1964 Palm Springs Golf Classic	T20	73	72	69	72	74	360	712.50

(5 round tournament)

Tournament	Place	R1	R2	R3	R4	Total	Earnings
1964 Phoenix Open	1	71	66	68	66	271	7,500.00
1964 Greater New Orleans Open	T2	70	70	72	72	284	3,400.00
1964 St. Petersburg Open	T4	71	69	68	70	278	1,400.00
1964 Doral Open	2	70	66	73	69	278	4,000.00
1964 Greater Greensboro Open	4	70	69	67	73	279	2,550.00
1964 **Masters**	T2	71	73	71	67	282	10,100.00
1964 Houston Classic	2	76	66	66	71	279	4,119.05
1964 Tournament of Champions	1	68	73	65	73	279	12,000.00
1964 Colonial National Invitation	T21	76	72	71	73	292	775.00
1964 Memphis Open	T12	72	70	66	66	274	1,110.00
1964 500 Festival Open	T18	72	69	68	71	280	916.66
1964 Thunderbird Classic	T11	73	69	68	72	282	2,000.00
1964 **U.S. Open**	T23	72	73	77	73	295	475.00
1964 Cleveland Open	T3	68	65	69	70	272	6,250.00
1964 Whitemarsh Open	1	69	70	70	67	276	24,042.01
1964 **PGA**	T2	67	73	70	64	274	9,000.00
1964 Western Open	T3	72	71	65	67	275	3,300.00
1964 American Golf Classic	4	73	69	70	73	285	2,900.00
1964 Carling World Open	T11	73	72	70	71	286	2,800.00
1964 Portland Open	1	68	72	68	67	275	5,800.00
1964 Sahara Invitational	T3	70	71	69	67	277	3,666.67
1964 Cajun Classic	T2	68	71	72	71	282	1,900.00
1964 Wills Masters	T2	72	68	70	70	280	1,000.00

International

Tournament	Place	R1	R2	R3	R4	Total	Earnings
1964 **British Open**	2	76	74	66	68	284	2,800.00
1964 Canadian Open	T5	70	72	71	69	282	2,080.00
1964 Piccadilly World Match-Play	(Eliminated in first round)						
1964 Canada Cup	1	72	69	65	70	276	2,000.00

(Partnered with Arnold Palmer; won individual title)

Tournament	Place	R1	R2	R3	R4	Total	Earnings
1964 Australia Open	1	75	71	74	67	287	–

1965

Tournament	Place	R1	R2	R3	R4	R5	Total	Earnings
1965 Bing Crosby National Pro-Am	T3	72	68	77	71		288	$3,100.00
1965 Bob Hope Desert Classic	T4	71	71	69	72	69	352	3,667.00

(5 round tournament)

Tournament	Place	R1	R2	R3	R4	Total	Earnings
1965 Phoenix Open	T8	70	69	70	71	280	2,075.00
1965 Pensacola Open	2	68	71	67	71	277	6,000.00
1965 Doral Open	T5	70	73	69	70	282	2,750.00
1965 Jacksonville Open	T2	72	69	73	72	286	3,575.00
1965 **Masters**	1	67	71	64	69	271	20,000.00
1965 Tournament of Champions	11	74	71	67	78	290	2,150.00
1965 Memphis Open	1	67	68	71	65	271	9,000.00
1965 Buick Open	4	70	71	70	73	284	5,000.00
1965 **U.S. Open**	T31	78	72	73	76	299	550.00
1965 St.Paul Open	T5	70	69	69	68	276	4,250.00
1965 National Challenge Cup	2	72	76	66	66	280	–
1965 Thunderbird Classic	1	67	66	69	68	270	20,000.00
1965 Philadelphia Golf Classic	1	71	65	73	68	277	24,300.00
1965 **PGA**	T2	69	70	72	71	282	12,500.00
1965 Carling World Open	T38	74	73	74	70	291	945.00
1965 American Golf Classic	T52	80	69	79	75	303	0.00
1965 World Series of Golf	2	71	71	–	–	142	–
1965 Portland Open	1	69	68	68	68	273	6,600.00
1965 Sahara Invitational	T6	71	67	70	68	276	3,600.00
1965 Cajun Classic	T3	69	67	71	69	276	1,900.00
1965 Greater New Orleans Open	T4	65	69	72	69	275	4,500.00
1965 Greater Seattle Open	T9	69	74	72	70	285	1,207.14
1965 PGA National 4-ball Championship	T7	67	66	65	68	266	2,100.00

(Partnered with Arnold Palmer)

International

Tournament	Place	R1	R2	R3	R4	Total	Earnings
1965 **British Open**	T12	73	71	77	73	294	371.00
1965 Canadian Open Championship	2	69	66	72	67	274	12,000.00
1965 Australian Open Championship	2	66	63	70	71	270	2,800.00
1965 Canada Cup	3/2	71	72	71	70	284	500.00

(Individual 2nd, team with Lema 3rd)

1966

Tournament	Place	R1	R2	R3	R4	Total	Earnings
1966 Bing Crosby National Pro-Am	T24	73	71	75	76	295	$730.00
1966 Doral Open	T14	77	66	70	70	283	1,850.00
1966 Florida Citrus Open	T2	70	73	68	70	281	8,833.33
1966 Jacksonville Open	T8	70	72	71	67	280	2,420.00
1966 **Masters**	1	68	76	72	72	288	20,000.00

(Won in playoff; Nicklaus 70, Jacobs 72, Brewer 78)

Tournament	Place	R1	R2	R3	R4	Total	Earnings
1966 Tournament of Champions	T5	76	71	69	72	288	4,250.00
1966 Greater New Orleans Open	T3	68	70	70	71	279	5,150.00
1966 Oklahoma City Open	3	73	70	65	71	279	3,700.00
1966 Memphis Open	T4	72	64	68	68	272	4,650.00
1966 **U.S. Open**	3	71	71	69	74	285	9,000.00
1966 **PGA**	T22	75	71	75	71	292	1,400.00
1966 Cleveland Open	T13	74	66	68	70	278	1,700.00
1966 Thunderbird Classic	2	71	72	66	70	279	12,000.00
1966 Philadelphia Golf Classic	2	72	70	70	67	279	13,000.00
1966 World Series of Golf	3	70	73	–	–	143	7,500.00
1966 Portland Open	T6	72	72	65	70	279	1,616.67
1966 Sahara Invitational	1	71	77	68	66	282	20,000.00
1966 Houston Champions International	T19	69	71	70	74	284	1,197.22
1966 PGA National Team Championship	1	63	66	63	64	256	25,000.00

(Partnered with Arnold Palmer)

International

Tournament	Place	R1	R2	R3	R4	Total	Earnings
1966 **British Open**	1	70	67	75	70	282	5,880.00
1966 Canadian Open	T27	73	72	72	75	292	651.94
1966 Piccadilly World Match-Play	Defeated in 36-hole final, 6 and 4						
1966 World Cup	1,3	69	68	67	69	273	1,300.00

(Partnered with Arnold Palmer; winner of team title; third in individual competition)

With Bob Hope in the pro am portion of the Bob Hope Desert Classic.

With Byron Nelson of the Metropolitan Golf Writers Association Dinner in 1972.

1967

1967	Bing Crosby National Pro-Am	1	69	73	74	68	284	$16,000.00
1967	Los Angeles Open	T51	69	74	72	71	286	0.00
		(5 round tournament)						
1967	Doral Open	4	68	71	66	72	277	5,000.00
1967	Florida Citrus Open	T7	71	69	69	69	278	3,565.00
1967	Pensacola Open	T33	71	69	70	67	277	468.75
1967	**Masters**	CUT	72	79	–	–	151	0.00
1967	Tournament of Champions	T4	68	68	75	73	284	4,700.00
1967	Houston Champions Int.	T38	77	71	72	71	291	553.92
1967	Greater New Orleans Open	2	70	68	69	71	278	12,000.00
1967	Colonial National Invitation	T8	72	71	72	70	285	3,258.34
1967	Memphis Open	T20	77	67	67	69	280	1,200.00
1967	**U.S. Open**	1	71	67	72	65	275	30,000.00
1967	Cleveland Open	T26	72	69	69	72	282	789.20
1967	**PGA**	T3	67	75	69	71	282	9,000.00
1967	Western Open	1	72	68	65	69	274	20,000.00
1967	American Golf Classic	T3	70	69	70	71	280	5,600.00
1967	World Series of Golf	1	74	70	–	–	144	50,000.00
1967	Westchester Classic	1	67	69	65	71	272	50,000.00
1967	Thunderbird Classic	T2	73	70	69	72	284	12,250.00
1967	Sahara Invitational	1	68	69	62	71	270	20,000.00
1967	Jacksonville Open	T34	72	74	74	72	292	678.00
1967	Houston Champions Intl.	T38	77	71	72	71	291	553.92

International

1967	Canadian Open	T3	69	72	70	69	280	10,037.90
1967	**British Open**	2	71	69	71	69	280	4,200.00
1967	World Cup	1,2	72	71	69	69	281	1,400.00
		(Partnered with Arnold Palmer; second in individual competition)						

1968

1968	Bing Crosby National Pro-Am	8	71	75	70	73	289	$2,480.00
1968	Andy Wiliams San Diego Open	5	67	69	69	72	277	6,450.00
1968	Phoenix Open	CUT	75	71	–	–	146	0.00

1968	Doral Open	T17	72	74	70	70	286	1,450.00
1968	Florida Citrus Open	3	67	68	73	68	276	8,625.00
1968	Jacksonville Open	T23	74	68	70	68	280	916.67
1968	**Masters**	T5	69	71	74	67	281	5,500.00
1968	Byron Nelson Golf Classic	10	73	67	70	69	279	2,600.00
1968	Houston Champions International	4	65	69	72	72	278	5,000.00
1968	Greater New Orleans Open	T13	71	71	71	68	281	1,900.00
1968	Memphis Open	T17	71	65	69	70	275	1,500.00
1968	Atlanta Classic	T16	69	73	75	71	288	1,725.00
1968	**U.S. Open**	2	72	70	70	67	279	15,000.00
1968	**PGA**	CUT	71	79	–	–	150	0.00
1968	Western Open	1	65	72	65	71	273	26,000.00
1968	American Golf Classic	1	70	69	72	69	280	25,000.00
1968	Westchester Classic	T2	67	68	72	66	273	20,416.70
1968	Philadelphia Golf Classic	T4	73	69	66	70	278	4,366.66
1968	Thunderbird Classic	T5	73	69	70	71	283	5,750.00
1968	Sahara Invitational	T12	67	70	68	74	279	2,033.34
1968	PGA Team Championship	T15	64	72	69	68	273	1,600.00

International

1968	Canadian Open	2	73	68	68	67	276	13,935.00
1968	**British Open**	T2	76	69	73	73	291	4,171.20
1968	Australian Open	1	71	64	68	67	270	2,800.00
1968	Australian PGA	2	71	67	72	72	282	–

1969

1969	Bing Crosby National Pro-Am	6	71	73	73	70	287	$4,500.00
1969	Andy Williams San Diego Open	1	68	72	71	73	284	30,000.00
1969	Bob Hope Desert Classic	T13	72	71 74 68 69				354	1,350.00
		(5 round tournament)						
1969	Doral Open	T4	72	71	64	72	279	6,600.00
1969	Florida Citrus Open	T10	70	71	71	71	283	2,438.00
1969	Greater Jacksonville Open	T28	69	72	70	75	286	642.50
1969	National Airlines Open	CUT	73	75	–	–	148	0.00
1969	**Masters**	T24	68	75	72	76	291	1,800.00
1969	Western Open	T36	71	72	75	73	291	663.00
1969	**U.S. Open**	T25	74	67	75	73	289	1,300.00
1969	Cleveland Open	T52	73	68	74	74	289	191.31
1969	American Golf Classic	T6	66	66	71	75	278	4,250.00
1969	Westchester Classic	T14	71	73	69	70	283	3,277.27
1969	**PGA**	T11	70	68	74	71	283	3,543.75
1969	Greater Hartford Open	7	68	68	69	68	273	3,200.00
1969	Sahara Invitational	1	69	68	70	65	272	20,000.00
1969	Kaiser Invitational	1	66	67	69	71	273	28,000.00
1969	Hawaiian Open	2	63	71	74	70	278	14,300.00
1969	Heritage Golf Classic	T6	71	72	71	75	289	3,250.00
1969	Tournament of Champions	T16	73	80	76	67	296	2,816.67

Jack won the Andy Williams Tournament in 1969.

Reading a putt on 13 at Augusta in 1968.

Year	Tournament	Pos	R1	R2	R3	R4	Total	Money
1969	Greater New Orleans Open	CUT	74	70	–	–	144	0.00
1969	Colonial National Invitational	T4	68	70	73	71	282	5,487.50
1969	Atlanta Classic	T47	70	77	73	72	292	230.00

International

Year	Tournament	Pos	R1	R2	R3	R4	Total	Money
1969	**British Open**	T6	75	70	68	72	285	3,300.00
1969	Ryder Cup Matches	(U.S. retained Cup after 16-16 tie; Nicklaus 1, 2, 1)						

1 9 7 0

Year	Tournament	Pos	R1	R2	R3	R4	Total	Money
1970	Bing Crosby National Pro-Am	2	70	72	72	65	279	$14,300.00
1970	Andy Williams San Diego Open	3	65	68	70	73	276	10,650.00
1970	Florida Citrus Invitational	T19	69	70	71	70	280	1,662.00
1970	Greater Jacksonville Open	T5	70	71	72	70	283	3,850.00
1970	**Masters**	8	71	75	69	69	284	4,500.00
1970	Tournament of Champions	T7	71	69	72	74	286	4,766.67
1970	Byron Nelson Golf Classic	1	67	68	68	71	274	20,000.00
1970	Colonial National Invitation	T17	71	70	69	73	283	1,456.25
1970	Atlanta Classic	T7	69	69	68	72	278	3,412.00
1970	Kemper Open	CUT	–	–	–	–	–	0.00
1970	Western Open	T3	72	70	67	69	278	5,906.00
1970	**U.S. Open**	T51	81	72	75	76	304	900.00
1970	Philadelphia Golf Classic	WD	74	–	–	–	–	0.00
1970	National 4-ball Championship	1	61	67	64	67	259	20,000.00
	(Partnered with Arnold Palmer)							
1970	Westchester Classic	T2	72	67	67	68	274	23,125.00
1970	American Golf Classic	T2	73	67	69	69	278	11,600.00
1970	**PGA**	T6	68	76	73	66	283	6,800.00
1970	World Series of Golf	1	66	70	–	–	136	50,000.00
1970	Dow Jones Open	T12	73	68	69	74	284	4,833.00
1970	Kaiser International Open	CUT	–	–	–	–	–	0.00
1970	Sahara Invitational	T43	76	69	70	71	286	317.05
1970	Heritage Classic	T17	75	71	72	73	291	1,450.00

International

Year	Tournament	Pos	R1	R2	R3	R4	Total	Money
1970	**British Open**	1	68	71	71	73	283	$12,600.00
	(Won in playoff; Nicklaus 72, Sanders 73)							
1970	Piccadilly World Match Play	1		2 and 1				13,800.00

1 9 7 1

Year	Tournament	Pos	R1	R2	R3	R4	Total	Money
1971	Bing Crosby National Pro-Am	T34	72	75	69	76	292	$743.00
1971	Andy Williams San Diego Open	T3	69	71	71	66	277	7,312.00
1971	Hawaiian Open	T46	70	74	70	73	287	500.00
1971	**PGA**	1	69	69	70	73	281	40,000.00
1971	Doral Eastern Open	T9	74	68	67	73	282	3,900.00
1971	Greater Jacksonville Open	T9	71	75	72	69	287	2,295.00
1971	**Masters**	T2	70	71	68	72	281	17,500.00
1971	Tournament of Champions	1	69	71	69	70	279	33,000.00
1971	Byron Nelson Golf Classic	1	69	71	68	66	274	25,000.00
1971	Atlanta Classic	2	67	68	70	70	275	14,300.00
1971	**U.S. Open**	2	69	72	68	71	280	15,000.00
1971	Westchester Classic	T9	72	69	72	67	280	6,500.00
1971	National Team Championship	1	62	64	65	66	257	20,000.00
	(Partnered with Arnold Palmer)							
1971	American Golf Classic	4	73	68	69	70	280	7,050.00
1971	IVB-Philadelphia Classic	3	66	73	70	67	276	10,650.00
1971	U.S. Match Play Championship	(Eliminated first round)						
1971	World Series of Golf	2	71	71	–	–	142	15,000.00
1971	Heritage Classic	T3	71	69	71	70	281	6,515.00
1971	Walt Disney World Open	1	67	68	70	68	273	30,000.00

International

Year	Tournament	Pos	R1	R2	R3	R4	Total	Money
1971	**British Open**	T5	71	71	72	69	283	5,520.00
1971	Ryder Cup Matches	(U.S. won 18½-13½; Nicklaus 4, 1, 0)						
1971	Piccadilly World Match Play	Defeated in final, 5 and 4						10,800.00
1971	Australian Open	1	68	65	66	70	269	4,320.00
1971	Dunlop International	1	69	62	73	70	274	4,480.00
1971	World Cup	1	68	69	63	71	271	2,000.00
	(Partnered with Lee Trevino; won individual title)							

1 9 7 2

Year	Tournament	Pos	R1	R2	R3	R4		Total	Money
1972	Bing Crosby National Pro-Am	1	66	74	71	73		284	$28,000.00
1972	Andy Williams San Diego Open	T32	73	68	72	72		285	808.53
1972	Hawaiian Open	T44	70	71	73	71		285	585.00
1972	Bob Hope Desert Classic	T10	70	72	68	71	70	351	3,190.00
	(5 round tournament)								

Year	Tournament	Pos	R1	R2	R3	R4	Total	Earnings
1972	Jackie Gleason's Inverrary Classic	2	73	68	71	67	279	29,640.00
1972	Doral Eastern Open	1	71	71	64	70	276	30,000.00
1972	Florida Citrus Open	T10	70	72	70	69	281	3,600.00
1972	Greater New Orleans Open	T2	66	70	71	73	280	11,575.00
1972	**Masters**	1	68	71	73	74	286	25,000.00
1972	Tournament of Champions	2	70	71	67	72	280	19,000.00
1972	Byron Nelson Golf Classic	T29	69	71	73	71	284	800.00
1972	Atlanta Golf Classic	T18	70	64	75	76	285	1,452.85
1972	**U.S. Open**	1	71	73	72	74	290	30,000.00
1972	**PGA**	T13	72	75	68	72	287	4,167.00
1972	Westchester Classic	1	65	67	70	68	270	50,000.00
1972	U.S. Match Play Championship	1	(Won final, 2 and 1)					40,000.00
1972	World Series of Golf	T2	75	69	–	–	144	11,250.00
1972	Kaiser International	T9	69	71	69	72	281	3,900.00
1972	Sahara Invitational	T5	66	69	73	68	276	5,197.50
1972	Walt Disney World Open	1	68	68	67	64	267	30,000.00

International

Year	Tournament	Pos	R1	R2	R3	R4	Total	Earnings
1972	**British Open**	2	70	72	71	66	279	10,000.00

1973

Year	Tournament	Pos	R1	R2	R3	R4	Total	Earnings
1973	Glen Campbell LA Open	T6	69	70	71	70	280	$4,860.00
1973	Bing Crosby National Pro-Am	1	71	69	71	71	282	36,000.00
1973	Bob Hope Desert Classic	T2	64 70 71 68 72				345	14,800.00
			(5 round tournament)					
1973	Jackie Gleason's Inverrary Classic	T6	73	69	70	71	283	8,092.50
1973	Doral Eastern Open	T16	69	74	73	69	285	2,175.00
1973	Greater Jacksonville Open	T26	69	73	75	71	288	903.00
1973	Greater New Orleans Open	1	68	72	71	69	280	25,000.00
1973	**Masters**	T3	69	77	73	66	285	12,500.00
1973	Tournament of Champions	1	70	70	68	68	276	40,000.00
1973	Atlanta Golf Classic	1	67	66	66	73	272	30,000.00
1973	IVB-Philadelphia Classic	T5	73	70	70	67	280	5,201.55
1973	**U.S. Open**	T4	71	69	74	68	282	9,000.00
1973	American Golf Classic	T9	69	70	73	68	280	3,680.00
1973	**PGA**	1	72	68	68	69	277	45,000.00
1973	U.S Professional Match Play	–	–	–	–	–	–	7,000.00
			(Eliminated in quarter finals)					

At The Players Championship in 1978.

Year	Tournament	Pos	R1	R2	R3	R4	Total	Earnings
1973	Westchester Classic	T9	70	68	69	69	276	6,250.00
1973	World Series of Golf	T2	71	69	–	–	140	11,250.00
1973	Ohio King's Island Open	1	68	69	62	72	271	25,000.00
1973	Walt Disney World Open	1	70	71	67	67	275	30,000.00

International

Year	Tournament	Pos	R1	R2	R3	R4	Total	Earnings
1973	**British Open**	4	69	70	76	65	280	7,150.00
1973	Ryder Cup Matches		(U.S. won 19-13; Nicklaus 3, 1, 1)					
1973	World Cup	1,3	69	68	73	71	281	1,300.00
		(Partnered with Johnny Miller, third in individual competition)						

1974

Year	Tournament	Pos	R1	R2	R3	R4	Total	Earnings
1974	Bing Crosby National Pro-Am	T24	74	73	71	–	218	$1,051.00
1974	Hawaiian Open	1	65	67	69	70	271	44,000.00
1974	Glen Campbell LA Open	T11	66	73	71	75	285	3,450.00
1974	Jackie Gleason's Inverrary Classic	T4	74	73	69	65	281	10,140.00
1974	Doral Eastern Open	T14	71	72	66	70	279	2,100.00
1974	Greater New Orleans Open	T6	66	71	70	70	277	4,875.00
1974	**Masters**	T4	69	71	72	69	281	10,833.00
1974	Tournament of Champions	T9	72	71	69	75	287	6,200.00
1974	Colonial National Invitation	2	71	69	69	68	277	28,500.00
1974	Kemper Open	T15	70	69	69	70	278	3,375.00
1974	**U.S. Open**	T10	75	74	76	69	294	3,750.00
1974	**PGA**	2	69	69	70	69	277	25,000.00
1974	Westchester Classic	T5	68	69	68	70	275	9,625.00
1974	The Players Championship	1	66	71	68	67	272	50,000.00
1974	World Open	T2	68	71	70	72	281	23,200.00
1974	Ohio King's Island Open	T7	71	71	69	73	284	4,256.25
1974	National Team Championship	T14	67	64	64	66	261	2,410.00
		(Partnered with Tom Weiskopf)						

International

Year	Tournament	Pos	R1	R2	R3	R4	Total	Earnings
1974	**British Open**	3	74	72	70	71	287	7,800.00
1974	Canadian Open	T13	70	65	72	70	277	3,400.00
1974	Dunlop Phoenix Tournament	T13	70	73	71	75	289	–

1975

Year	Tournament	Pos	R1	R2	R3	R4	Total	Earnings
1975	Bing Crosby National Pro-Am	T6	71	74	72	72	289	$5,318.67
1975	Hawaiian Open	T14	68	74	70	69	281	3,300.00
1975	Glen Campbell LA Open	3	69	75	71	65	280	10,650.00
1975	Jackie Gleason's Inverrary Classic	3	67	69	66	73	275	18,460.00
1975	Doral Eastern Open	1	69	70	69	68	276	30,000.00
1975	Heritage Classic	1	66	63	74	68	271	40,000.00
1975	**Masters**	1	68	67	73	68	276	40,000.00
1975	MONY Tourn. of Championship	T9	70	72	71	74	287	5,945.00
1975	Danny Thomas Memphis Classic	T3	66	70	73	68	277	10,325.00
1975	Atlanta Classic	T4	68	73	67	69	277	9,300.00
1975	**U.S. Open**	T7	72	70	75	72	289	7,500.00
1975	**PGA**	1	70	68	67	71	276	45,000.00
1975	Tournament Players Championship	T18	67	75	70	75	287	3,250.00
1975	World Open	1	70	71	70	69	280	40,000.00
1975	Kaiser International	6	72	67	69	69	277	6,300.00

International

Year	Tournament	Pos	R1	R2	R3	R4	Total	Earnings
1975	Canadian Open	2	65	71	70	68	274	22,800.00
1975	**British Open**	T3	69	71	68	72	280	8,507.40
1975	Ryder Cup Matches		(U.S. won 21-11; Nicklaus 2, 2, 1)					
1975	Australian Open	1	67	70	70	72	279	8,820.00

1976

Year	Tournament	Pos	R1	R2	R3	R4	Total	Earnings
1976	Bing Crosby National Pro-Am	T18	67	72	70	82	291	$2,220.00
1976	Bob Hope Desert Classic	T7	69 70 72 69 72				352	5,535.00
			(5 round tournament)					
1976	The Players Championship	1	66	70	68	65	269	60,000.00
1976	Doral Eastern Open	T2	69	71	68	68	276	18,500.00

1977	World Series of Golf	T5	69	73	68	68	278	11,166.66
1977	Ohio King's Island Open	CUT	73	72	—	—	145	0.00

International

1977	Canadian Open	T4	68	70	74	74	286	7,970.00
1977	**British Open**	2	68	70	65	66	269	4,100.00
1977	Ryder Cup Matches	(U.S. won 12½-7½; Nicklaus 1, 2, 0)						
1977	Australian Open	T14	77	67	72	80	296	—

1 9 7 8

1978	Bing Crosby National Pro-Am	T29	77	74	66	73	290	$1,465.00
1978	Glen Campbell LA Open	2	72	66	70	72	280	22,800.00
1978	Jackie Gleason's Inverrary Classic	1	70	75	66	65	276	50,000.00
1978	Doral Eastern Open	2	67	69	72	65	273	22,800.00
1978	The Players Championship	1	70	71	73	75	289	60,000.00
1978	**Masters**	7	72	73	69	67	281	10,000.00
1978	MONY Tourn. of Champions	T15	72	69	73	77	291	4,925.33
1978	Memorial Tournament	T4	67	76	71	74	288	10,333.33
1978	Atlanta Classic	CUT	73	74	–	–	147	0.00
1978	**U.S. Open**	T6	73	69	74	73	289	7,548.33
1978	IVB-Philadelphia Classic	1	66	64	72	68	270	50,000.00
1978	**PGA**	CUT	79	74	–	–	153	0.00
1978	Westchester Classic	T10	67	69	71	72	279	6,150.00
1978	World Series of Golf	7	72	76	70	67	285	6,900.00

International

1978	Canadian Open	T15	73	72	72	72	289	3,750.00
1978	**British Open**	1	71	72	69	69	281	23,750.00
1978	Australian Open	1	73	66	74	71	284	50,600.00

1 9 7 9

1979	Bob Hope Desert Classic	T11	71 69 69 72 69				350	$6,325.00

(5 round tournament)

1979	Bay Hill Citrus Classic	T30	68	70	72	78	288	1,485.71
1979	Jackie Gleason's Inverrary Classic	T66	74	72	73	75	294	615.00
1979	Doral Eastern Open	T53	73	74	75	72	294	573.00
1979	The Players Championship	T33	67	73	82	78	300	2,310.00
1979	**Masters**	4	69	71	72	69	281	15,00.00
1979	MONY Tourn. of Champions	T15	72	72	77	73	294	6,250.00
1979	Memorial Tournament	T27	73	73	74	79	299	2,220.00
1979	**U.S. Open**	T9	74	77	72	68	291	7,500.00
1979	IVB-Philadelphia Classic	T3	72	70	67	65	274	13,000.00
1979	**PGA**	T65	73	72	78	71	294	515.00

International

1979	Canadian Open	T22	70	75	71	77	293	3,640.00
1979	British Open	T2	72	69	73	72	286	23,625.00

1 9 8 0

1980	Bing Crosby National Pro-Am	T11	69	76	66	73	284	$7,200.00
1980	Glen Campbell LA Open	T16	73	70	69	71	283	3,875.00
1980	Jackie Gleason's Inverrary Classic	T53	69	76	72	73	290	691.20
1980	Doral Eastern Open	2	72	67	71	69	279	27,000.00
1980	The Players Championship	T14	69	73	69	73	284	6,400.00
1980	**Masters**	T33	74	71	73	73	291	1,860.00
1980	Byron Nelson Classic	T43	70	74	74	71	289	1,110.00
1980	Memorial Tournament	T20	71	73	71	73	288	3,250.00
1980	Atlanta Classic	CUT	78	67	–	–	145	0.00
1980	**U.S. Open**	1	63	71	70	68	272	55,000.00
1980	**PGA**	1	70	69	66	69	274	60,000.00
1980	World Series of Golf	WD	68	72	71	–	211	0.00

International

1980	Canadian Open	T13	71	68	70	73	282	6,000.00
1980	**British Open**	T4	73	67	71	69	280	22,200.00

Jack and Jackie at the 1981 U.S. Open at Merion. USGA official, and later USGA president, Grant Spaeth looks on.

1976	Heritage Classic	T11	72	69	68	73	282	4,353.75
1976	**Masters**	T3	67	69	73	73	282	16,250.00
1976	Greater New Orleans Open	T4	68	67	74	69	278	5,937.57
1976	Byron Nelson Golf Classic	T8	71	68	71	71	281	4,487.50
1976	Memorial Tournament	T8	71	75	73	73	292	6,560.00
1976	**U.S. Open**	T11	74	70	75	68	287	4,000.00
1976	Westchester Classic	T23	70	73	69	68	280	2,286.00
1976	**PGA**	T4	71	69	69	74	283	9,750.00
1976	World Series of Golf	1	68	70	69	68	275	100,000.00
1976	World Open	CUT	72	74	–	–	146	0.00
1976	Ohio King's Island Open	T6	71	69	69	67	276	4,668.75

International

1976	Canadian Open	2	67	67	72	65	271	22,800.00
1976	**British Open**	T2	74	70	72	69	285	9,450.00
1976	Australian Open	1	72	71	72	71	286	40,000.00
1976	Dunlop Phoenix Tournament	T37	76	67	76	75	294	—

1 9 7 7

1977	Bing Crosby National Pro-Am	11	69	69	70	73	281	$4,600.00
1977	Hawaiian Open	CUT	73	72	–	–	145	0.00
1977	Jackie Gleason's Inverrary Classic	1	70	66	69	70	275	50,000.00
1977	Doral Eastern Open	T11	72	70	70	71	283	3,920.00
1977	The Players Championship	T5	73	74	72	74	293	10,900.00
1977	Heritage Classic	T7	68	72	70	70	280	6,641.67
1977	**Masters**	2	72	70	70	66	278	30,000.00
1977	MONY Tourn. of Champions	1	71	69	70	71	281	45,000.00
1977	Houston Open	T6	69	75	67	71	282	5,980.00
1977	Memorial Tournament	1	72	68	70	71	281	45,000.00
1977	Atlanta Classic	5	70	73	67	68	278	8,200.00
1977	**U.S. Open**	T10	74	68	71	72	285	4,100.00
1977	Pleasant Valley Classic	2	68	67	70	67	272	28,500.00
1977	**PGA**	3	69	71	70	73	283	15,000.00
1977	Westchester Classic	T8	71	74	68	66	279	7,530.00

1 9 8 1

1981	Bob Hope Desert Classic	T28	68	67 74 71 69	349	$1,920.00
				(5 round tournament)		
1981	Bing Crosby National Pro-Am	T11	71	68	72	–	211	4,612.50
1981	Glen Campbell LA Open	T15	71	70	67	70	278	4,800.00
1981	American Motors Classic	2	65	73	69	68	275	32,400.00
1981	Doral Eastern Open	CUT	74	73	–	–	147	0.00
1981	The Players Championship	T29	75	68	74	76	293	2,600.00
1981	Masters	T2	70	65	75	72	282	30,500.00
1981	MONY Tourn. of Champions	T11	72	69	74	71	286	8,375.00
1981	Memorial Tournament	T12	71	71	74	72	288	7,700.00
1981	Atlanta Classic	T9	68	72	69	72	281	8,100.00
1981	U.S. Open	T6	69	68	71	72	280	9,920.00
1981	Western Open	7	75	72	70	69	286	9,037.50
1981	PGA	T4	71	68	71	69	279	13,146.43
1981	World Series of Golf	T10	71	67	71	74	283	11,500.00
1981	Hall of Fame Tournament	T25	67	71	71	75	284	1,867.85

International

1981	Canadian Open	T2	70	70	70	71	281	31,733.33
1981	British Open	T23	83	66	71	70	290	2,437.50
1981	Ryder Cup Matches		(U.S. won 18½-9½; Nicklaus 4, 0, 0)					

1 9 8 2

1982	Wickes-Andy Williams Open	2	69	68	70	64	271	$32,400.00
1982	Bing Crosby National Pro-Am	T3	69	70	71	70	280	13,530.00
1982	Doral Eastern Open	T11	67	71	72	74	284	6,150.00
1982	Bay Hill Classic	T2	69	67	67	75	278	26,400.00
1982	Honda Inverrary Classic	CUT	73	71	–	–	144	0.00
1982	Thet Players Championship	CUT	73	78	–	–	151	0.00
1982	Masters	T15	69	77	71	75	292	5,850.00
1982	USF&G Classic	T67	71	76	–	–	147	564.00

1982	Colonial National Invitation	1	66	70	70	67	273	63,000.00
1982	Memorial Tournament	T11	74	68	72	72	286	7,420.00
1982	Kemper Open	T3	72	65	72	74	283	23,200.00
1982	U.S. Open	2	74	70	71	69	284	34,506.00
1982	PGA	T16	74	70	72	67	283	4,625.00
1982	World Series of Golf	T6	71	75	72	67	285	15,00.00

International

1982	Canadian Open	CUT	73	73	–	–	146	0.00
1982	British Open	T10	77	70	72	69	288	12,495.00

1 9 8 3

1983	Bob Hope Desert Classic	T25	72 68 69 69 71	349	$2,862.50
				(5 round tournament)		
1983	Bing Crosby National Pro-Am	6	71	71	66	72	280	11,700.00
1983	Doral Eastern Open	T8	70	70	69	71	280	9,000.00
1983	Honda Inverrary Classic	2	72	72	70	66	280	43,200.00
1983	Bay Hill Classic	T5	72	72	73	70	287	12,293.00
1983	The Players Championship	T19	73	76	68	74	291	8,785.00
1983	Masters	WD	73					0.00
1983	MONY Tourn. of Champions	T10	65	72	77	73	287	12,500.00
1983	Byron Nelson Classic	T23	69	74	70	69	282	3,840.00
1983	Colonial National Invitation	T28	66	75	74	69	284	2,720.00
1983	Memorial Tournament	T33	76	72	70	73	291	2,610.00
1983	U.S. Open	T43	73	74	77	76	300	2,847.00
1983	PGA	2	73	65	71	66	275	60,000.00
1983	World Series of Golf	2	67	73	69	65	274	60,000.00
1983	Chrysler Team Championship	1	61	65	65	–	191	54,175.00
				(Partnered with Johnny Miller)		

International

1983	British Open	T29	71	72	72	70	285	2,197.50
1983	Canadian Open	3	73	68	70	67	278	23,800.00
1983	Ryder Cup Matches		(Captain; U.S. won 14½-13½)					

Jack and Seve in an exhibition at St. Andrews.

1984

1984	Bing Crosby National Pro-Am	T17	72	73	71	70	286	$4,720.00
1984	Los Angeles Open	3	73	71	70	69	283	27,200.00
1984	Honda Classic	T19	77	70	70	71	288	5,642.86
1984	Doral Eastern Open	2	67	69	70	68	274	43,200.00
1984	Bay Hill Classic	T9	69	72	73	66	280	9,600.00
1984	The Players Championship	T33	78	70	75	69	292	4,050.00
1984	Masters	T18	73	73	70	70	286	8,400.00
1984	Memorial Tournament	1	69	70	71	70	280	90,000.00
1984	U.S. Open	T21	71	71	70	77	289	6,575.50
1984	PGA	T25	77	70	71	69	287	4,506.25
1984	NEC World Series of Golf	10	72	73	69	66	280	18,900.00
1984	Southern Open	T11	70	68	70	66	274	6,600.00
1984	Chrysler Team Championship	T12	62	66	69	66	263	3,463.00

(Partnered with Johnny Miller)

International

1984	Canadian Open	2	73	69	69	69	280	43,200.00
1984	British Open	T31	76	72	68	72	288	3,377.40

1985

1985	Bob Hope Desert Classic	T53	71	69	72	71	71	354	$1,141.43

(5 round tournament)

1985	Los Angeles Open	T17	67	71	70	71	279	5,800.00
1985	Bing Crosby National Pro-Am	T15	76	72	73	67	288	8,500.00
1985	Doral Eastern Open	T3	76	68	69	74	287	23,200.00
1985	Honda Classic	T27	70	68	73	73	284	3,328.25
1985	USF&G Classic	T35	68	72	74	–	214	1,847.50
1985	The Players Champions	T17	71	70	71	76	288	12,600.00
1985	Masters	T6	71	74	72	69	286	22,663.00
1985	MONY Tourn. of Champions	T21	74	72	72	74	292	5,700.00
1985	Memorial Tournament	T54	71	76	74	78	299	1,638.75
1985	U.S. Open	CUT	76	73	–	–	149	0.00
1985	Western Open	T61	76	72	74	76	298	1,085.00
1985	PGA	T32	66	75	74	74	289	3,408.34
1985	Greater Milwaukee Open	2	70	69	67	71	277	32,400.00
1985	Chrysler Team Championship	T23	65	65	70	66	266	–

(Partnered with Johnny Miller)

International

1985	Canadian Open	T2	70	73	66	72	281	42,144.21
1985	British Open	CUT	77	75	–	–	152	0.00

1986

1986	Phoenix Open	T60	72	69	69	72	282	$1,085.00
1986	AT&T National Pro-Am	CUT	73	80	74	–	227	0.00
1986	Hawaiian Open	T39	70	69	71	74	284	2,050.00
1986	Honda Classic	CUT	73	76	–	–	149	0.00
1986	Doral Eastern Open	T47	70	70	73	75	288	1,268.75
1986	The Players Championship	CUT	74	73	–	–	–	0.00
1986	Masters	1	74	71	69	65	279	144,000.00
1986	Houston Open	T42	72	73	72	73	290	1,700.00
1986	Memorial Tournament	T5	66	70	72	69	277	21,100.00
1986	U.S. Open	T8	77	72	67	68	284	14,500.00
1986	PGA	T16	70	68	72	75	285	8,500.00
1986	The International	T23	–	–	–	–	–	6,000.00
1986	NEC World Series of Golf	T9	71	69	69	73	282	16,800.00
1986	Chrysler Team Championship	T4	65	63	63	65	256	13,655.00

(Partnered with Jack Nicklaus II)

International

1986	Canadian Open	T16	74	69	70	74	287	9,000.00
1986	British Open	T46	78	73	76	71	298	3,712.50
1986	Suntory International Open	T23	71	74	72	67	284	–

1987

1987	AT&T National Pro-Am	T15	72	72	70	71	285	$8,715.00
1987	Doral-Ryder Open	T22	69	74	73	70	286	8,775.00
1987	Honda Classic	71	74	77	73	76	300	1,188.00
1987	The Players Championship	CUT	70	74	–	–	144	0.00
1987	Masters	T7	74	72	73	70	289	26,200.00
1987	Memorial Tournament	T66	73	73	72	75	293	2,552.50
1987	Hanover Westchester Classic	CUT	77	76	–	–	153	0.00
1987	U.S. Open	T46	70	68	76	77	291	4,240.00
1987	PGA	T24	76	73	74	73	296	5,975.00
1987	The International	T60	–	–	–	–	–	2,180.00
1987	Izuzu Kapalua International	T36	73	70	75	71	289	2,375.00
1987	Chrysler Team Championship	CUT	64	66	70		200	0.00

(Partnered with Jack Nicklaus II)

International

1987	Canadian Open	T24	72	70	72	73	287	4,860.00
1987	British Open	T72	74	71	81	76	302	2,560.00
1987	Ryder Cup Matches	(Captain; U.S. lost 13-15)						

1988

1988	AT&T National Pro-Am	T64	73	73	73	–	219	$1,456.00
1988	Doral-Ryder Open	T24	68	69	71	75	283	7,912.28
1988	The Players Championship	CUT	73	74	–	–	147	0.00
1988	Masters	T21	75	73	72	72	292	11,200.00
1988	Memorial Tournament	CUT	74	76	–	–	150	0.00
1988	U.S. Open	CUT	74	73	–	–	147	0.00
1988	PGA	CUT	72	79	–	–	151	0.00
1988	The International	T34	–	–	–	–	–	5,275.00

International

1988	British Open	T25	75	70	75	68	288	9,350.00
1988	Canadian Open	T38	68	74	76	67	285	3,000.00

1989

1989	AT&T National Pro-Am	T45	69	69	80	71	289	$2,928.00
1989	Doral-Ryder Open	CUT	78	76	–	–	154	0.00
1989	Players Championship	T29	71	72	68	78	289	8,775.00
1989	USG&G Classic	T25	73	69	70	72	284	5,850.00
1989	Masters	T18	73	74	73	71	291	14,00.00
1989	Memorial Tournament	67	72	78	77	75	302	3,550.00
1989	U.S. Open	T43	67	74	74	75	290	6,281.00
1989	PGA	T27	68	72	73	72	285	7,535.72
1989	The International	9	–	–	–	–	–	29,000.00
1989	Children's Charities Invitational	T4	74	65	58		197	–

(Partnered with Greg Norman)

International

1989	Canadian Open	T10	68	69	69	70	276	18,675.00
1989	British Open	T13	74	71	71	70	286	7,537.00

1990

1990	AT&T National Pro-Am	61	72	71	78	78	299	$2,180.00
1990	Doral-Ryder Open	T68	68	72	75	74	289	2,814.00
1990	Players Championship	CUT	75	78	–	–	153	0.00
1990	Masters	6	72	70	69	74	285	45,000.00
1990	USF&G Classic	WD	78					0.00
1990	Memorial Tournament	T26	78	73	73	–	224	7,550.00
1990	U.S. Open	T33	71	74	68	76	289	8,221.16
1990	PGA	CUT	78	74	–	–	152	0.00
1990	The International	T54	–	–	–	–	–	2,284.00
1990	Children's Charities Invitational	9	65	70	62	–	197	–

(Partnered with Greg Norman)

1990	Sazale Classic	CUT	–	–	–	–	–	0.00

Champions Tour

Year	Tournament	Finish	R1	R2	R3	R4	Total	Earnings
1990	The Tradition	1	71	67	68	–	206	120,000.00
1990	PGA Seniors	T3	68	78	67	72	285	25,00.00
1990	Mazda Seniors Championship	1	65	68	64	64	261	150,00.00
1990	U.S Senior Open	2	71	69	67	70	277	45,000.00

International

Year	Tournament	Finish	R1	R2	R3	R4	Total	Earnings
1990	**British Open**	T63	71	70	77	71	289	5,339.50

1991

Year	Tournament	Finish	R1	R2	R3	R4	Total	Earnings
1991	AT&T National Pro-Am	CUT	70	77	75	–	222	$0.00
1991	Doral-Ryder Open	T5	71	63	75	70	279	53,200.00
1991	USF&G Classic	T14	68	69	74	71	282	18,500.00
1991	**Masters**	T35	68	72	72	76	288	6,371.00
1991	Memorial Tournament	T15	71	68	69	74	282	20,400.00
1991	**U.S. Open**	T46	70	76	77	74	297	6,875.00
1991	**PGA**	T23	71	72	73	71	287	11,500.00
1991	Shark Shootout	2	68	66	59	–	193	–

(Partnered with Greg Norman)

Champions Tour

Year	Tournament	Finish	R1	R2	R3	R4	Total	Earnings
1991	The Tradition	1	71	73	66	67	277	120,000.00
1991	PGA Seniors	1	66	66	69	70	271	85,00.00
1991	Mazda Seniors Championship	T22	77	70	69	73	289	–
1991	Kroger Senior Classic	T7	71	66	70	–	207	17,134.00
1991	U.S Senior Open	1	72	69	70	71	282	110,000.00

International

Year	Tournament	Finish	R1	R2	R3	R4	Total	Earnings
1991	**British Open**	T43	70	75	69	71	285	7,114.00
1991	Canadian Open	T27	74	68	74	67	283	6,950.00

1992

Year	Tournament	Finish	R1	R2	R3	R4	Total	Earnings
1992	AT&T National Pro-Am	CUT	76	73	70	–	219	$0.00
1992	Doral-Ryder Open	CUT	71	75	–	–	146	0.00
1992	Honda Classic	T29	70	70	69	72	281	6,150.83
1992	**Masters**	T42	69	75	69	74	287	5,450.00
1992	Memorial Tournament	T48	74	69	70	71	284	3,267.00
1992	**U.S. Open**	CUT	77	74	–	–	151	0.00
1992	**PGA**	CUT	72	78	–	–	150	0.00
1992	The International	CUT	–	–	–	–	–	0.00

Champions Tour

Year	Tournament	Finish	R1	R2	R3	R4	Total	Earnings
1992	The Tradition	2	65	72	69	69	275	69,000.00
1992	PGA Seniors	T10	73	68	74	76	291	14,500.00
1992	U.S Senior Open	T3	70	68	75	67	280	27,207.00
1992	Nationwide Championship	T39	73	75	–	–	148	3,840.00

International

Year	Tournament	Finish	R1	R2	R3	R4	Total	Earnings
1992	**British Open**	CUT	75	73	–	–	148	0.00

1993

Year	Tournament	Finish	R1	R2	R3	R4	Total	Earnings
1993	AT&T National Pro-Am	CUT	73	76	72	–	221	$0.00
1993	Doral-Ryder Open	T10	69	68	67	73	277	31,033.33
1993	Honda Classic	CUT	73	80	–	–	153	0.00
1993	Nestle Invitational	CUT	72	78	–	–	150	0.00
1993	**Masters**	T27	67	75	76	71	289	12,350.00
1993	Memorial Tournament	72	70	75	81	72	298	2,744.00
1993	**U.S. Open**	T72	70	72	76	71	289	5,405.00
1993	**PGA**	CUT	71	73	–	–	144	0.00
1993	The International	CUT	–	–	–	–	–	0.00

Champions Tour

Year	Tournament	Finish	R1	R2	R3	R4	Total	Earnings
1993	The Tradition	T9	72	69	70	67	278	22,950.00
1993	PGA Seniors	T9	69	71	73	71	284	16,00.00
1993	Bell Atlantic Classic	T28	72	71	75	–	218	4,930.71
1993	Ford Senior Players Championship	T22	67	75	78	71	291	12,068.57
1993	U.S Senior Open	1	68	73	67	70	278	135,330.00
1993	Nationwide Championship	T16	68	73	72	–	213	14,748.75

International

Year	Tournament	Finish	R1	R2	R3	R4	Total	Earnings
1993	**British Open**	CUT	69	75	–	–	144	0.00
1993	Canadian Open	CUT	76	73	–	–	149	0.00

1994

Year	Tournament	Finish	R1	R2	R3	R4	Total	Earnings
1994	AT&T National Pro-Am	CUT	74	73	73	–	220	$0.00
1994	Nissan Los Angeles Open	CUT	73	77	–	–	150	0.00
1994	Doral-Ryder Open	CUT	80	73	–		153	0.00
1994	Nestle Invitational	CUT	75	77	–	–	152	0.00
1994	**Masters**	CUT	78	74	–	–	152	0.00
1994	Memorial Tournament	CUT	75	77	–	–	152	0.00
1994	**U.S. Open**	T28	69	70	77	76	292	11,514.00
1994	**PGA**	CUT	79	71	–	–	150	0.00
1994	Lincoln-Mercury Kapalua Intl.	T31	69	71	76	78	294	–
1994	Mercedes Championship	1	73	69	69	68	279	100,000.00

Champions Tour

Year	Tournament	Finish	R1	R2	R3	R4	Total	Earnings
1994	The Tradition	T4	70	71	69	68	278	41,933.34
1994	PGA Seniors	9	71	71	72	72	286	20,500.00
1994	Ford Senior Players Championship	T6	68	72	73	67	280	50,400.00
1994	U.S Senior Open	T7	69	68	70	72	279	21,651.00
1994	Northville Long Island Classic	T13	70	74	72	–	216	4,793.75
1994	Diners Club Matches	(Defeated in final at 19th hole, partnered with Arnold Palmer)						

International

Year	Tournament	Finish	R1	R2	R3	R4	Total	Earnings
1994	**British Open**	CUT	72	73	–	–	145	
1994	Dunlop Phoenix Tournament	T28	70	71	70	–	211	

1995

Year	Tournament	Finish	R1	R2	R3	R4	Total	Earnings
1995	AT&T National Pro-Am	T6	71	70	67	70	278	$46,900.00
1995	Doral-Ryder Open	CUT	77	67	–	–	144	0.00
1995	Nestle Invitational	WD	79	78	–	–	157	0.00
1995	The Players Championship	CUT	76	79	–	–	155	0.00
1995	**Masters**	T35	67	78	70	75	290	10,840.00
1995	Memorial Tournament	CUT	78	75	–	–	153	0.00
1995	**U.S. Open**	CUT	71	81	–	–	152	0.00
1995	**PGA**	T67	69	71	71	76	287	3,262.50
1995	Senior Tournament of Champions	9	75	72	68	–	215	27,500.00
1995	GTE Suncoast Classic	T5	69	70	68	–	207	31,000.00
1995	Sprint International	CUT	–	–	–	–	–	–

Champions Tour

Year	Tournament	Finish	R1	R2	R3	R4	Total	Earnings
1995	The Tradition	1	69	71	69	67	276	150,000.00
1995	PGA Seniors	8	76	66	68	74	284	30,000.00
1995	Bell Atlantic Classic	3	72	69	68	–	209	64,800.00
1995	U.S Senior Open	2	71	71	70	67	279	103,500.00
1995	Ford Senior Players Ch.	2	71	68	66	67	272	132,000.00
1995	Diners Club Matches	(Defeated in first round, partnered with Arnold Palmer)						

International

Year	Tournament	Finish	R1	R2	R3	R4	Total	Earnings
1995	**British Open**	T79	78	70	77	71	296	7,177.50

1996

Year	Tournament	Finish	R1	R2	R3	R4	Total	Earnings
1996	AT&T National Pro-Am	CUT	71	72	–	–	143	$0.00
	(Tournament flooded out)							
1996	Doral-Ryder Open	CUT	72	75	–	–	147	0.00
1996	**Masters**	T41	70	73	76	78	297	10,050.00
1996	Memorial Tournament	CUT	77	75	–	–	152	0.00

1996	U.S. Open	T27	72	74	69	72	287	17,809.40
1996	PGA	CUT	77	69	–	–	146	0.00
1996	Office Depot Father-Son Challenge	6	65	67	–	–	132	–

(Partnered with Gary Nicklaus)

1996	Puerto Rico Senior Tournament of Champions	T7	70	72	68	–	210	36,500.00
1996	GTE Suncoast Classic	1	76	68	67	–	211	112,500.00
1996	Legends of Golf	T2	66	69	65	–	200	–

Champions Tour

1996	The Tradition	1	68	74	65	65	272	150,00.00
1996	PGA Seniors	T22	77	72	74	70	293	19,536.00
1996	U.S Senior Open	16	77	72	68	73	290	19,536.00
1996	Ford Senior Players Championship	T24	74	70	72	71	287	–
1996	Northville Long Island Classic	T12	69	70	71	–	210	–

International

1996	British Open	T44	69	66	77	73	285	9,920.00
1996	Dunlop Phoenix Tournament	CUT	–	–	–	–	–	0.00

1997

1997	AT&T Pebble Beach	CUT	73	74	67	–	214	$0.00
1997	Doral-Ryder Open	CUT	76	71	–	–	147	0.00
1997	Masters Tournament	T39	77	70	74	78	299	11,610.00
1997	Memorial Tournament	T8	69	70	69		208	57,000.00
1997	U.S. Open	T52	73	71	75	74	293	7,138.84
1997	PGA	CUT	74	76	–	–	150	0.00

International

1997	British Open	T60	73	74	71	75	293	9634.13

1998

1998	AT&T Pebble Beach National	W/D	71	72	–	–	143	$0.00
1998	Doral-Ryder Open	T58	70	74	72	77	293	4,420.00
1998	Masters	T6	73	72	70	68	283	111,200.00
1998	Memorial Tournament	CUT	74	77	–	–	151	0.00
1998	U.S. Open	T43	73	74	73	75	295	12,537.00

1999

1999	Memorial Tournament	T70	74	74	76	73	297	$5,074.50
1999	U.S. Open	CUT	78	75	–	–	153	0.00
1999	Wendy's Three Tour Challenge	T1	–	–	–	–	–	10,0000.00

2000

2000	AT&T Pebble Beach National	CUT	74	76	72	–	222	$0.00
2000	Doral-Ryder Open	CUT	75	75	–	–	150	0.00
2000	Masters	T54	74	70	81	78	303	10,672.00
2000	COMPAQ Classic of New Orleans	CUT	70	77	–	–	147	0.00
2000	Memorial Tournament	T64	75	73	72	73	293	6,572.00
2000	U.S. Open	CUT	73	82	–	–	155	0.00
2000	PGA	CUT	77	71	–	–	148	0.00
2000	Franklin Templeton Shootout	T9	–	–	–	–	–	50,000.00

International

2000	British Open	CUT	77	73	–	–	150	0.00

2001

2001	Genuity Championship	CUT	70	73	–	–	143	$0.00
2001	Masters	CUT	73	75	–	–	148	0.00
2001	Compaq Classic of New Orleans	CUT	73	72	–	–	145	0.00
2001	Memorial Tournament	CUT	75	73	–	–	148	0.00

2002

2002	Memorial Tournament	71	71	74	71	79	295	$8,910.00

2003

2003	Ford Championship at Doral	CUT	73	73	–	–	146	$0.00
2003	Bay Hill Invitational	CUT	82	76	–	–	158	0.00
2003	Masters	CUT	85	77	–	–	162	0.00
2003	The Memorial Tournament	CUT	76	72	–	–	148	0.00

2004

2004	Masters	CUT	75	75	–	–	150	$0.00
2004	The Memorial Tournament	T63	74	73	77	71	295	11,130.00

2005

2005	Masters	CUT	77	76	–	–	153	$0.00
2005	The Memorial Tournament	CUT	75	77	–	–	152	0.00

International

2005	British Open	CUT	75	72	–	–	147	0.00

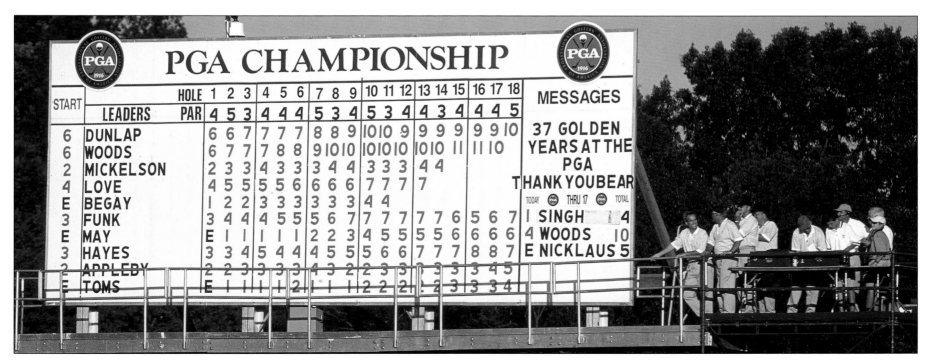

A "thank you" from the PGA of America in 2000.

The Nicklaus Record in the Professional Majors

MASTERS TOURNAMENT

Year	Venue	Place	1st	2nd	3rd	4th	Score	Earnings
2005	Augusta National GC	CUT	77	76	–	–	153	$5,000.00
	Par 72 / 7,290 yards							
2004	Augusta National GC	CUT	75	75	–	–	150	5,000.00
2003	Augusta National GC	CUT	85	77	–	–	162	5,000.00
2001	Augusta National GC	CUT	73	75	–	–	148	5,000.00
	Par 72 / 6,925 yards							
2000	Augusta National GC	T-54	74	70	81	78	303	10,672.00
	Par 72 / 6,985 yards.							
1999	Augusta National GC	Par 3 Contest						5,000.00
	(Recovering from hip replacement surgery)							
1998	Augusta National GC	T-6	73	72	70	68	283	111,200.00
	Par 72 / 6,925 yards							
1997	Augusta National GC	T-39	77	70	74	78	299	11,610.00
1996	Augusta National GC	T-41	70	73	76	78	297	10,050.00
1995	Augusta National GC	T-35	67	78	70	75	290	10,840.00
1994	Augusta National GC	CUT	78	74	–	–	152	1,500.00
1993	Augusta National GC	T-27	67	75	76	71	289	12,350.00
1992	Augusta National GC	T-42	69	75	69	74	287	5,450.00
1991	Augusta National GC	T-35	68	72	72	76	288	6,371.00
1990	Augusta National GC	6	72	70	69	74	285	45,000.00
1989	Augusta National GC	T-18	73	74	73	71	291	14,000.00
1988	Augusta National GC	T-21	75	73	72	72	292	11,200.00
1987	Augusta National GC	T-7	74	72	73	70	289	26,200.00
1986	Augusta National GC	1	74	71	69	65	279	144,000.00
1985	Augusta National GC	T-6	71	74	72	69	286	22,663.00
1984	Augusta National GC	T-18	73	73	70	70	286	8,400.00
1983	Augusta National GC	WD	73	–	–	–	–	1,500.00
1982	Augusta National GC	T-15	69	77	71	75	292	5,850.00
1981	Augusta National GC	T-2	70	65	75	72	282	30,500.00
1980	Augusta National GC	T-33	74	71	73	73	291	1,860.00
1979	Augusta National GC	4	69	71	72	69	281	15,000.00
1978	Augusta National GC	7	72	73	69	67	281	10,000.00
1977	Augusta National GC	2	72	70	70	66	278	30,000.00
1976	Augusta National GC	T-3	67	69	73	73	282	16,250.00
1975	Augusta National GC	1	68	67	73	68	276	40,000.00
1974	Augusta National GC	T-4	69	71	72	69	281	10,833.00
1973	Augusta National GC	T-3	69	77	73	66	285	12,500.00
1972	Augusta National GC	1	68	71	73	74	286	25,000.00
1971	Augusta National GC	T-2	70	71	68	72	281	17,500.00
1970	Augusta National GC	8	71	75	69	69	284	4,500.00
1969	Augusta National GC	T-24	68	75	72	76	291	1,800.00
1968	Augusta National GC	T-5	69	71	74	76	281	5,500.00
1967	Augusta National GC	CUT	72	79	–	–	151	1,000.00
1966	Augusta National GC	1	68	76	72	72	288	20,000.00
	(Playoff: Nicklaus 70, Jacobs 72, Brewer 78)							
1965	Augusta National GC	1	67	71	64	69	271	20,000.00
1964	Augusta National GC	T-2	71	73	71	67	282	10,100.00
1963	Augusta National GC	1	74	76	74	72	286	20,000.00
1962	Augusta National GC	T-14	74	75	70	72	291	1,160.00
1961	Augusta National GC	T-7	70	75	70	72	287	*
1960	Augusta National GC	T-13	75	71	72	75	293	*
1959	Augusta National GC	CUT	76	74	–	–	150	*

*Amateur

Total Earnings: $777,359.00

Masters Recap

Won	1963, 1965, 1966, 1972, 1975, 1986*
Masters Played	44
Rounds Played	161
Times Finished 72 Holes	37*
Scoring Average	71.93*
Top 3 Finishes	12*
Top 5 Finishes	15*
Top 10 Finishes	22*
Top 25 Finishes	29*
Rounds Under Par	71*
Lowest Masters Score:	64
Birdies	502*
Eagles	24*
Earnings	$777,359

*Record

1963

1965

1966

1972

1975

1986

U.S. OPEN

Year	Venue	Place	1st	2nd	3rd	4th	Score	Earnings
2000	Pebble Beach Golf Links Pebble Beach, CA Par 71 / 6,846 yards	CUT	73	82	–	–	155	$1,000.00
1999	Pinehurst CC (No 2) Pinehurst, NC Par 70 / 7,175 yards	CUT	78	75	–	–	153	1,000.00
1998	The Olympic Club San Francisco, CA Par 70 / 6,797 yards	T-43	73	74	73	75	295	12,537.00
1997	Congressional CC Bethesda, MD Par 70 / 7,213 yards	T-52	73	71	75	74	293	7,138.84
1996	Oakland Hills CC Birmingham, MI Par 70 / 6,974 yards	T-27	72	74	69	72	287	17,809.40
1995	Shinnecock Hills GC Southampton, NY Par 70 / 6,944 yards	CUT	71	81	–	–	152	1,000.00
1994	Oakmont CC Oakmont, PA Par 71 / 6,946 yards	T-28	69	70	77	76	292	11,514.20
1993	Baltusrol GC Springfield, NJ Par 70 / 7,152 yards	T-72	70	72	76	71	289	5,405.00
1992	Pebble Beach Golf Links Pebble Beach, CA Par 72 / 6,809 yards	CUT	77	74	–	–	151	1,000.00
1991	Hazeltine National GC Chaska, MN Par 72 / 7,149 yards	T-46	70	76	77	74	297	6,875.67
1990	Medinah CC (No 3) Medinah, IL Par 72 / 6,996 yards	T-33	71	74	68	76	289	8,221.16
1989	Oak Hill CC Rochester, NY Par 70 / 6,902 yards	T-43	67	74	74	75	290	6,281.00
1988	The Country Club Brookline, MA Par 71 / 7,010 yards	CUT	74	73	–	–	147	1,000.00
1987	The Olympic Club San Francisco, CA Par 70 / 6,714 yards	T-46	70	68	76	77	291	4,240.00
1986	Shinnecock Hills GC Southampton, NY Par 70 / 6,912 yards	T-8	77	72	67	68	284	14,500.75
1985	Oakland Hills CC Birmingham, MI Par 70 / 6,996 yards	CUT	76	73	–	–	149	600.00
1984	Winged Foot GC (West) Mamaroneck, NY Par 70 / 6,930 yards	T-21	71	71	70	77	289	6,575.50
1983	Oakmont CC Oakmont, PA Par 71 / 6,972 yards	T-43	73	74	77	76	300	2,847.20
1982	Pebble Beach Golf Links Pebble Beach, CA Par 72 / 6,815 yards	2	74	70	71	69	284	34,506.00
1981	Merion GC Ardmore, PA Par 70 / 6,544 yards	T-6	69	68	71	72	280	9,920.00
1980	Baltusrol GC Springfield, NJ Par 70 / 7,076 yards	1	63	71	70	68	272	55,000.00
1979	Inverness Club Toledo, OH Par 71 / 6,982 yards	T-9	74	77	72	68	291	7,500.00
1978	Cherry Hills CC Englewood, CO Par 71 / 7,083 yards	T-6	73	69	74	73	289	7,548.33
1977	Southern Hills CC Tulsa, OK Par 70 / 6,873 yards	T-10	74	68	71	72	285	4,100.00
1976	Atlanta Athletic Club Duluth, GA Par 70 / 7,015 yards	T-11	74	70	75	68	287	4,000.00
1975	Medinah CC (No 3) Medinah, IL Par 71 / 7,032 yards	T-7	72	70	75	72	289	7,500.00
1974	Winged Foot GC (West) Mamaroneck, NY Par 70 / 6,961 yards	T-10	75	74	7	69	294	3,750.00
1973	Oakmont CC Oakmont, PA Par 71 / 6,921 yards	T-4	71	69	74	68	282	9,000.00
1972	Pebble Beach G.L. Pebble Beach, CA Par 72 / 6,815 yards	1	71	73	72	74	290	30,000.00
1971	Merion GC Ardmore, PA Par 70 / 6,544 yards (Playoff: Trevino 68, Nicklaus 71)	2	69	72	68	71	280	15,000.00
1970	Hazeltine National GC Chaska, MN Par 72 / 7,151 yards	T-51	81	72	75	76	304	900.00
1969	Champions GC Houston, TX Par 70 / 6,967 yards	T-25	74	67	75	73	289	1,300.00

1962

1967

1972

1980

Year	Venue	Place	1st	2nd	3rd	4th	Score	Earnings
1968	Oak Hill CC Rochester, NY Par 70 / 6,962 yards	2	72	70	70	67	279	15,000.00
1967	Baltusrol GC Springfield, NJ Par 70 / 7,015 yards	1	71	67	72	65	275	30,000.00
1966	The Olympic Club San Francisco, CA Par 70 / 6,719 yrds	3	71	71	69	74	285	9,000.00
1965	Bellerive CC St. Louis, MO Par 70 / 7,191 yards	T-31	78	72	73	76	299	550.00
1964	Congressional CC Washington, DC Par 70 / 7,053 yards	T-23	72	73	77	73	295	475.00
1963	The Country Club Brookline, MA Par 71 / 6,870 yards	CUT	76	77	–	–	133	150.00
1962	Oakmont CC Oakmont, PA Par 71 / 6,894 yards (Playoff: Nicklaus 71, Palmer 74)	1	72	70	72	69	283	17,500.00
1961	Oakland Hills CC Birmingham, MI Par 70 / 6,907 yards	T-4	75	69	70	70	284	*
1960	Cherry Hills CC Englewood, CO Par 71 / 7,004 yards	2	71	71	69	71	282	*
1959	Winged Foot GC Mamaroneck, NY Par 70 / 6,873 yards	CUT	77	77	–	–	154	*
1958	Southern Hills CC Tulsa, OK Par 70 / 6,907 yards	T-41	79	75	73	77	304	*
1957	Inverness Club Toledo, OH Par 70 / 6,919 yards	CUT	80	80	–	–	160	*
1956	Oak Hill CC Rochester, NY Par 70 / 6,902 yards	(Second alternate; missed championship)*						

*Amateur

Total Earnings: $372,245.05

U.S. Open Recap

Won	1962. 1967, 1972, 1980*
Events	44
Rounds Played	160
Times Finished 72 Holes	35
Scoring Average	72.59
Low Round	63
Top 3 Finishes	9*
Top 5 Finishes	11*
Top 10 Finishes	18*
Top 25 Finishes	22*
Rounds in 60s	29*
Rounds Under Par	37*
Sub-par 72 Hole Total	7*
First to Last Victory	18 years*
Consecutive Opens Started	44*
Opens Completed 72 Holes	35*
Earnings	$372,245.05

*Record

BRITISH OPEN

Year	Venue	Place	1st	2nd	3rd	4th	Score	Earnings
2005	Old Course at St. Andrews	CUT	75	72	–	–	147	$0.00
	St. Andrews, Fife, Scotland Par 72 / 7,279 yards							
2000	Old Course at St. Andrews	CUT	77	73	–	–	150	0.00
	St. Andrews, Fife, Scotland Par 72 / 7,115 yards							
1997	Royal Troon GC	T-60	73	74	71	75	293	9,634.13
	Troon, Ayrshire, Scotland Par 71 / 7,079 yards							
1996	Royal Lytham & St. Annes GC	T-44	69	66	77	73	285	9,920.00
	Lytham, Lancashire, England Par 71 / 6,892 yards							
1995	Old Course at St. Andrews	T-79	78	70	77	71	296	7,177.50
	Lytham, Lancashire, England Par 71 / 6,892 yards							
1994	Turnberry (Ailsa Course)	CUT	72	73	–	–	145	0.00
	Turnberry, Ayrshire, Scotland Par 70 / 6,957 yards							
1993	Royal St. George's GC	CUT	69	75	–	–	144	0.00
	Sandwich, Kent, England Par 70 / 6,860 yards							
1992	Honourable Company of Edinburgh Golfers	CUT	75	73	–	–	148	0.00
	Muirfield, East Lothian, Scotland Par 71 / 6,970 yards							
1991	Royal Birkdale GC	T-44	70	75	69	71	285	7,114.16
	Southport, Lancashire, England Par 70 / 6,940 yards							
1990	Old Course at St. Andrews	T-63	71	70	77	71	289	5,339.50
	St. Andrews, Fife, Scotland Par 72 / 6,933 yards							
1989	Royal Troon GC	T-30	74	71	71	70	286	7,537.60
	Troon, Ayrshire, Scotland Par 72 / 7,067 yards							
1988	Royal Lytham & St. Annes GC	T-25	75	70	75	68	288	9,350.00
	Lytham, Lancashire, England Par 71 / 6,857 yards							
1987	Honourable Company of Edinburgh Golfers	T-72	74	71	81	76	302	2,560.00
	Muirfield, East Lothian, Scotland Par 71 / 6,963 yards							
1986	Turnberry (Ailsa Course)	T-46	78	73	76	71	298	3,712.50
	Turnberry, Ayrshire, Scotland Par 70 / 6,957 yards							
1985	Royal St. George's GC	CUT	77	75	–	–	152	0.00
	Sandwich, Kent, England Par 70 / 6,857 yards							
1984	Old Course at St. Andrews	T-31	76	72	68	72	288	3,377.40
	St. Andrews, Fife, Scotland Par 72 / 6,933 yards							

1966

1970

1978

British Open Recap

Won	1966, 1970, 1978
Second Place Finishes	1964, 1967, 1968, 1972, 1976, 1977, 1979*
Events	38
Rounds Played	140
Times Finished 72 Holes	24
Scoring Average	71.96
Top 3 Finishes	13*
Top 5 Finishes	16*
Top 10 Finishes	18*
Top 25 Finishes	21*
Rounds Under 70	33*
Rounds Under Par	56
Lowest British Open Score	65
Earnings	$246,327.59

*Record

Year	Venue	Place	1st	2nd	3rd	4th	Score	Earnings
1983	Royal Birkdale GC	T-29	71	72	72	70	285	2,197.50
	Southport, Lancashire, England Par 71 / 6,968 yards							
1982	Royal Troon GC	T-10	77	70	72	69	288	12,495.00
	Troon, Ayrshire, Scotland Par 72 / 7,067 yards							
1981	Royal St. George's GC	T-23	83	66	71	70	290	2,437.50
	Sandwich, Kent, England Par 70 / 6,829 yards							
1980	Honourable Company of Edinburgh Golfers	T-4	73	67	71	69	280	22,200.00
	Muirfield, East Lothian, Scotland Par 71 / 6,926 yards							
1979	Royal Lytham & St. Annes GC	T-2	72	69	73	72	286	23,625.00
	Lytham, Lancashire, England Par 71 / 6,822 yards							
1978	Old Course at St. Andrews	1	71	72	69	69	281	23,750.00
	St. Andrews, Fife, Scotland Par 72 / 6,933 yards							
1977	Turnberry (Ailsa Course)	2	68	70	65	66	269	13,600.00
	Turnberry, Ayrshire, Scotland Par 70 / 6,875 yards							
1976	Royal Birkdale GC	T-2	74	70	72	69	285	9,450.00
	Southport, Lancashire, England Par 72 / 7,001 yards							
1975	Carnoustie GC	T-3	69	71	68	72	280	8,507.40
	Carnoustie, Angus, Scotland Par 72 / 7,065 yards							
1974	Royal Lytham & St. Annes GC	3	74	72	70	71	287	7,800.00
	Lytham, Lancashire, Scotland Par 71 / 6,822 yards							
1973	Royal Troon GC	4	69	70	76	65	280	7,150.00
	Troon, Ayrshire, Scotland Par 72 / 7,064 yards							
1972	Honourable Company of Edinburgh Golfers	2	70	72	71	66	279	10,000.00
	Muirfield, East Lothian, Scotland Par 71 / 6,892 yards							
1971	Royal Birkdale GC	T-5	71	71	72	69	283	5,520.00
	Southport, Lancashire, England Par 72 / 7,001 yards							
1970	Old Course at St. Andrews	1	68	69	73	73	283	12,600.00
	St. Andrews, Fife, Scotland Par 72 / 6,951 yards (Playoff: Nicklaus 72, Sanders 73)							
1969	Royal Lytham & St. Annes GC	T-6	75	70	68	72	285	3,300.00
	Lytham, Lancashire, England Par 71 / 6,822 yards							
1968	Carnoustie GC	T-2	76	69	73	73	291	4,171.20
	Carnoustie, Angus, Scotland Par 72 / 7,065 yards							
1967	Royal Liverpool GC	2	71	69	71	69	280	4,200.00
	Holyoke, England Par 70 / 6,995 yards							
1966	Honourable Company of Edinburgh Golfers	1	70	67	75	70	282	2,100.00
	Muirfield, East Lothian, Scotland Par 71 / 6,887 yards							
1965	Royal Birkdale GC	T-12	73	71	77	73	294	371.00
	Southport, Lancashire, England Par 73 / 7,037 yards							
1964	Old Course at St. Andrews	2	76	74	66	68	284	2,800.00
	St. Andrews, Fife, Scotland Par 72 / 7,115 yards							
1963	Royal Lytham & St. Annes GC	3	71	67	70	70	278	2,240.00
	Lytham, Lancashire, England Par 71 / 6,836 yards							
1962	Royal Troon GC	T-34	80	72	74	79	305	90.20
	Troon, Scotland Par 72 / 7,045 yards							

Total Earnings: $246,327.59

PGA CHAMPIONSHIP

Year	Venue	Place	1st	2nd	3rd	4th	Score	Earnings
2000	Valhalla GC Louisville, KY Par 72 / 7,167 yards	CUT	77	71	–	–	148	$2,000.00
1997	Winged Foot GC (West) Mamaroneck, NY Par 70 / 6,987 yards	CUT	74	76	–	–	150	1,300.00
1996	Valhalla GC Louisville, KY Par 72 / 7,144 yards	CUT	77	69	–	–	146	1,300.00
1995	Riviera CC Pacific Palisades, CA Par 71 / 6,956 yards	T-67	69	71	71	76	287	3,262.50
1994	Southern Hills CC Tulsa, OK Par 70 / 6,824 yards	CUT	79	71	–	–	150	1,200.00
1993	Inverness Club Toledo, OH Par 71 / 7,024 yards	CUT	71	73	–	–	144	1,200.00
1992	Bellerive CC St Louis, MO Par 71 / 7,024 yards	CUT	72	78	–	–	150	1,200.00
1991	Crooked Stick GC Carmel, IN Par 72 / 7,295 yards	T-23	71	72	73	71	287	11,500.00
1990	Shoal Creek CC Birmingham, AL Par 72 / 7,145 yards	CUT	78	74	–	–	152	1,000.00
1989	Kemper Lakes GC Hawthorn Woods, IL Par 72 / 7,217 yards	T-27	68	72	73	72	285	7,535.72
1988	Oak Tree GC Edmond, OK Par 71 / 7,015 yards	CUT	72	79	–	–	151	1,000.00
1987	PGA National GC (Ch.) Palm Beach Gardens, FL Par 72 / 7,002 yards	T-24	76	73	74	73	296	5,975.00
1986	Inverness Club Toledo, OH Par 71 / 6,982 yards	T-16	70	68	72	75	285	8,500.00
1985	Cherry Hills CC Englewood, CO Par 71 / 7,089 yards	T-32	66	75	74	74	289	3,408.34
1984	Shoal Creek CC Birmingham, AL Par 72 / 7,145 yards	T-25	77	70	71	69	287	4,506.25
1983	Riviera CC Pacific Palisades, CA Par 71 / 6,946 yards	2	73	65	71	66	275	60,000.00
1982	Southern Hills CC Tulsa, OK Par 70 / 6,862 yards	T-16	74	70	72	67	283	4,625.00
1981	Atlanta Athletic Club Duluth, GA Par 70 / 7,070 yards	T-4	71	68	71	69	279	13,146.43
1980	Oak Hill CC Rochester, NY Par 70 / 6,964 yards	1	70	69	66	69	274	60,000.00
1979	Oakland Hills CC Birmingham, MI Par 70 / 7,014 yards	T-65	73	72	78	71	294	515.00
1978	Oakmont CC Oakmont, PA Par 71 / 6,989 yards	CUT	79	74	–	–	153	303.00
1977	Pebble Beach Golf Links Pebble Beach, CA Par 72 / 6,804 yards	3	69	71	70	73	283	15,000.00
1976	Congressional CC Bethesda, MD Par 70 / 7,054 yards	T-4	71	69	69	74	283	9,750.00

1963

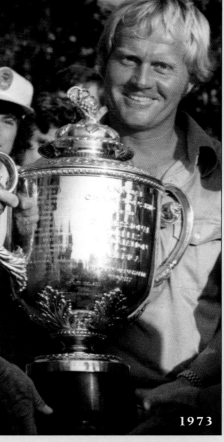

1973

1971

1975

1980

PGA Championship Recap

Won	1963, 1971, 1973, 1975, 1980*
Events	37*
Rounds Played	128*
Scoring Average	71.37*
Cuts Made	27*
Top 3	12*
Top 5	14*
Top 10	15*
Top 25	23*
Lowest Score	64
Largest Winning Margin	7 shots*
Rounds in the 60s	41*
Earnings	$436,788

*Record

Year	Venue	Place	1st	2nd	3rd	4th	Score	Earnings
1975	Firestone CC (South) Akron, OH Par 70 / 7,180 yards	1	70	68	67	71	276	45,000.00
1974	Tanglewood GC Clemmons, NC Par 70 / 7,050 yards	2	69	69	70	69	277	25,700.00
1973	Canterbury GC Cleveland, OH Par 71 / 6,852 yards	1	72	68	68	69	277	45,000.00
1972	Oakland Hills CC Birmingham, MI Par 70 / 6,815 yards	T-13	72	75	68	72	287	4,167.00
1971	PGA National GC Palm Beach Gardens, FL Par 72 / 7,096 yards	1	69	69	70	73	281	40,000.00
1970	Southern Hills CC Tulsa, OK Par 70 / 6,962 yards	T-6	68	76	73	66	283	6,800.00
1969	NCR CC Dayton, OH Par 71 / 6,915 yards	T-11	70	68	74	71	283	3,543.75
1968	Pecan Valley CC San Antonio, TX Par 70 / 7,096 yards	CUT	71	79	–	–	150	0.00
1967	Columbine CC Denver, CO Par 72 / 7,436 yards	T-3	67	75	69	71	282	9,000.00
1966	Firestone CC Akron, OH Par 70 / 7,180 yards	T-22	70	68	74	71	283	1,400.00
1965	Laurel Valley CC Ligonier, PA Par 71 / 7,090 yards	T-2	69	70	72	71	282	12,500.00
1964	Columbus CC Columbus, OH Par 70 / 6,851 yards	T-2	67	73	70	64	274	9,000.00
1963	Dallas Athletic Club Dayton, OH. Par 71 / 7,046 yards	1	69	73	69	68	279	13,000.00
1962	Aronimink CC Newton Square, PA Par 70 / 7,045 yards	T-3	71	74	69	67	281	3,450.00

Total Earnings: $436,788.00

The Golf Courses of Nicklaus Design

At work on Harbour Town Golf Links on Hilton Head Island, South Carolina, with Pete Dye (kneeling, far right).

1969	Harbour Town Golf Links (Hilton Head Island, SC)
1970	Grand Geneva Resort (Lake Geneva, WI)
1970	John's Island – South Course (Vero Beach, FL)
1972	Wabeek Country Club (Bloomfield Hills, MI)
1973	Golf Center at Kings Island – Bruin (Mason, OH)
1973	Golf Center at Kings Island – Grizzly (Mason, OH)
1973	Mayacoo Lakes Country Club (West Palm Beach, FL)
1973	New Saint Andrews Golf Club (Otawara, Tochigi, Japan)
1974	Muirfield Village Golf Club (Dublin, OH)
1976	Glen Abbey Golf Club (Oakville, Ontario, Canada)
1976	La Moraleja Golf Club (Alcobendas, Madrid, Spain)
1976	Shoal Creek (Shoal Creek, AL)
1977	Australian Golf Club, Rosebery (New South Wales, Australia)*
1978	The Greenbrier (White Sulphur Springs, WV)*
1980	Bear's Paw Country Club (Naples, FL)
1980	Lochinvar Golf Club (Houston, TX)
1981	Annandale Golf Club (Madison, MS)
1981	Castle Pines Golf Club (Castle Rock, CO)
1981	The Club at Morningside (Rancho Mirage, CA)
1981	The Hills of Lakeway – The Hills Country Cub Course (Austin, TX)
1981	Sailfish Point Golf Club (Stuart, FL)
1981	Turtle Point Golf Club (Charleston, SC)
1982	Bear Creek Golf Club (Murrieta, CA)
1982	The Country Club at Muirfield Village (Dublin, OH)
1983	Atlanta Country Club (Marietta, GA)*
1983	Park Meadows Country Club (Park City, UT)

1984	Country Club of the Rockies (Edwards, CO)
1984	Desert Highlands Golf Club (Scottsdale, AZ)
1984	Elk River Golf Club (Banner Elk, NC)
1984	Grand Cypress Golf Club – North, South, East (Orlando, FL)
1984	Grand Traverse Resort – The Bear (Acme, MI)
1984	La Paloma Country Club (Tucson, AZ)
1984	The Loxahatchee Club (Jupiter, FL)
1984	Meridian Golf Club (Englewood, CO)
1985	Bear Lakes Country Club – Lakes Course (West Palm Beach, FL)
1985	Britannia Golf Course (Georgetown, Grand Cayman, British West Indies)
1985	Saint Andrew's Golf Club (Hastings-on-Hudson, NY)*
1986	The Country Club at Castle Pines (Castle Rock, CO)
1986	The Country Club of Louisiana (Baton Rouge, LA)
1986	Dallas Athletic Club – Blue Course (Mesquite, TX)*
1986	St. Mellion Hotel Golf & Country Club (Cornwall, England)
1986	Valhalla Golf Club (Louisville, KY)
1987	Breckenridge Golf Club (Breckenridge, CO)
1987	Country Club of The South (Alpharetta, GA)
1987	Daufuskie Island Club & Resort – Melrose Course (Hilton Head Island, SC)
1987	Desert Mountain – Renegade (Scottsdale, AZ)
1987	PGA West – Private Course (La Quinta, CA)
1987	PGA West – Resort Course (La Quinta, CA)
1988	Bear Lakes Country Club – Links Course (West Palm Beach, FL)
1988	Desert Mountain – Cochise (Scottsdale, AZ)
1988	English Turn Golf & Country Club (New Orleans, LA)
1988	Golf Club Crans-Sur-Sierre (Crans-Sur-Sierre, Valais, Switzerland)
1988	Golf Club Gut Altentann (Henndorf, Salzburg, Austria)
1988	Grand Cypress Golf Club – New Course (Orlando, FL)
1988	Kauai Lagoons – Kiele Course (Lihue, HI)
1988	Pawleys Plantation (Pawleys Island, SC)
1988	Ptarmigan Golf & Country Club (Fort Collins, CO)
1988	Richland Country Club (Nashville, TN)
1988	Sunny Field Golf Club (Gozenyama, Ibaraki, Japan)

The 17th hole at The Loxahatchee Club in Jupiter, Florida.

*Redesign

The Country Club of the Rockies course utilizes much of the natural terrain.

1989   Avila Golf & Country Club (Tampa, FL)*
1989   Dallas Athletic Club – Gold Course (Mesquite, TX)*
1989   Desert Mountain – Geronimo (Scottsdale, AZ)
1989   Eagle Oaks Golf Club (Farmingdale, NJ)
1989   Kauai Lagoons – Mokihana Course (Lihue, HI)
1989   The Long Bay Club (Longs, SC)
1989   National Golf Club (Village of Pinehurst, NC)
1989   Sherwood Country Club (Thousand Oaks, CA)
1989   Shimonoseki Golden Golf Club (Shimonoseki, Yamaguchi, Japan)
1989   St. Creek Golf Club (Asuke, Aichi, Japan)
1989   Sycamore Hills Golf Club (Fort Wayne, IN)
1989   Wynstone Golf Club (North Barrington, IL)

1990   PGA National – Champion Course (Palm Beach Gardens, FL)*
1990   Country Club of Landfall (Wilmington, NC)
1990   Governers Club (Chapel Hill, NC)
1990   Japan Memorial Golf Club (Yakawa-cho, Hyogo-ken, Japan)
1990   Oakmont Golf Club (Yamazoe, Nara, Japan)
1990   TPC Michigan (Dearborn, MI)

1991   Dove Canyon Country Club (Dove Canyon, CA)
1991   Hanbury Manor Golf & Country Club (Ware, Hertfordshire, England)
1991   Hokkaido Classic Golf Club (Hayakita, Hokkaido, Japan)
1991   Ibis Golf & Country Club – Heritage (West Palm Beach, FL)
1991   Ibis Golf & Country Club – Legend (West Palm Beach, FL)
1991   Legacy Golf Links (Aberdeen, NC)
1991   Mission Hills Golf Club – Kanchanaburi (Thamuang, Kanchanaburi, Thailand)
1991   Mount Juliet (Thomastown, County Kilkenny, Ireland)
1991   Paris International Golf Club (Paris, France)

1992   The Club at Nevillewood (Nevillewood, PA)
1992   Colleton River Plantation – Nicklaus Course (Bluffton, SC)
1992   Damai Indah Golf & Country Club (Jakarta, Banten, Indonesia)
1992   Glenmoor Country Club (Canton, OH)
1992   Great Waters at Reynolds Plantation (Greensboro, GA)
1992   Hananomori Golf Club (Ohira, Miyagi, Japan)
1992   Huis Ten Bosch Country Club (Seihi, Nagasaki, Japan)
1992   Komono Golf Club (Komono, Mie, Japan)
1992   Manila Southwoods Golf & Country Club – Legends
          (Carmona, Cavite, Philippines)
1992   Natural Park Ramindra Golf Club (Klongsamwa, Bangkok, Thailand)
1992   New Albany Country Club (New Albany, OH)

1993   The Challenge at Manele (Lanai City, HI)
1993   Chang An Golf & Country Club (Hukou, Hsinchu, Taiwan)
1993   Chung Shan Hot Spring Golf Club (Zhongshan City, Guangdong, China)
1993   Country Club of the North (Beavercreek, OH)
1993   Gleneagles Hotel – The PGA Centenary Course
          (Auchterarder, Perthshire, Scotland)

1993   Golden Bear Golf Club at Indigo Run (Hilton Head Island, SC)
1993   Laem Chabang International Country Club (Sriracha, Chonburi, Thailand)
1993   Las Campanas – Sunrise (Santa Fe, NM)
1993   Leo Palace Resort Manenggon Hills (Barrigada, GMF, Guam)
1993   Manila Southwoods Golf & Country Club – Masters
          (Carmona, Cavite, Philippines)
1993   Medallion Club (Westerville, OH)
1993   Mission Hills Khao Yai Golf Club (Pak Chong, Nakhon Ratchasima, Thailand)
1993   Palmilla Golf Club (Los Cabos, Baja California Sur, Mexico)
1993   Santa Lucia River Club at Ballantrae (Port St. Lucie, FL)
1993   Sendai Minami Golf Club (Shibat-gun, Miyagi-ken, Japan)
1993   Springfield Royal Country Club (Cha-Am, Phetchaburi, Thailand)
1993   Sungai Long Golf & Country Club (Kajang, Selangor, Malaysia)

1994   Barrington Golf Club (Aurora, OH)
1994   Cabo del Sol – Ocean Course (Cabo San Lucas, Baja California Sur, Mexico)
1994   Castlewoods Country Club – The Bear (Brandon, MS)
1994   Ishioka Golf Club (Ogawa, Ibaraki, Japan)
1994   London Golf Club – The Heritage (Ash, Kent, England)
1994   London Golf Club – The International Course (Ash, Kent, England)
1994   Miramar Linkou Golf & Country Club (Linkou Hsiang, Taipei, Taiwan)
1994   Mission Hills Golf Club – World Cup Course
          (Guanlan Town, Shenzhen, China)
1994   Montecastillo Hotel & Golf Resort (Jerez, Cadiz, Spain)
1994   The Zenzation (Pak Chong, Nakhon Ratchasima, Thailand)

Describing a new development, Britania Golf Course in Grand Cayman.

1995   Borneo Golf & Country Club (Bongawan, Sabah, Malaysia)
1995   Bukit Darmo Golf Club (Surabaya, Indonesia)
1995   Eagle Bend Golf Club – Championship Course (Big Fork, MT)
1995   Emeralda G & CC – Plantation North Course (Cimanngis, Bogor, Indonesia)
1995   La Gorce Country Club (Miami Beach, FL)*
1995   Le Robinie Golf & Sporting Club (Solbiate Olona, Varese, Italy)
1995   Mission Hills Golf Club – Valley Course (Guanlan Town, Shenzhen, China)
1995   President Country Club (Tochigi, Tochigi, Japan)
1995   Sanyo Golf Club (Okayama, Japan)
1995   Tamarin Santana Golf Club (Batam, Riau, Indonesia)
1995   Williamsburg National (Williamsburg, VA)

1996   Bearpath Golf & Country Club (Eden Prairie, MN)
1996   Bukit Barisan Country Club at Medan (Medan, Sumatera Utara, Indonesia)
1996   Country Club Bosques (Hidalgo, Distrito Federal, Mexico)
1996   Desert Mountain – Apache (Scottsdale, AZ)
1996   Golf Club at Indigo Run (Hilton Head Island, SC)
1996   The Golf Club of Purchase (Purchase, NY)
1996   Hammock Creek Golf Club (Palm City, FL)
1996   Hertfordshire Golf & Country Club (Hertfordshire, England)
1996   Hibiki no Mori Country Club (Kurabuchi, Gunma, Japan)
1996   Hualalai Golf Club (Kailua-Kona, HI)
1996   Lakelands Golf Club (Robina, Queensland, Australia)
1996   Nicklaus North Golf Course (Whistler, British Columbia, Canada)

1996	Rokko Kokusai (Kobe, Hyogo, Japan)
1996	Ruby Hill Golf Club (Pleasanton, CA)
1996	Southshore at Lake Las Vegas (Henderson, NV)
1996	Sun Belgravia Golf Club (Nukata, Aichi, Japan)
1996	Top of the Rock Golf Course (Ridgedale, MO)
1997	Aspen Glen Golf Club (Carbondale, CO)
1997	Bintan Lagoon – Seaview Course (Bintan, Riau, Indonesia)
1997	Forest Hills Golf & Country Club (Inarawan, Antipolo, Philippines)
1997	Golf Platz Gut Larchenhof (Cologne, Germany)
1997	Great Bear Golf & Country Club (East Stroudsburg, PA)
1997	Legends Golf & Country Resort (Kulai, Johor, Malaysia)
1997	Montreux Golf & Country Club (Reno, NV)
1997	Old Works Golf Course (Anaconda, MT)
1997	Ruitoque Country Club (Bucaramanga, Santander, Spain)
1997	Salem Glen Country Club (Clemmons, NC)
1997	Spring City Resort (Kunming City, Yunnan, China)
1997	Stonewolf Golf Club (Fairview Heights, IL)
1997	Suzhou Sunrise Golf Club (Suzhou, Jiangsu, China)
1997	Taman Dayu Club (Pandaan, East Java, Indonesia)

Superstition Mountain's Lost Gold Course was co-designed with Jack II.

1998	Arzaga Golf Club (Drugolo di Lonato, Brescia, Italy)
1998	Bear Trace at Cumberland Mountain (Crossville, TN)
1998	Carden Park (Chesire, England)
1998	Classic Golf Resort – Basant Lok (Vasant Vihar, New Delhi, India)
1998	Empire Hotel and Country Club (Negara Brunei Darussalam, Jerudong, Brunei)
1998	Grand Haven Golf Club (Palm Coast, FL)
1998	J&P Golf Club (Utsonomiya, Tochigi, Japan)
1998	Laurel Springs Golf Club (Suwanee, GA)
1998	Legends West at Diablo Grande (Patterson, CA)
1998	Nanhu Country Club (Guangzhou, Guangdong, China)
1998	Pecanwood Estate (Hartebeespoort Dam, Guateng, South Africa)
1998	Phoenix Park Golf Club (Pyeongchang, Gangwon-do, South Korea)
1998	Reflection Bay Golf Club at Lake Las Vegas (Henderson, NV)
1998	Sherwood Hills Golf & Country Club (Trece Martires, Cavite, Philippines)
1998	Superstition Mountain G & CC – Prospector (Superstition Mountain, AZ)
1998	Westlake Golf & Country Club (Hangzhou, Zhejiang, China)

1999	Alabang Country Club (Alabang, Muntinlupa, The Phillipines)
1999	Aliso Viejo Golf Club (Aliso Viejo, CA)
1999	Aston Oaks (North Bend, OH)
1999	Bear Trace at Harrison Bay (Harrison, TN)
1999	Bear Trace at Tims Ford (Winchester, TN)
1999	Camp John Hay (Bagio, Benguet, Philippines)
1999	The Club at TwinEagles – Talon (Naples, FL)
1999	Coyote Creek Golf Club – Tournament Course (San Jose, CA)
1999	Desert Mountain – Chiricahua (Scottsdale, AZ)
1999	El Dorado Golf & Beach Club (San Jose del Cabo, Baja California Sur, Mexico)

1999	Estrella Mountain Ranch Golf Club (Goodyear, AZ)
1999	Four Seasons Golf Club Punta Mita (Punta Mita, Nayarit, Mexico)
1999	The Golden Bear Club at Keene's Pointe (Windermere, FL)
1999	The Golf Club at Mansion Ridge (Monroe, NY)
1999	Grand Bear Golf Course (Saucier, MS)
1999	New Capital Golf Club (Yamaoka, Gifu, Japan)
1999	Okanagan Golf Club (Kelowna, British Columbia, Canada)
1999	Palm Island Golf Club (Hui Yang City, Guangdong, China)
1999	Palmilla Ocean Nine (San Jose del Cabo, BCS, Mexico)
1999	Roaring Fork Club (Basalt, CO)
1999	Rocky Gap Lodge & Golf Resort (Flintstone, MD)
1999	Shanghai Links Golf & Country Club (Pudong New Area, Shanghai, China)
1999	Spring Creek Ranch (Collierville, TN)
1999	Superstition Mountain G & CC – Lost Gold (Superstition Mountain, AZ)
1999	TPC Snoqualmie Ridge (Snoqualmie, WA)
1999	Vermont National Country Club (South Burlington, VT)

Working on plans for the fourth hole at Moon Palace Golf Club in Cancun, Mexico.

2000	Bear Creek Golf Course at Chandler (Chandler, AZ)
2000	Bear Trace at Chickasaw State Park (Henderson, TN)
2000	The Bear's Club (Jupiter, FL)
2000	Bear's Paw Japan Country Club (Kouga-gun, Shiga-ken, Japan)
2000	The Club at Porto Cima (Lake Ozark, MO)
2000	Country Club of Landfall II (Wilmington, NC)
2000	Gapyeong Benest Golf Club (Gapyeong-gun, Kyonggi-do, South Korea)
2000	Gapyeong Benest Golf Club – Nicklaus Design Course (Gapyeong-gun, Kyonggi-do, South Korea)
2000	Heritage Golf & Country Club (Melbourne, Victoria, Australia)
2000	King & Bear (St. Augustine, FL)
2000	Las Campanas – Sunset (Santa Fe, NM)
2000	Achasta Golf Club (Dahlonega, GA)
2000	Ocean Course at Hammock Beach (Palm Coast, FL)
2000	Pasadera Country Club (Monterey, CA)
2000	Whispering Pines Golf Club (Trinity, TX)
2000	Winghaven Country Club (O'Fallon, MO)

2001	Bear Creek Golf Course at Chandler – Short Course (Chandler, AZ)
2001	Bear Trace at Ross Creek Landing (Clifton, TN)
2001	Bear's Best Las Vegas (Las Vegas, NV)

The Outlaw Course at Desert Mountain in Scottsdale, Arizona.

2001	Breckenridge – Elk Nine (Breckenridge, CO)
2001	The Club at Carlton Woods (The Woodlands, TX)
2001	Coyote Creek Golf Club (Bartonville, IL)
2001	Coyote Creek Golf Club – Valley Course (San Jose, CA)
2001	Cozumel Country Club (Cozumel, Quintana Roo, Meixco)
2001	Ibis Golf and Country Club – Tradition (West Palm Beach, FL)
2001	Mayacama Golf Club (Santa Rosa, CA)
2001	Montreux – 3 Holes (Reno, NV)
2001	Nicklaus Golf Club at LionsGate (Overland Park, KS)
2001	Olympic Staff Ashikaga Golf Course (Ashikaga, Tochigi, Japan)
2001	Pine Valley Golf & Country Club – Golden Bear Course (Beijing, Changping, China)
2001	The Summit Course at Cordillera (Edwards, CO)
2001	Vista Vallarta Golf Club (Puerto Vallarta, Jalisco, Mexico)
2001	WuYi Fountain Palm Golf Club (Jiangmen, Guangdong, China)

2002	Bear's Best Atlanta (Suwanee, GA)
2002	Canadas De Santa Fe (Mexico City, C.P., Distrito Federal, Mexico)
2002	Cherry Creek Country Club (Denver, CO)
2002	Cimarron Hills Country Club (Georgetown, TX)
2002	Dalhousie Golf Club (Cape Girardeau, MO)
2002	The Hills of Lakeway – The Flintrock Fans Course (Austin, TX)
2002	Hokulia Golf Club (Kailua-Kona, HI)
2002	Lost Tree Club (North Palm Beach, FL)*
2002	Moon Palace Golf Club (Cancun, Quintana Roo, Mexico)
2002	Northern Bear Golf Club (Sherwood Park, Alberta, Canada)
2002	Pinehills Golf Club (Plymouth, MA)
2002	The Reserve at Lake Keowee (Sunset, SC)
2002	Reserve Club at Woodside Plantation (Aiken, SC)
2002	The Ritz-Carlton Golf Club & Spa (Jupiter, FL)
2002	Takaraike Golf Course (Nara, Japan)
2002	The Tradition Golf Club (Okazaki-shi, Aichi, Japan)

Jack on site at The Bear's Club with son Jack II (middle).

2003	Bear Mountain Golf & Country Club (Victoria, British Columbia, Canada)
2003	The Bear's Club Par 3 (Jupiter, FL)
2003	Bull at Pinehurst Farms (Sheboygan Falls, WI)
2003	The Club at Longview (Weddington, NC)
2003	Desert Mountain – Outlaw (Scottsdale, AZ)
2003	Mayan Palace – Riviera Maya (Riviera Maya, Quintana Roo, Mexico)
2003	Pearl Valley Golf Estate & Spa (Franschhoek, Western Cape, South Africa)
2003	Royal Palm Yacht & Country Club (Boca Raton, FL)*
2003	Sagamore Club (Noblesville, IN)

2004	Angeles National Golf Club (Sunland, CA)
2004	Chapelco Golf & Resort (San Martin de los Andes, Neuquen, Argentina)
2004	The Cliffs at Walnut Cove (Arden, NC)
2004	The Club at Pronghorn (Bend, OR)
2004	Laguna Del Mar (Puerto Penasco, Sonora, Mexico)
2004	May River Club (Bluffton, SC)

2004	Mission Hills Phuket Golf Resort & Spa (Talang, Phuket, Thailand)
2004	Old Greenwood (Truckee, CA)
2004	Toscana Country Club (Indian Wells, CA)
2004	Traditions Club (Bryan, TX)
2004	Tres Marias Residencial Golf Club (Morelia, Michoacan, Mexico)

The eleventh hole at The Ritz-Carlton Golf Club and Spa in Jupiter, FL.

2005	Bay Creek (Cape Charles, VA)
2005	Bay Point Golf Club (Panama City Beach, FL)*
2005	Bayside Resort Golf Club (Selbyville, DE)
2005	The Bridges Golf & Country Club (Montrose, CO)
2005	Champions Retreat Golf Club – Bluffs Course (Augusta, GA)
2005	Club Polaris Golf Resort (Seoul, South Korea)
2005	Escena (Palm Springs, CA)
2005	Machynys Peninsula Golf Club (Carmarthenshire, Wales, England)
2005	Moon Palace – 3rd nine (Cancun, Quintana Roo, Mexico)
2005	Olympic Country Club – Lake Tsuburada (Misato-cho, Saitama Prefecture, Japan)
2005	Palisades Country Club (Charlotte, NC)
2005	Simola Golf and Country Lodge (Knysna, South Africa)
2005	Toscana Country Club – North (Indian Wells, CA)

2006	Broadmoor Golf Club (Colorado Springs, CO)
2006	The Concession (Bradenton, FL)
2006	Cordillera Ranch (Boerne, TX)
2006	Dismal River Club (Mullen, NE)
2006	La Loma (San Luis Potosi, Mexico)
2006	La Torre (Torre Pacheco, Murcia, Spain)
2006	Sherwood Lake Club (Thousand Oaks, CA)
2006	North Palm Beach Country Club (North Palm Beach, FL)*
2006	The Peninsula (Puerto Penasco, Sonora, Mexico)
2006	The Peninsula Golf and Country Club (Millsboro, DE)
2006	Punta Espada (Punta Cana, La Alta Gracia, Dominican Republic)
2006	Puntiro Golf Club (Mallorca, Spain)
2006	Real de Faula (Benidorm, Valencia, Spain)
2006	Reserve Club at St. James Plantation (Southport, NC)
2006	The Retreat Golf and Country Club (Corona, CA)
2006	Reunion Resort & Club – The Tradition Course (Kissimmee, FL)
2006	Scarlet Golf Course at Ohio State University (Columbus, OH)*
2006	Sebonack Golf Club (Southhampton, NY)
2006	St Francis Links (St.Francis Bay, South Africa)

2007	The Cliffs at Keowee Falls (Keowee Falls, SC)
2007	The Kinloch Club/Jack Nicklaus Golf Club New Zealand (Kinloch, Noan Island, New Zealand)
2007	Oak Valley (Kangwan-Do, South Korea)
2007	Old Corkscrew Golf Club (Estero, FL)
2007	Pine Valley Golf & Country Club – Nicklaus Course (Beijing, Changping, China)
2007	Real de Faula II(Benidorm, Valencia, Spain)
2007	Whispering Oak at Verandah Club (Ft. Myers, FL)

*Redesign